Caribbean Examinations Council®

Economics

CAPE®

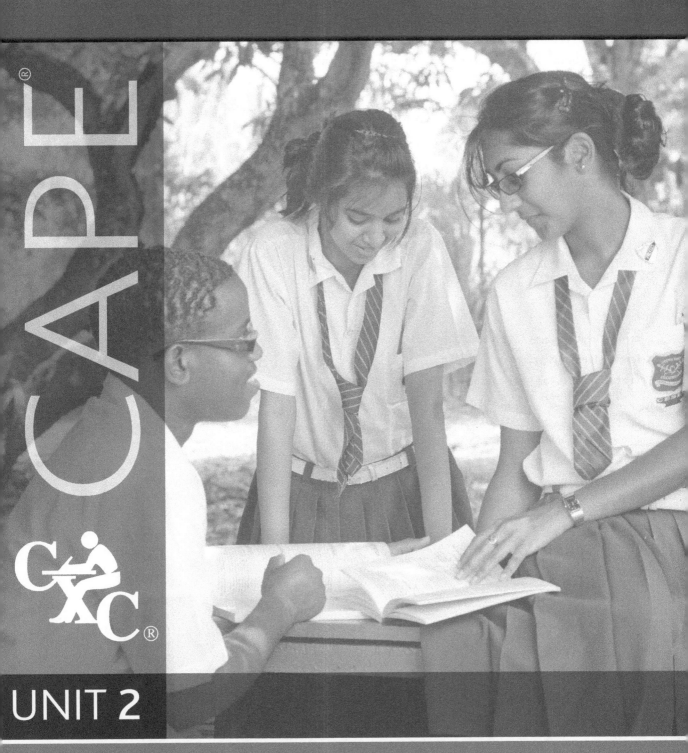

C X C®

UNIT 2

for self-study and distance learning

OXFORD
UNIVERSITY PRESS

Great Clarendon Street, Oxford, OX2 6DP, United Kingdom

Oxford University Press is a department of the University of Oxford.
It furthers the University's objective of excellence in research, scholarship,
and education by publishing worldwide. Oxford is a registered trade mark of
Oxford University Press in the UK and in certain other countries

First published by the Caribbean Examinations Council in association with
The Commonwealth of Learning in 2006
Second edition published by Nelson Thornes Ltd in 2012
This edition published by Oxford University Press in 2015

British Library Cataloguing in Publication Data
Data available

978-1-4085-0908-1

10 9 8 7 6 5

Printed in Great Britain by CPI Group (UK) Ltd., Croydon CR0 4YY

Acknowledgements

Cover image: Mark Lyndersay, Lyndersay Digital, Trinidad
www.lyndersaydigital.com
Page make-up: The OKS Group

Caribbean Examinations Council would like to acknowledge Roger Hosein
and Rebecca Gookol for their assistance in preparing the content for this
Self-Study Guide.

Although we have made every effort to trace and contact all
copyright holders before publication this has not been possible in all
cases. If notified, the publisher will rectify any errors or omissions at
the earliest opportunity.

Links to third party websites are provided by Oxford in good faith
and for information only. Oxford disclaims any responsibility for
the materials contained in any third party website referenced in
this work.

Contents

Chapter 1

National income accounting   5

Chapter 2

Classical models of the
macroeconomy   24

Chapter 3

Basic Keynesian models   39

Chapter 4

Investment   59

Chapter 5

Unemployment and inflation   65

Chapter 6

Monetary theory and policy   81

Chapter 7

Fiscal policy   97

Chapter 8

Public debt   107

Chapter 9

Growth and sustainable
development   115

Chapter 10

International trade   134

Chapter 11

Balance of payments and
exchange rates   146

Chapter 12

Economic integration   158

Chapter 13

International economic relations   172

References   181

Acknowledgements   184

1 National income accounting

General objective

On completion of this Study Guide you should have:

developed an understanding of national income accounting.

Specific objectives

You should have an understanding of:

economic agents

Gross Domestic Product (GDP), Gross National Product (GNP) and other measures

calculation of GDP, GNP and their components (personal income, disposable income), Net National Income (NNI), and per capita income; avoidance of double counting

total measures: GDP at market prices and GDP at factor costs

use of national income accounts to measure economic performance over time and to make inter-country comparisons

calculation of real and nominal GDP using the price deflator

limits of national income accounts as a measure of well-being:

- non-inclusion of the informal sector (the underground economy, illegal activities)

- non-payment for do-it-yourself activities

Economic agents in a two-sector, or private, closed economy model

The circular flow of income in macroeconomics refers to the flow of incomes and expenditures among the principal economic agents in an economy. In a two-sector economy, the economic agents are households and firms.

One of the basic assumptions of this model is that households own all the factors of production, while firms undertake the production of all goods and services. The other fundamental assumptions are that all incomes received by households are either spent or saved, and only firms undertake investment. Savings is a withdrawal from the circular flow of income while investment is an injection into the system.

A withdrawal refers to any income received by households, which is not returned to the circular flow of income.

Injections, on the other hand, refer to any additional spending that does not come from domestic households.

In the two-sector circular flow model, households offer factor services to firms in the form of labour time, capital use, talent and experience, as well as the use of land premises. Firms utilise these factors, in conjunction with their own entrepreneurial time, in the production of goods and services.

Households receive factor incomes from firms for the use of the factors of production, in the form of wages, interest, profits and rents respectively. This income is then either spent on the purchase of goods and services or is saved.

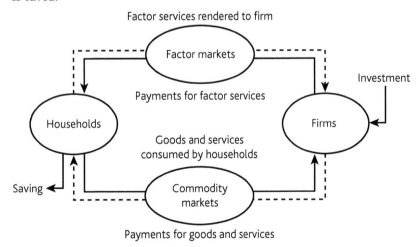

Figure 1.1 *Circular flow of income for a two-sector economy*

In Figure 1.1 solid arrows represent real flows between the agents while the broken arrows represent financial flows.

Economic agents in a four-sector, or open, economy model

In a four-sector economy, the economic agents include households, firms, the government and the international sector. The flows between households and firms remain the same as in the two-sector scenario, but with the introduction of the government and the international sectors other transactions arise between and among the agents. Note that the financial sector enables some of the economic transactions between the economic agents.

As can be seen in Figure 1.2, government spending is one of the additional injections, and refers to spending by the government on locally produced goods and services. The other injection that arises, exports, refers to the spending by foreign consumers on locally produced goods and services.

There are also two additional withdrawals from the circular flow of income. These are taxes, or income taxes that households pay, and imports. Imports, in the context of the circular flow model, refer to spending by households on foreign-produced goods and services.

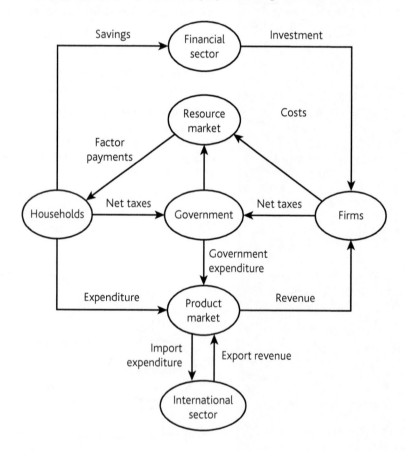

Figure 1.2 *Circular flow of income in an open economy*

From Figures 1.1 and 1.2 it is clear that the payments made to the owners of factors of production are equal to the value of goods and services and also to the payments for those goods and services. Clearly national output, national income and national expenditure are therefore equal. In this regard, one can use three methods to calculate national income: the output approach, the income approach and the expenditure approach. A discussion of each of these alternative methods is presented later in this chapter.

Key terms associated with the circular flow of income model

Consumption of goods and services (C)

Consumption, in the macroeconomic context, refers to the total level of expenditure by households on domestically produced goods and services. There is a variety of theoretical explanations of the consumption behaviour of households. For the purposes of this reader, the Keynesian type consumption function will be considered. Keynes assumed that the level of consumption was directly related to the level of current household income.

The Keynesian consumption function can, therefore, be expressed as follows:

$$C = C_0 + c_1 Y$$

where

C_0 = autonomous consumption

$c_1 Y$ = induced consumption

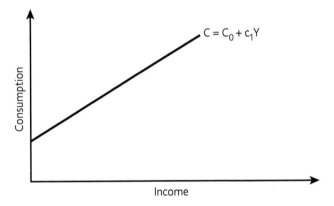

Figure 1.3 *Keynesian consumption function*

The theory of consumption will be detailed more thoroughly later in this Study Guide.

Saving (S)

Saving refers to that portion of disposable income (income less income taxes) that is not spent on the consumption of goods and services; saving is treated as a residual. In this regard, savings can be expressed as:

$$S = Y - C$$

where

S = savings

Y = income

C = consumption

Note the following distinction between saving and savings. Saving refers to the residual of income less consumption in a given period, while savings refers to the total amount saved as at a particular point in time. It can, therefore, be said that *saving* is a flow concept and *savings* a stock concept.

Taxes (T)

In the circular flow model, households and firms pay taxes to the government. This tax revenue is then used by the government to fund its affairs. The topic of taxation will be covered in more detail later in Chapter 7, on fiscal policy.

In the circular flow of income model context, taxes refer to income or direct taxes, in which case tax paid to the government is equal to a given proportion of the household's income level. The level of taxes paid can, therefore, be derived as follows:

$$T = t_1 Y$$

where

t_1 = the proportion of income paid in taxes

Note that when the tax rate is proportional the average rate of taxation is the same as the marginal rate of taxation.

With $T = t_1 Y$

$$\text{Average rate of taxation} = \frac{t_1 Y}{Y} = t_1$$

$$\text{Marginal rate of taxation} = \frac{t_1 \Delta Y}{\Delta Y} = t_1$$

Figure 1.4 illustrates this direct relationship between income and taxes paid.

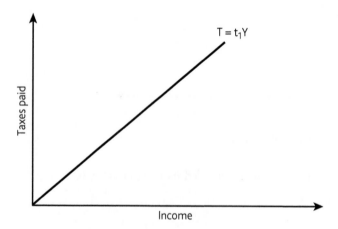

Figure 1.4 *Taxes paid*

Imports (M)

In the study of macroeconomics, and in the context of the circular flow model, imports refer to the expenditure of local consumers on foreign-produced goods and services. Imports are, therefore, regarded as a withdrawal from the circular flow system in that monies flow out of the domestic economy to the foreign sectors in order to cover the purchase of these foreign-produced goods and services.

The total value of imports can be determined in two ways. Consider the alternative import functions below:

$$M = M_0 + m_1 Y \qquad (1)$$

$$M = m_1 Y \qquad (2)$$

The total level of imports expressed by equation (1) shows that imports comprise two components: autonomous imports (M_0) and induced imports (m_1Y). In equation (2), the level of imports is equal to the level of induced imports.

For the economies of the Caribbean region, the import function most representative of the structure of imports is that of equation (1): there is an autonomous component to imports. The other component of imports m1Y varies with the level of income, in which case m1 is referred to as the marginal propensity to import (mpm). The marginal propensity to import refers to the fraction of a change in income that is spent on imports. This differs from the average propensity to import (apm), which measures the fraction of total expenditure on imports to income. The apm is calculated as:

$$apm = \frac{total\ expenditure\ on\ imports}{national\ income}$$

Table 1.1 *Average and marginal propensity to import*

Income $ (a)	Import expenditure $ (b)	apm = (b) / (a)	mpm = Δ (b) / Δ (a)
1000	300	0.3	
2000	600	0.3	0.3
3000	900	0.3	0.3
4000	1200	0.3	0.3
5000	1500	0.3	0.3

The last three variables discussed – saving, taxes and imports – are defined as withdrawals from the circular flow of income for the four-sector economy. The rest of this section provides some basic details on the three injections into the four-sector economy: investment, exports and government expenditures.

Investment (I)

The term 'investment' is related to saving or deferred consumption. Investment expenditure refers to spending on capital goods, with the aim of increasing the productive capacity of firms. In economics the capital stock of an economy is represented by K, which changes over time. Specifically, the difference between the capital stock in time period t and the capital stock of the previous year, (t–1), is equal to the level of investment spending undertaken in time period t.

Algebraically, this can be represented as:

$$K_t - K_{t-1} = \Delta K$$

Investment undertaken in any time period can take two forms, specifically:

- Investment undertaken to replace the loss in capital stock for the given period. This is known as replacement investment and covers the cost of depreciated capital over the period. Replacement investment helps to keep the capital stock unchanged for the given period.
- Addition to the capital stock or new investment. New investments increase the stock of capital, *ceteris paribus*.

Net investment is equal to new minus replacement investment.

In the circular flow model, investment is undertaken by firms and is regarded as an injection into the system. Investment is also assumed to be exogenous: the level of investment undertaken is independent of the level of income in the circular flow system.

Exports (X)

In the circular flow of income model, exports refers to the total expenditure by foreign consumers on locally produced goods and services. Exports is regarded as an injection, in that incomes flow into the economy from abroad. In addition to this, the level of exports is exogenously determined: the volume of exports is not dependent on local incomes and taste conditions but rather on foreign income and taste conditions.

Government spending (G)

Government spending refers to the total expenditure by the government on locally produced goods and services. Specifically government expenditure can take two forms:

- Government expenditure is an injection into the circular flow of income.
- Government expenditure is also regarded as constant or independent of domestic income.

In summary, therefore, for the four-sector economy there are three withdrawals: saving, taxes and imports, all of which are directly related to the level of domestic income; and three injections: investment, exports and government spending.

Gross Domestic Product, Gross National Product and other measures of national income

The terms used to describe national income include Gross Domestic Product (GDP), Gross National Product (GNP), National Disposable Income (NDI) and Net National Product (NNP). These terms are often used interchangeably in the literature.

- **GDP:** This refers to the sum of all final goods and services produced in an economy in a given year.
- **GNP:** This refers to the sum of all final goods and services produced by nationals of a country in a given year. The concept of GNP can be further explained using the following illustrations:
  1 Income earned by a Trinidad and Tobago nurse working in the United States on a short-term contract.
  2 Income earned by British Petroleum Trinidad and Tobago (bpTT) as a result of commercial operations in Trinidad and Tobago.
  3 Income generated by branches of the commercial bank Republic Bank (Trinidad and Tobago Ltd) located in CARICOM countries.

In situations 1 and 3, productive activity by Trinidad and Tobago's resources outside of the country generates income. This income is recorded as property income from abroad and adds to the domestic output. The income generated flows into the Trinidad and Tobago economy. In situation 2, however, productive activity is undertaken by non-Trinidad and Tobago resources. The income generated in this situation flows out of the Trinidad and Tobago economy, and is known as property income going abroad. Income, which flows out of the economy, reduces the value of domestic output.

The GNP of an economy is therefore calculated as follows:

$$\text{GNP} = \text{GDP} + (\text{property income from abroad} - \text{property income going abroad})$$

Note that net property income from abroad = property income from abroad – property income going abroad.

- **NNP:** This refers to the sum of all final goods and services produced by the resources of a country in a given year less capital consumption in the same year. Capital consumption is also known as depreciation or the loss in the value of capital as a result of operations. NNP is therefore calculated as:

$$\text{NNP} = \text{GNP} - \frac{\text{capital consumption}}{\text{depreciation}}$$

- **GDP per capita:** One of the primary tools for determining the level of development in a country over time and across countries is to understand underlying trends in the GDP per capita. GDP per capita measures the average distribution of income per unit of the country's population. It is calculated as:

$$\text{GPD per capita} = \frac{\text{GDP}}{\text{population}}$$

An increase in GDP per capita infers, other things being constant, that the average income earned by each citizen increases.

National income

National income can be adjusted to get GDP. National income represents all income earned by the citizens of a country, whether the income is earned locally or abroad. In order to calculate the output produced within the physical boundaries of the country three adjustments are made.

- **Indirect taxes:** The market value of goods and services includes indirect taxes like licence fees and sales taxes. For example, a good is produced and retailed for $100. The production and sale of the good creates $100 of factor incomes. If the government imposes a 15% sales tax to the price, the tax is added and passed along to consumers. However, the $15 that was added is not earned income, since the government does not contribute to the production of the good. National income accounts will, therefore, add indirect taxes to national income.

- **Net foreign factor income:** National income includes all income earned by citizens of a country, whether it is supplied locally or abroad. However, GDP includes output produced within a country whether the resources are supplied by local people or foreigners. Hence, in moving from national income to GDP, the income earned abroad from local resources must be subtracted and the income that foreigners earn in the local economy must be added. This difference is called net foreign factor income.

- **Consumption of fixed capital:** In the production process, fixed capital will be used well beyond the initial year of purchase. The fixed capital will become obsolete or wear out as time goes by. Accountants will therefore estimate how much of the fixed capital is being used up and make an allowance for it. This is called consumption of fixed capital or depreciation. Depreciation is the cost of production that will be reflected in the market price but it does not add to income. It is therefore added to national income.

$$GDP = \text{national income} + \text{indirect taxes}$$
$$+ \text{net foreign factor income}$$
$$+ \text{consumption of fixed capital}$$

Calculating GDP

The output method/approach

In understanding this approach to determining the value of national income it is necessary to understand the following concepts.

Market values

The market value of goods and services is its market price. Whereas price is determined via the interaction of market demand and market supply, there are some goods and services for which markets do not exist and hence market prices cannot be observed. Some of these services include homemaking and illegal or black market transactions.

Final goods and services: avoidance of double counting

In considering national output, consideration should be given to the concept of final goods and services. These are the goods and services that are utilised or consumed by the final consumer. Evaluating national income accounts using final goods and services avoids the problems associated with double counting. To illustrate this, consider the following diagrammatic analysis of the production stages of a chair.

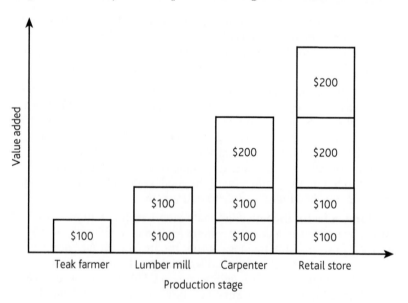

Figure 1.5 *Stages of production and value added in the manufacture of a chair*

In Figure 1.5, in the first stage of production the teak farmer engages in the production of teak trees. Each tree produced is valued at $100. A key assumption at this point is that the land utilised in the production of teak trees was not previously utilised, in which case, the value added by the teak farmer's action is equal to $100.

A teak tree is then sold to the lumber mill. The activity undertaken at this stage is the preparation of lumber from the teak tree. The prepared lumber is worth $200, but the value of the intermediary good – the teak tree – is $100. This, therefore, implies that the value added at the lumber mill stage is $100.

The prepared lumber is then sold to the carpenter who proceeds to fashion a chair from the lumber slabs. The value of the chair produced by the carpenter is $400, but the value of the lumber used to produce the chair is $200. At this stage, therefore, the value added by the carpenter is $200.

At the final stage, the furniture retail store, the chair is painted and cushions are added. At the furniture store this chair is sold for $600. However, at this stage the value of the intermediary good is $400, with the value added by the furniture retail store being $200.

In this example, assuming that the analyst wanted to determine the value of national output, does she sum the total output at every stage of production? If this was done, then the value of the national output would be $100 + $200 + $400 + $600 = $1 300. The problem with this method of reasoning is that the initial value added by the farmer is added four times at each of the respective stages, the value added at the lumber mill is added three times, and the value added by the carpenter is added twice. This problem can severely overstate the value of national output. To avoid this problem, national income analysts usually sum the value added at each stage of production as a gauge for national output; in which case it is equal to $100 + $100 + $200 + $200 = $600. From this example, therefore, it can be shown that the sum of the value added at each stage of production is equal to the value of the final good: $600. In this example also, it can be shown that $400 is the total value of the intermediary goods used in the production of the chair.

Value Added Tax

Value Added Tax (VAT) is an indirect tax – that is, a tax applied to goods and services. The tax is supposed to be levied on the value added at every stage of production. Hence if the tax rate is 15% then the total amount of tax generated should be $600 × 0.15 = $90. However, what can actually happen is that the VAT is paid on the price paid by each individual consumer.

	Value of goods purchased	VAT reflected on receipt
Lumber mill	$100	$15
Carpenter	$200	$30
Retail store	$400	$60
Customer	$600	$90
Total	$1300	$195

Feedback

	Intermediate good	Final good
Output	Used as input by other firms in production process	Not used as input by other firms but consumed by customers

Activity 1.1

Distinguish between a 'final good' and an 'intermediate good'.

Factor cost

Implicit in the definition of national output is the concept of factor cost. Market prices in reality do not always reflect equilibrium conditions; the market price/market value may reflect the effects of distortions such as taxes and subsidies. In this regard, therefore, the national output of an economy is determined using market prices less these distortions – that is, at factor prices.

Feedback

Specifically, in 1990, the most dominant sector of the Trinidad and Tobago economy was the services subsector which accounted for 64% of economic output. By 2006, however, although the services sector still accounted for the largest share of economic activity, the relative proportion fell to 57%.

As for petroleum, the relative size of this subsector increased by some 16 percentage points with attendant contraction in the agriculture and the manufacturing subsectors by 2 and 1 percentage points respectively.

Activity 1.2

Consider the two pie charts below and discuss the structural changes in output between 1990 and 2006.

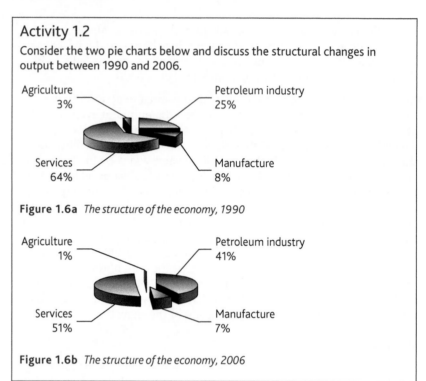

Figure 1.6a *The structure of the economy, 1990*

Figure 1.6b *The structure of the economy, 2006*

The income method/approach

This method of national income determination involves the summation of all factor incomes earned in an economy, where factor incomes refer to the rewards earned by employed factors of production. Specifically, the income approach sums wages and other payments made to labour; interest payments made to owners of capital; rent payments made to owners of land; and profit payments to entrepreneurs and other risk takers.

Consider Table 1.2, which shows the trends in the various income components of GDP. Notice that compensation of employees, a measure of the reward to labour, increased by 53% between 2000 and 2005. Additionally, operating surplus – a measure of the reward paid to entrepreneurial activity – increased by over 120%. Over the defined period 2000–05, Gross National Income (GNI) expanded by 85%.

Table 1.2 *Income components of GDP, 2000–05 TT$mn*

	2000	2001	2002	2003	2004	2005
Compensation of employees[1]	19177.1	21265.4	21508.0	23890.1	26526.8	29323.1
Operating surplus[2]	23263.9	23673.8	24073.2	33155.1	40006.3	51584.0
Consumption of fixed capital[3]	5692.1	6370.6	6678.6	9475.7	8597.0	10025.5

Indirect taxes[4]	1931.6	2071.4	2244.4	2581.9	2457.8	2891.0
(less) subsidies[5]	721.4	552.7	615.1	748.4	1229.7	1714.7
(plus) Value Added Tax	2027.3	2178.7	2400.6	2364.3	3170.9	2948.4
Gross National Income	**51370.6**	**55007.2**	**56290.0**	**70718.7**	**79826.1**	**95057.0**

Notes

[1] According to the Central Statistical Office of Trinidad and Tobago, compensation of employees is defined as 'all payments in cash or kind by producers to their employees, and consists of wages and salaries, employers' contribution to social security schemes and contributions to private pensions or similar allowances'.

[2] The Central Statistical Office defines operating surplus as 'the excess of value added over the sum of compensation of employees, consumption of fixed capital and indirect taxes reduced by subsidies. It is the amount remaining for remuneration for the production capital and in the case on unincorporated enterprises, remuneration of the owner and other unpaid labour which were not included under compensation of employees'.

[3] The consumption of fixed capital refers to the 'provision for that part of the fixed assets used up during the process of production during the period of account'.

[4] These are 'taxes assessed on producers in respect of the production, sale, purchase and use of goods and services which are charged to the expenses of production'.

[5] These refer to 'grants on current account made to private industries and public corporations by government to compensate for losses resulting from the pricing policies of government or as in the case of public corporations, to compensate for operating losses'.

Source: Central Statistical Office of Trinidad and Tobago

■ **Personal income (PI):** Personal income refers to the level of income, which is adjusted for net transfers. In particular, there are three main types of income/transfers that have been earned but not received; this includes contributions to social security or national insurance programmes, corporate profits and undistributed corporate profits. Incomes received but not earned include social security or national insurance payments, unemployment and other welfare benefits. These payments, which essentially augment household incomes, can also be regarded as transfers from the government sector.

Personal income can be calculated as:

$$PI = \text{national income} + \left(\frac{\text{incomes}}{\text{transfers earned but not received}} - \frac{\text{incomes}}{\text{transfers received but not earned}} \right)$$

i.e. PI = national income + net transfers

■ **Disposable income (Y^d):** Disposable income is defined as the residual personal income after taxes have been removed from gross income. Disposable income can be calculated as:

$$Y^d = \text{gross income} - \text{taxes}$$

The expenditure method/approach

The expenditure approach sums the total of all expenditures on domestic goods and services. In particular, the expenditure method sums expenditure undertaken by the following categories of economic agents:

1 Domestic consumers: this is known as consumption expenditure (C).
2 Local investors: this is known as investment expenditure (I).
3 Government: this is known as government expenditures (G).
4 Foreigners: this is known as exports (X).
5 Less expenditure by local people on foreign produced goods and services: this is known as imports (M).

The expenditure approach to determining GDP can be expressed in the form of the identity shown below:

$$E = C + I + G + (X - M)$$

where:

E = national expenditure

C = aggregate consumption expenditure

I   = aggregate investment expenditure

G = aggregate government expenditure

X = exports

M = imports

Table 1.3 illustrates the trends in the various components of expenditure. Over the period 2000 to 2005, government expenditure increased by 93%, private final consumption by 64%, gross capital formation by 71%, exports by over 100% and imports by 77%. Aggregate expenditure expanded by 85% over the period 2000 to 2005.

Table 1.3 *GDP by expenditure, 2000–05 TT$mn*

	2000	2001	2002	2003	2004	2005
Government final consumption expenditure (G)	6140.5	7548.0	7652.3	9042.0	9584.5	11884.7
Private final consumption expenditure (C)	29480.2	26864.4	32786.4	33690.5	43869.3	48431.5
Gross capital formation (I)	8622.7	14694.2	12735.7	17926.3	13906.3	14748.7
Exports of goods and services (X)	30421.0	30428.4	28299.0	36872.1	45480.7	61315.3
(less) Imports of goods and services (M)	23293.8	24527.8	25183.4	26812.2	33014.7	41323.2
Expenditure on GDP	**51370.6**	**55007.2**	**56290.0**	**70718.7**	**79826.1**	**95057.0**

Source: Central Statistical Office of Trinidad and Tobago

Real and nominal GDP

GDP, as defined previously, refers to the market value of all final goods and services produced within an economy in a given year. Value is measured in money terms, which implies that the market value of goods and services has two elements: the market price and the quantity produced. Assume, for example, that an economy produces toy cars, the market price of which is $10 per car. If in a given year the economy produces 10 cars then the market value of GDP for that year will be $100 ($10 × 10). The value $100 is referred to as the nominal GDP or the dollar value of output. Real GDP, however, refers to the GDP adjusted for changes in the domestic price level or the inflation rate. Eliminating the influence of price changes implies that economists use a base year, against which all other years are compared. Consider the previous example where in year 1 the price per unit was $10 and the quantity produced was 10. Assume that year 1 is the base year, which means that to calculate real GDP in year 2 the analyst uses the base year price of $10 per unit even if the market price of the good changes. Therefore, if in year 2 output produced increases to 12 units and the market price increases to $12, the real GDP would be calculated as $(12 \times \$10) = \$120$. The change in real GDP from year 1 to year 2 reveals that output of the economy has increased, that the economy has experienced real growth. Nominal GDP in year 2 has also increased to $144. It can be concluded that nominal GDP would change if both price and quantity changes but real GDP changes only when quantity or real changes in output occur in the economy.

Table 1.4 illustrates the concepts of real and nominal GDP in a multi-sector economy.

$$\text{Price per unit} \times \text{quantity produced} = \text{GDP}$$

Table 1.4 *Illustration of nominal and real GDP*

	Year 1 (base year)			Year 2				Year 3			
	Qty	Price ($)	Value ($)	Qty	Price ($)	Nominal value (Q × P) ($)	Real value = (Q × base year price) ($)	Qty	Price ($)	Nominal value (Q × P) ($)	Real value = (Q × base year price) ($)
Crude oil	100 barrels	25	2 500	110 barrels	25	2 750	2 750	100 barrels	27.50	2 750	2 500
Natural gas	100 btu	20	2 000	110 btu	20	2 200	2 200	100 btu	22	2 200	2 000
Methanol	100 mmt	15	1 500	110 mmt	15	1 650	1 650	100 mmt	16.50	1 650	1 500
Total GDP			6 000			6 600	6 600			6 600	6 000

Table 1.4 clearly illustrates that nominal GDP changes with changes in both price and quantity, but real GDP is only affected by changes in the level of production in an economy. In year 2, the output increased resulting in an increase in real GDP (calculated as quantity of year 2 × price of year 1). Nominal GDP also increased (calculated as quantity in year 2 × prices of year 2). In year 3, however, real GDP remained constant at the year 1 level, as output produced was unchanged.

Calculating real and nominal GDP using the price deflator

Using the information in Table 1.4, it can be shown that given nominal GDP, real GDP can be calculated by adjusting the nominal values to reflect some base year prices, removing the inflation effects.

To do this economists employ the use of a deflator. This tool essentially removes the effect of inflation or price changes that may have occurred between the base year and the year for which real GDP is to be determined. Real GDP is calculated as follows:

$$\text{Real GDP} = \left(\frac{\text{nominal GDP}}{\text{GDP deflator}}\right) \times 100$$

The most commonly used deflator is the retail price index or the consumer price index, which measures the change in the general price level. However, to deflate nominal GDP a national income deflator can be also be used.

Consider Table 1.5 which illustrates this operation.

Table 1.5 *The calculation of real GDP from nominal GDP for Trinidad and Tobago, 1990–2006*

Year	Nominal GDP TT million ($)	National income deflator (2000 = 100)	Real GDP TT million ($)
1990	21 539.3	57	38 052.8
1991	22 558.6	59	38 376.4
1992	23 117.6	63	36 938.2
1993	24 490.5	69	35 327.8
1994	29 311.7	75	38 858.2
1995	31 697	79	39 903.6
1996	34 586.6	82	42 156.5
1997	35 870.8	85	42 120.7
1998	38 065.1	89	42 802.5
1999	42 889.1	95	45 116.8
2000	51 370.7	100	51 370.7
2001	55 007.2	106	52 139.4
2002	55 365.6	110	50 363.3
2003	71 169	114	62 375.6
2004	82 838.6	119	69 344.1
2005	95 399.4	128	74 704.2
2006	120 556	136	88 558.6

Source: Adapted from Review of the Economy

Activity 1.3

Use the information below to answer the following questions.

Year	Price of milk ($)	Quantity of milk (litres)	Price of honey ($)	Quantity of honey (quarts)
2001	1	100	2	50
2002	2	150	3	100
2003	3	200	4	150

1 Using 2001 as the base year, compute the following for each year:
   a Nominal GDP
   b Real GDP
   c GDP deflator

2 Compute the percentage change from 2001 to 2002 and from 2002 to 2003 for the following:

a Nominal GDP

b Real GDP

c GDP deflator

Feedback

1 a Nominal GDP = (quantity $\times$ price of milk) + (quantity $\times$ price of honey)

$$2001 = (100 \times 1) + (50 \times 2) = 200$$

$$2002 = (150 \times 2) + (100 \times 3) = 600$$

$$2003 = (200 \times 3) + (150 \times 4) = 1200$$

b Real GDP = (quantity of milk $\times$ base year price of milk) + (quantity of honey $\times$ base year price of honey)

$$2001 = (100 \times 1) + (50 \times 2) = 200$$

$$2002 = (150 \times 1) + (100 \times 2) = 350$$

$$2003 = (200 \times 1) + (150 \times 2) = 500$$

c GDP deflator $= \dfrac{\text{nominal GDP}}{\text{real GDP}}$

$$2001 = \frac{200}{200} \times 100 = 100$$

$$2002 = \frac{600}{350} \times 100 = 171.4$$

$$2003 = \frac{1200}{500} \times 100 = 240$$

2 Changes in nominal GDP, real GDP and GDP deflator:

Period	Nominal GDP (% change)	Real GDP (% change)	GDP deflator (% change)
2001–02	67	75	71.4
2002–03	100	43	68.6

Using national income accounts

Comparing national income over time

National income accounts can be used to evaluate a country's economic performance. A number of problems arise, however, when comparing national incomes over time.

- **Rising prices:** When the price level increases over time, this decreases the purchasing power of money. For example, while J$100.00 may have been able to purchase one box of lunch four years ago in Jamaica, today it would be insufficient. The simple point here is that the general increase in the price level erodes the purchasing power of money over time. To overcome this problem, economists calculate real per capita GDP, which deflates the nominal GDP by the Retail Price Index to get real GDP. When real GDP is divided by the population we get real GDP per capita. Note though that real GDP per capita may conceal variations in the distribution of income which, although increasing, may become more inequitable.

■ **Quality of goods and services over time:** It is also possible that as an economy matures the quality of goods and services produced can change. In the Trinidad and Tobago economy, for example, the level of real GDP increased from TT\$42 802.5 million in 1998 to TT\$88 558.6 million in 2006, an increase of 130%. In this same interval of time, however, there was an increase in the amount of kidnappings and so many people now live inside 'caged houses'. In this type of economic environment, although people are materially better off, the extent of their fear may actually lead to a reduction in their overall welfare.

Example

Crime and economic growth: kidnappings in Trinidad and Tobago

The Trinidad and Tobago economy has been blessed with some 13 years of consecutive real economic growth. This has been complemented by an expansion in per capita GDP, an expansion in production, an expansion in the level of industrial diversification, and increase in the level of exports, persistent current account surpluses and an attendant fall in the unemployment rate.

These basic macroeconomic fundamentals suggest that the Trinidad and Tobago economy is on the upswing of a boom. However, a closer look at the realities of daily life may suggest that the economic buoyancy may soon be overshadowed by the negative trends in criminal activity, especially kidnapping.

Since 2002, the number of kidnappings has increased. Table 1.6 gives an indication of the trend.

If left unchecked, the spate in criminal activity has the potential to seriously deter private sector investment and hence compromise the long-term growth potential of the Trinidad and Tobago economy. Although some progress has been made by the protective services, more still needs to be done in order to alleviate the underlying sense of constant panic among Trinidadians and Tobagonians.

Table 1.6 *Trends in kidnappings*

2002	29
2003	51
2004	28
2006	17
2007	155

Comparing national income between economies

When comparing national income between economies we need to be considerate of differences in the level of sophistication of the collecting machinery between the relevant economies. Differences in the value of national incomes between economies may arise because of the absence of uniformity in comparing and classifying national incomes internationally.

Another problem in comparing national incomes is how different goods and services are consumed. Thus if a greater amount of heating fuel is consumed in colder economies compared with warmer economies, this would manifest as a higher expenditure for the colder economies but does not necessarily indicate a higher standard of living in these economies.

In comparing incomes between, say, economies A and B, a common method is to convert the incomes in both economies to US\$ using an appropriate exchange rate index. This, however, presumes that the bilateral exchange rate between country A and the US, and country B and the US, is correctly valued in the sense that what US\$1 can buy in country A is properly comparable with what US\$1 can buy in country B. However, a limitation with this method is that not all goods are traded internationally. In particular, these criticisms arise because conversion to a common currency does not always account for the differences in the domestic price levels for non-tradeable goods or differences in the consumption patterns in different countries.

Example

SWOT analysis of Trinidad and Tobago

The Business Monitor International (BMI) Ltd has projected that Trinidad and Tobago would experience a favourable trend in its GDP growth in the medium term, averaging approximately 4% annually. It is also expected that other macroeconomic indicators would improve. Inflation rates are anticipated to taper off and begin to decline while current account balances, foreign exchange reserves and fiscal surpluses are expected to increase.

Their favourable expectations are premised on the buoyancy in prices of Trinidad and Tobago's key exports, namely crude oil, natural gas, urea, ammonia and methanol. However, analysts are concerned that all this economy's 'eggs' are in one 'basket'. The BMI has therefore prepared a SWOT analysis for the Trinidad and Tobago economy. This shows the internal strengths and weaknesses and the external opportunities and threats.

Strengths	Strong growth in international petrochemical markets
	Implementation of revenue stabilisation fund to protect against unexpected drops in the price of oil
Weaknesses	Increasing dependence of economy on the petroleum sector
	Rising real effective exchange rate
Opportunities	Initiation of some degree of structural diversification
Threats	Commanding eights dominated by foreign multinationals

Source: BMI (2007)

Based on these, projections as per the macroeconomic indicators of the Trinidad and Tobago economy have been undertaken. These projected statistics are given in Table 1.7.

Table 1.7 *Macroeconomic forecasts for Trinidad and Tobago, 2008–11*

	2008	2009	2010	2011
Nominal GDP (US$ billion)	19.86	21.25	22.63	24.19
Real GDP growth (%)	4.3	3.5	3.0	3.4
Unemployment (%)	5.5	5.5	5.6	5.8
Inflation (%)	7.5	6.8	6.0	5.2
Trade balance (US$ billion)	4.0	4.3	4.3	4.2
Current account (% of GDP)	17.1	11.8	8.8	9.5

Source: BMI (2006)

Limits of national income accounts as a measure of well-being

The use of national income accounts as a measure of economic welfare is limited in several regards.

- **The non-inclusion of the informal sector:** In many developing economies a significant amount of economic activity is generated by the informal sector. In such economies the true value of goods and services generated by domestic factors of production is understated by the formal national accounting mechanism. Informal activities also includes illegal activities as well as 'do-it-yourself' activities. To get a good idea of the size of the informal sector you could look at the difference between GDP measured by the expenditure approach, and GDP measured by the income approach. GDP measured by the income approach will only reflect incomes that are reported for income tax purposes. Incomes 'earned' in the informal sector will not be reflected in the GDP figures. However, the incomes 'earned' in the informal sector will be spent on goods and services produced in the formal sector and this will, therefore, be reflected in the expenditure approach to calculating GDP.

- **The presence of externalities:** The national accounting mechanism does not account for the externalities that arise out of domestic economic activities. Externalities may include pollution, environmental degradation and criminal activities. These externalities have a negative impact on the standard of living of people and are not measured by the formal national accounts. Countries like Trinidad, which engage in the extraction of fossil fuels and by-products, will have reduced air quality because of the presence of chlorofluorocarbons (CFCs) in the atmosphere.

As mentioned above, the formal national accounting mechanism does not account for environmental degradation and resource depletion as a result of economic activity. In this regard, the concept of green GDP was advanced by Mäler (National Accounts and Environmental Resources, *Environmental and Resource Economics* 1(1):1–15, 1991), Grambsch, Michaels and Peskin (Taking Stock of Nature: Environmental Accounting for Chesapeake Bay, *Toward Improved Accounting for the Environment*, 184–7, 1993) and Peskin and Angeles (Accounting for Environmental Services: Contrasting the SESA and the ENRAP Approaches, *Review of Income and Wealth* 47(2):203–219, 2001), and later developed into an index as a measure of economic growth, having adjusted for the environmental consequences of that growth.

Another limitation associated with the use of national income accounts as a measure of well-being relates to the fact that national income accounts measure changes in the value of output over time and are not an accurate representative of changes in the population's quality of life. For example, GDP figures give no indication of the trends in crime or the impact of criminal activity on people's well-being.

End test

1   What is the circular flow of income?

2   List the economic agents in a four-sector model of the circular flow of income.

3   In the context of the circular flow of income, what is a withdrawal?

4   In the context of the circular flow of income, what is an injection?

5   What are the three methods of calculating GDP?

6   Is Value Added Tax (VAT) a direct or an indirect tax?

7   List FIVE limitations of the use of national income accounts as a measure of economic development.

8   List any 10 indices that can be used together with national income accounts in order to describe a country's human development position.

End test feedback

1   The circular flow of income in macroeconomics refers to the flow of incomes and expenditures among the principal economic agents in an economy.

2   The economic agents in a four-sector model of the circular flow of income include households, firms, government, the financial sector and the international sector.

3   A withdrawal refers to any income received by households that is not returned to the circular flow of income. In a four-sector model of the circular flow of income there are three withdrawals: savings, taxes and imports.

4   Injections refer to any additional spending that does not come from domestic households. In the four-sector model of the circular flow of income there are three injections: investment, government spending and exports.

5   Economists use three approaches to the calculation of GDP: the income approach, output approach and expenditure approach.

6   VAT is an indirect tax that is generally levied on the consumption of goods and services.

7   There are several limitations to the use of national income accounts as a measure of economic development:

   •   National income accounts do not include informal sector activities. The implication of this is that national income tends to be understated in countries with a large informal sector.

   •   National income accounts generally give no indication of the level of human development. As such, national income accounts are often used together with other indicators such as the Human Development Index (HDI).

   •   National income accounts generally give no indication as to the distribution of income in an economy.

   •   National income accounts do not reflect the real quality of life of the population in terms of the impact of pollution, resource depletion, environmental degradation and criminal activities, for example.

   •   National income accounts generally give no indication of the nature of the local market, the cost of living or the role of the state in the provision of goods and services.

8   Answers could include the following:

   •   Human Development Index (HDI)

   •   Gender Development Index (GDI)

   •   Gender Empowerment Index (GEI)

   •   Human Poverty Index (HPI)

   •   Gini coefficient

   •   Corruption Perception Index (CPI)

   •   Global Competitiveness Index (GCI)

   •   Logistics Performance Index (LPI)

   •   World Governance Indices (WGI)

   •   Genuine savings

2 Classical models of the macroeconomy

Specific objectives

You should have an understanding of:

flexibility of wages and prices

the role of wage price and interest rate flexibility

the factors that influence aggregate demand:

- consumer spending
- investment spending
- government spending
- net export spending

factors that influence aggregate supply including changes in input prices and incomes

the assumptions of the vertical aggregate supply curve

the interaction of the classical aggregate demand and supply curves

shifts in the aggregate demand and aggregate supply curves.

The classical approach

The classical approach utilises the concepts of aggregate demand and aggregate supply to explain unemployment and price fluctuations. A discussion of the aggregate demand curve and the aggregate supply curve will first be presented, after which the price and output determination process will be addressed.

The classical model of the economy was developed and refined during the period 1850–1950. The general perception of economists from this era is that government interference should be minimal in the running of the economy. The model assumes that the economic system is characterised by sufficient flexibility to allow the system to always clear. The classical system, based on the work of Jean Baptiste Say, assumes that supply always creates its own demand.

Example

Jean Baptiste Say (1767–1832)

Jean Baptiste Say was a French economist and businessman. His doctrines were largely premised on classical fundamentals of non-intervention, free market and free trade. He is best known for 'Say's law' which states that supply creates its own demand.

His literary history began with the publication of a pamphlet on the liberties of the free press, published in 1789. Say continued to publish and study, improving on his most famous publication *A Treatise on Political Economy or the Production Distribution and Consumption of Wealth*, published in 1804. Revisions to this manuscript were published in 1814 and 1817. In 1817 a chair was established for him at the Conservatoire des Arts et Métiers. Later, in 1831, he was made professor of political economy at the Collège de France.

Say was one of the first economists to argue that money had a neutral effect on the economy, given that money is not demanded of its own sake but rather for what it can purchase. Say argued that as the amount of money in circulation increased, this would cause the price of goods to increase but the relative prices and quantities of goods would remain unchanged. These thoughts were later developed into the Quantity Theory of Money.

The classical model is founded on a number of assumptions including the following:

1 Wages are flexible both upwards and downwards so that prices and wages continuously rise and fall.
2 Perfect competition prevails, and both product and factor markets always clear. All firms produce homogenous goods using identical factors of production.
3 In the short term the economy is in equilibrium with D = S.
4 The economy is closed so that imports and exports are not explicitly considered.
5 Labour is homogenous and all other factor inputs except capital are in abundant supply, identical and fully employed.

These five assumptions specify the conditions under which full employment always occurs when all the available labour is employed in the economy.

Aggregate demand

The classical economists' argument is not dissimilar to that of the microeconomic explanation of the relationship between price and quantity demanded, in that they propose that as the general price level falls, the aggregate level of demand for goods and services will increase. Classical theorists argue that as the general price level falls, the purchasing power of money increases – the amount of goods and services that a given level of income can command increases. Economists refer to this as real income.

The aggregate demand curve will slope downwards from left to right like the demand curve in microeconomic analysis. In microeconomic analysis the demand curve slopes downward because of the income and substitution effects. The aggregate demand curve slopes downward because of the wealth effect, the foreign purchases effect and the interest rate effect.

The wealth effect occurs when prices increase. This reduces the purchasing power of financial assets. The balances of both financial and physical assets are diminished. Individuals will reduce consumption. The foreign purchases effect occurs when prices increase locally. This results in foreigners switching purchases to cheaper substitutes elsewhere. Additionally, local consumers will switch to cheaper foreign imports resulting in increased imports. Net exports will decrease and so too will real output. The interest rate effect occurs when price levels increase. This results in an increase in demand for money. As the demand for money increases, with a fixed supply of money interest rates will tend to increase.

According to the classical theorists, the primary factors influencing the willingness and ability of people to purchase goods and services are the level of income and the purchasing power of income. That is, aggregate demand is dependent on the general price level and the level of income.

Aggregate demand, in turn, is influenced by a number of factors. Figure 2.1 shows aggregate demand curves for an economy, one version of which is shifted to the left and the other of which is shifted to the right.

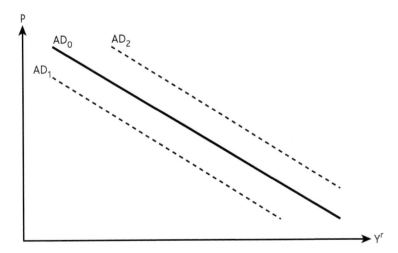

Figure 2.1 *Aggregate demand*

AD_0 = original aggregate demand curve
AD_1 = aggregate demand curve shifted to the left
AD_2 = aggregate demand curve shifted to the right

Basically the aggregate demand curve in an economy provides an illustration of aggregate expenditures at different price levels. The factors that can lead to a shift are: expectations, government policy, and foreign income and price levels.

- **Expectations:** Both consumption and investment patterns in an economy are influenced by expectations. Thus when consumers expect income in the economy to improve, they generally buy more at every price level so that the aggregate demand curve shifts to the right. When people expect the economy to enter into recession, consumption will drop and the aggregate demand curve will move from AD_0 to AD_1.

  Expectations are also important for investors. If a firm expects that future economic conditions are likely to be buoyant then they will invest today and aggregate demand will rise. If the business community takes the view that the economy will enter into a recession then profits will fall and both investment and aggregate demand will decline.

- **Government policy:** Changes in government policy also affect the level of aggregate demand. For example, expansionary fiscal policy would result in a rightward shift of the aggregate demand curve, while contractionary fiscal policy would result in a leftward shift of the aggregate demand curve.

- **Foreign income and price levels:** As foreign incomes increase, the amount of consumption expenditure that takes place in the foreign economy will increase, some of which will be on imported goods. A rise in imports by the foreign economy will lead to a rise in exports from the domestic economy and its aggregate demand curve will shift to the right.

  Similarly, a fall in foreign income will precipitate a decline in imports by the foreign economy from the domestic economy, the consequence of which is a fall in the aggregate demand of the domestic economy.

  If the foreign price level increases, then foreign consumers will increase their consumption of goods from overseas markets – that is, the imports of goods from the domestic economy by the foreign economy will increase.

Aggregate supply

Short run aggregate supply

Classical economists point out that real Gross Domestic Product (GDP) is determined by the intersection of aggregate supply and aggregate demand. The long run aggregate supply curve of the classical school is influenced by a number of factors and as such changes in any of these factors would result in shifts of the AS curve. These factors include:

- the price of resources
- technology
- expectations
- the quality of the labour force.

These are summarised in Figure 2.2 (opposite).

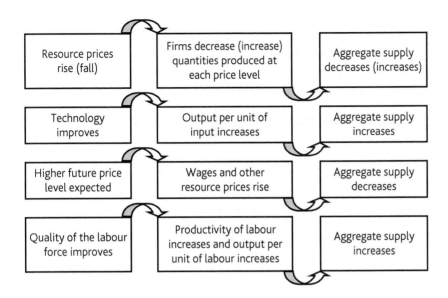

Figure 2.2 *The determinants of supply*

Long run aggregate supply

The classical theorists propose that the long run aggregate supply curve is vertical at the full employment output level. This is one of the distinguishing features of the classical model. At the full employment level firms are assumed to be operating at optimal capacity and productive efficiency. This is illustrated in Figure 2.3.

Classical economists argue that if the general price level increases (one of the components of which is the price of labour, or wages) then the relative wage differences between workers as well as the relative prices of goods and services would remain unchanged. In addition to this, the productive capacity of firms would also remain unchanged, and as such the quantity of goods and services brought to the market remains constant at the full employment level of output.

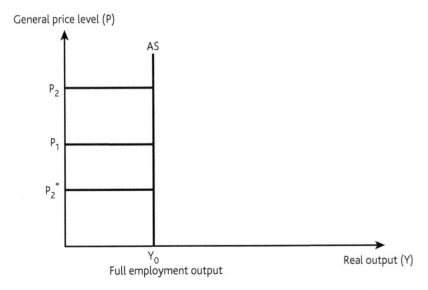

Figure 2.3 *Aggregate supply*

Assuming therefore that all prices in the economy increase from P_1 to P_2, given that relative prices remain unchanged there is no motivation for the level of productivity to change. Output produced remains at Y_0. If prices fall, however, to P_2^* the same would occur in that the level of output produced would remain unchanged.

Equilibrium: interaction of aggregate demand and aggregate supply

The equilibrium levels of national output and prices are determined in much the same way as with individual commodity / factor markets in microeconomics, through the interaction of demand and supply. As highlighted in the first part of this chapter, classical economists believe that markets will clear and that the interaction of market forces will result in the optimal employment of all factors of production at the full employment level.

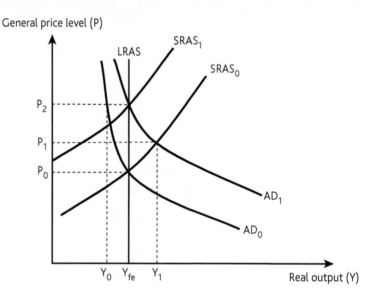

Figure 2.4 *Macroeconomic equilibrium*

Consider Figure 2.4, in which the equilibrium price and quantity level settles at Y_{fe}, full employment output at P_0, and where the AD curve, the SRAS curve and the LRAS curve intersect. To illustrate, assume that the government initiates expansionary fiscal policy. This is shown as a rightward shift of the aggregate demand curve from AD_0 to AD_1. This causes a rise in the general price level from P_0 to P_1 as well as a rise in the level of economic activity from Y_{fe} to Y_1.

As all prices in the economy rise, firms would face higher costs in terms of raw material inputs. Additionally, labour employed would begin to demand higher wages in order to maintain the purchasing power of their income. As such, over time, wages would also tend to increase. The increase in production costs would have a negative effect on firms' willingness to supply. The evidence of this fall in willingness is a leftward shift of the short run aggregate curve from $SRAS_0$ to $SRAS_1$. Notice that the SRAS curve would shift leftward until the full employment equilibrium is restored at Y_{fe}, the original equilibrium quantity, but at a higher domestic price level P_2.

Activity 2.1

Study Figure 2.5, which illustrates a series of events ultimately resulting in a rise in the domestic price level (inflation). The economy is initially at point A where AD_1 and AS_1 intersect.

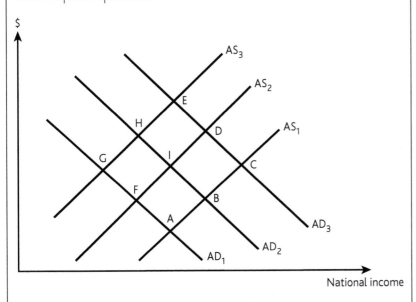

Figure 2.5

Assuming that the following events occur in a sequence, identify the point of intersection after each event.

a   The government initialises several large infrastructural development projects.

b   The government then reduces the level of income taxes.

c   Production costs throughout all industries begin to rise.

d   Through trade union lobbying, workers begin to collectively bargain for higher wage rates.

Feedback

a   B

b   C

c   D

d   E

Flexibility of wages and prices

Supply and demand for labour

The classical model assumes full employment in the labour market:

$$L^d = L^s$$

where

L^d = demand for labour

L^s = supply of labour

Both the demand and supply of labour are influenced by real wages.

$L^d = f(w_0)$, $f'(W_0) < 0$ indicates that the gradient on the demand curve for labour is negative (less than 0), which implies a downward-sloping demand curve. This downward-sloping demand curve for labour shows that as real wages increase – that is, the price of labour increases – the quantity of labour demanded falls. Additionally, as the real wage falls the demand for labour increases. In other words, there is an inverse relationship between real wages and the quantity demanded of labour.

$L^s = g(w_0)$, $g'(w_0) > 0$ indicates that the gradient of the supply curve for labour is positive (greater than 0) which implies an upward-sloping labour supply curve. This upward-sloping supply curve shows that as real wages increase the quantity of labour supplied also increases. Additionally, as the real wage falls the quantity of labour supplied also falls. In other words, there is a positive relationship between real wages and the quantity of labour supplied.

If, for some reason, the labour market is brought into disequilibrium then the real wage rate adjusts immediately to bring it back into equilibrium. In this regard the labour market is always in full employment equilibrium.

To illustrate the mechanics of the labour market, consider Figure 2.6. Initial conditions carry a labour supply curve L^s, and L^d is a labour demand curve. Real equilibrium wages occur at the point where $w_0 = w_0/P_0$ with L_e workers employed.

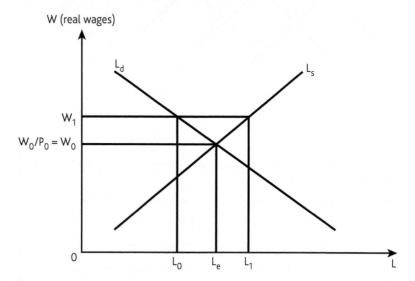

Figure 2.6 *Demand and supply of labour*

w_0 = nominal wages
P_0 = price level
W_0 = real wages
L^s = labour supply
L^d = labour demand

As real wages increase, the labour market is thrown into disequilibrium where the quantity of labour supplied exceeds the quantity demanded. The result is that there is a surplus of labour resources on the market at the real wage level W_1. This surplus of labour on the market puts a downward pressure on wages and hence real wages fall. As real wages fall, the quantity of labour demanded increases and the quantity supplied decreases until equilibrium employment is re-attained.

From a classical point of view, full employment in the labour market implies that long run national output is fixed at the full employment level of employment. The associated production function in the classical market may be drawn as shown in Figure 2.7. This shows that at a level of employment L_{fe} the classical model would produce a national level of output Y_{fe}. This full employment level of income does not change as the full employment level of labour remains L_{fe}.

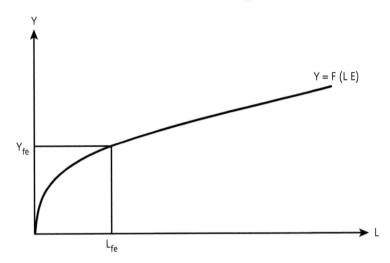

Figure 2.7 *The classical production function*

Interest rate flexibility

In the classical model, the forces of savings and investment are what determine the rate of interest. In Figure 2.8 (overleaf), r_0 is the equilibrium rate of interest motivated by a savings schedule of S_0 and an investment schedule of I_0. Both S_0 and I_0 are functions of the rate of interest.

$S_0 = h(r)$, $h'(r) > 0$ indicates that the gradient of the savings function is positive (greater than 0), which implies that the saving curve is an upward-sloping curve. The upward-sloping function implies that as the rate of interest increases, the level of savings would also increase – that is, there is a positive relationship between the interest rate and the level of savings. Interest in this regard is essentially the opportunity cost of consumption. As the rate of interest increases, consumption becomes relatively more expensive so that individuals would tend to consume less and save more.

$I_0 = m(r)$, $m'(r) < 0$ indicates that the gradient of the investment function is negative (less than 0), which implies that the investment curve is a downward-sloping curve. This downward-sloping function implies that there is a negative relationship between the interest rate and the level of investment. The interest rate in this regard represents the cost of investing. As this cost increases, firms would tend to invest less and as such the level of investment would fall. On the other hand as the interest rate falls, firms would tend to increase the amount of investment they engage.

These functions are plotted in Figure 2.8, where the S_0 and I_0 curves intersect the equilibrium rate of interest r_0.

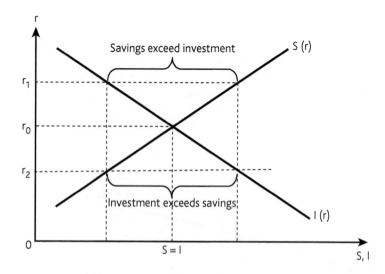

Figure 2.8 *Interest rate determination: the classical approach*

Notice that if the interest rate rises above or even falls below the equilibrium interest rate, these markets are thrown into disequilibrium where savings exceed investment or vice versa. When interest rates rise above the equilibrium level, savings exceed the level of investments. Downward pressure is exerted on the interest rate and consequently the level of savings decreases while the amount of investments engaged increases. Equilibrium is eventually restored.

As the rate of interest falls below the equilibrium level, the amount of investments engaged exceeds that of the level of savings. Consequently, upward pressure is exerted on the interest rate and eventually the level of savings and investment would equalise.

The Keynesian approach

John Maynard Keynes is undoubtedly one of the most influential figures in the history of economics, so much so that an entire branch of economic theory is named after him. Keynesian economic theory represented a complete paradigm shift in the school of thought of his day.

John Maynard Keynes, born in Cambridge, England in 1883 obtained his first degree in Mathematics at King's College, Cambridge University in 1905.

He was particularly known for advocating the necessity of government intervention in situations where the market mechanism failed. His most famous publication was *The General Theory of Employment Interest and Money* (1935), in which Keynes's macroeconomic theories were presented.

In this publication, Keynes proposed two primary concepts, which would eventually form the basis of understanding how modern economies operate. Specifically, Keynes highlighted that aggregate demand was the sum of household consumption, domestic investment, and government spending. In addition to this, Keynes showed that full employment could only be attained through government intervention and furthermore the adverse effects of the recession, depression and slums characteristic of the business cycle could be mitigated through the intentional use of fiscal and monetary policies.

Over his lifetime Keynes published 122 books, articles and pamphlets. A significant number of his articles were included in the prestigious *Economic Journal* of which he was made the editor in 1911.

Keynes's writings virtually revolutionised the economic conventions of his time and indeed made a 'splash in the economic and political circles' of his day. Even today Keynesian economics remain entrenched in the workings of many economies.

In his book *The General Theory of Employment, Interest and Money* (1935), John Maynard Keynes highlighted the inability of the classical school of economics to deal effectively with the adverse economic conditions associated with the Great Depression. In his book he highlighted certain concerns.

- **Unemployment equilibrium:** Keynes argued that markets did not always clear in the manner alluded to by the classical school, and as such large pockets of unemployment could persist. This phenomenon Keynes defined as 'unemployment equilibrium'. He also advocated that reaching full employment was a matter of chance and that the economy could not indefinitely sustain that level of output. Keynes also suggested that if full employment was always the goal of the government then prevailing economic conditions would always be unstable.

  Keynes advocated that the primary cause of unemployment was an insufficient level of aggregate demand. Specifically, Keynes argued that the level of aggregate demand existing during the time of the Great Depression was insufficient to generate a level of economic activity that would increase employment levels. Keynes advocated that the government increase its own level of expenditure in order to expand the level of aggregate demand, thus creating the stimulus necessary to improve domestic employment conditions.

- **Government intervention:** According to Keynes, the cure for the high level of unemployment was an increase in government spending. This increase in expenditure would result in an increase in the aggregate level of demand and hence economic activity. Keynes argued that the government had the 'ability and the responsibility' to 'manage the level of aggregate demand'.

Factors that influence aggregate demand

Keynesian aggregate demand

Unlike the classical economists, who believed that the primary determinants of aggregate demand are the stock of money and the purchasing power of money, Keynes advocated that aggregate demand comprised four components:

- Household consumption expenditure (C)
- Investment expenditure (I)
- Government expenditure (G)
- Net exports (NX)

The Keynesian aggregate demand curve is downward sloping and shows a negative relationship between price and output (Figure 2.9, overleaf).

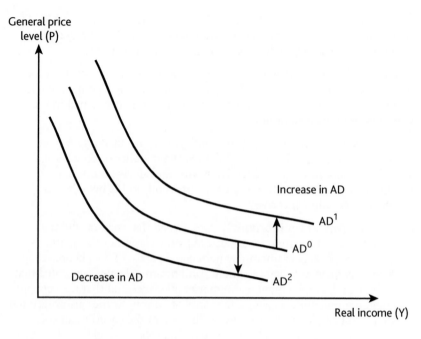

Figure 2.9 *Keynesian aggregate demand*

Aggregate demand would shift rightward in any component of aggregate spending increases. For example, if the government initiates an increase in infrastructure investment, the evidence would be a rightward shift of the AD curve. If the opposite occurs – that is, if any component of aggregate expenditure falls – then the AD curve will shift leftward. This is illustrated in Figure 2.9.

Other factors that may result in shifts of the aggregate demand curve include changes in:

- consumption
- taxation
- business confidence
- the exchange rate
- interest rates
- an economy's stock of wealth.

Factors that influence aggregate supply

Keynesian aggregate supply

Although the classical economists recognised that prices and wages were sticky downward, they still advocated that in the long run markets cleared; and that price stickiness was associated with the 'transitional periods' or the short run period. Keynes, however, strongly disagreed, placing more emphasis on the short run dynamics associated with wage and price stickiness. Keynes went on to show that workers tended to strongly resist wage cuts; and as such this resulted in some degree of rigidity of the system, a characteristic that perpetuated long periods of unemployment. Keynes, therefore, proposed that the aggregate supply curve was not vertical at the full employment level but rather had two distinct portions: a horizontal portion and a vertical portion. This is illustrated in Figure 2.10.

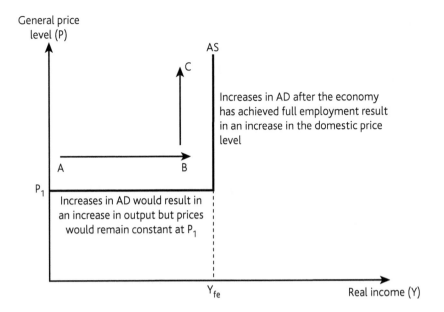

Figure 2.10 *Keynesian aggregate supply*

Along the horizontal portion of the aggregate supply curve AB, changes in the level of aggregate demand will have no effect on the general price level, which would remain constant at P_1, but the level of output produced will change. Over the portion AB, firms could effectively increase productivity without affecting cost as more and more of the previously unemployed resources become utilised. That is, the economy could effectively increase national output by employing more resources. The range AB is known as the Keynesian range. Beyond part B on the AS curve, where the economy has reached its full employment level of output, implying that all resources are efficiently employed, increases in the level of aggregate demand would cause domestic prices to increase (over the portion BC). The vertical portion of the Keynesian AS curve is the same as the classical AS curve. The horizontal/Keynesian portion and the vertical/classical portion of the aggregate supply curve combine to form an L-shaped supply curve.

Since the 1930s, however, the economic environment has changed. Specifically, it has been recognised that the aggregate supply function does not always result in a situation of the L-shaped supply curve. In reality, not all industries operate at full capacity, coupled with the fact that some industries achieve full employment before others. The implication of this for the AS curve is that for industries tending towards full employment, prices would rise, exerting an upward pressure on the average price level. This occurs regardless of the fact that some industries still operate at levels below the full employment level. This phenomenon results in a situation where both prices and output increase, the evidence of which is a curved rather than an L-shaped supply curve as illustrated in Figure 2.11 (overleaf).

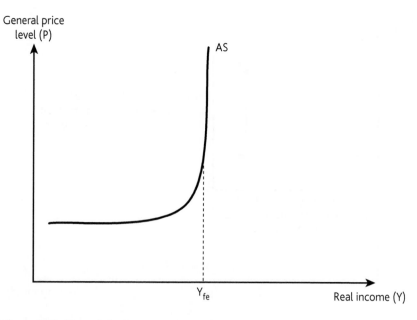

Figure 2.11 *Upward-sloping aggregate supply*

Activity 2.2

Read the following two extracts, taken from the publications of John Maynard Keynes. Then answer the questions that follow.

> We have, as a rule, only the vaguest idea of any but the most direct consequences of our acts … our knowledge of the future is fluctuating, vague and uncertain … the sense in which I am using the term (uncertain) is that in which the prospect of a European war is uncertain, or the price of copper and the rate of interest twenty years hence, or the obsolescence of a new invention, or the position of private wealth-owners in the social system in 1970. About these matters there is no scientific basis on which to form any calculable probability whatever. We simply do not know.
>
> *Source: Keynes (1937) in W. Hutton,* The Revolution that Never Was *(1986), p.95.*

> Many of the greatest economic evils of our time are the fruits of uncertainty, and ignorance. It is because particular individuals, fortunate in situation or in abilities, are able to take advantage of uncertainty and ignorance, and also because for the same reason big business is often a lottery, that great inequalities of wealth come about; and these same factors are also the cause of the unemployment of labour, or the disappointment of reasonable expectations, and of the impairment of efficiency and production. Yet the cure lies outside the operation of individuals; it may even be to the interest of individuals to aggravate the disease. I believe that the cure for these things is partly to be sought in the deliberate control of the currency and of credit by a central institution, and partly in the collection and dissemination on a great scale of data relating to the business situation, including the full publicity, by law if necessary, of all business facts which it is useful to know. These measures would involve society in exercising directive intelligence through some appropriate organ of action over many of the inner intricacies of private business, yet it would leave private initiative and enterprise unhindered. Even if these measures prove insufficient, nevertheless, they will furnish us with better knowledge than we have now for taking the next step.
>
> *Source: Keynes in A.P. Thirlwall,* Keynes and Laissez-Faire *(1978), pp.39–40.*

Think about what Keynes thought were the core problems facing macroeconomic management. How did he suggest that these problems might be countered?

End test

1   What are the fundamental assumptions on which the classical approach to economics is premised?

2   Why do aggregate demand curves slope downward?

3   What is meant by the wealth effect, the foreign purchases effect and the interest rate effect?

4   List and discuss the factors that result in a shift of the aggregate demand curve.

5   What factors result in the shift of the long run aggregate supply curve?

6   At the macroeconomic level, how is the equilibrium price level determined?

7   According to the Keynesian school of thought, what factors determine aggregate demand?

8   How is the Keynesian aggregate supply different from that of the classical school?

End test feedback

1   The classical model is founded on a number of assumptions including the following:

   a   Wages are flexible both upwards and downwards so that prices and wages continuously rise and fall.

   b   Perfect competition prevails, both product and factor markets always clear. All firms produce homogenous goods using identical factors of production.

   c   In the short run the economy is in equilibrium with D = S.

   d   The economy is closed so that imports and exports are not explicitly considered.

   e   Labour is homogenous and all other factor inputs except capital are in abundant supply, identical and fully employed.

   These five assumptions specify the conditions under which full employment always occurs when all the available labour is employed in the economy.

2   The aggregate demand curve slopes downward because of the wealth effect, the foreign purchases effect and the interest rate effect.

3   The wealth effect occurs when prices increase. This reduces the purchasing power of financial assets. The balances of both financial and physical assets are diminished. Individuals will reduce consumption. The foreign purchases effect occurs when prices increase locally. This results in foreigners switching purchases to cheaper substitutes elsewhere. Additionally, locally consumers will switch to cheaper foreign imports resulting in increased imports. Net exports will decrease and so too will real output. The interest rate effect occurs when price levels increase. This result is an increase in demand for money. As the demand for money increases, with a fixed supply of money interest rates will tend to increase.

4   Basically the aggregate demand curve in an economy provides an illustration of aggregate expenditures at different levels of price. The factors that can lead to a shift are:

   •   expectations

   •   government policy

   •   foreign income and price levels.

   Expectations: Both consumption and investment patterns in an economy are influenced by expectations. Thus when consumers expect income in the economy to improve, they generally buy more at every price level so that the aggregate demand curve shifts to the right. When people expect the economy to enter into recession, consumption will drop and the aggregate demand curve will shift leftward.

   Expectations are also important for investors. If a firm expects future economic conditions to be buoyant then they will invest today and aggregate demand will rise. If the business community believes that the economy will enter into a recession then profits will fall and both investment and aggregate demand will decline.

   Government policy: Changes in government policy also affect the level of aggregate demand. For example, expansionary fiscal policy would result in a rightward shift of the aggregate demand curve while contractionary fiscal policy would result in a leftward shift of the aggregate demand curve.

Foreign income and price levels: As foreign incomes increase, the amount of consumption expenditure that takes place in the foreign economy will increase, some of which will be on imported goods. A rise in imports by the foreign economy will lead to a rise in exports from the domestic economy and its aggregate demand curve will shift to the right.

Similarly, a fall in foreign income will precipitate a decline in imports by the foreign economy from the domestic economy, the consequence of which is a fall in the aggregate demand of the domestic economy.

If the foreign price level increases, then foreign consumers will increase their consumption of goods from overseas markets – that is, the imports of goods from the domestic economy by the foreign economy will increase.

5   The long run aggregate supply curve of the classical school is influenced by a number of factors and so changes in any of these factors would result in shifts of the AS curve. These factors include:

- the price of resources
- technology
- expectations
- the quality of the labour force.

6   The equilibrium levels of national output and prices are determined in much the same way as with individual commodity / factor markets in microeconomics: through the interaction of demand and supply.

7   Unlike the classical economists, who believed that the primary determinants of aggregate demand are

the stock of money and the purchasing power of money, Keynes advocated that aggregate demand comprised four components:

- Household consumption expenditure (C)
- Investment expenditure (I)
- Government expenditure (G)
- Net exports (NX)

8   Keynes proposed that the aggregate supply curve was not vertical at the full employment level but rather had two distinct portions: a horizontal portion and a vertical portion. This is illustrated in Figure 2.10 on page 35.

Along the horizontal portion of the aggregate supply curve, AB, changes in the level of aggregate demand will have no effect on the general price level which would remain constant at P_1 but the level of output produced will change. Over the portion AB, firms could effectively increase productivity without affecting cost as more and more of the previously unemployed resources become utilised – that is, the economy could effectively increase national output by employing more resources. The range AB is known as the Keynesian range. Beyond part B on the AS curve, where the economy has reached its full employment level of output, implying that all resources are efficiently employed, increases in the level of aggregate demand would cause domestic prices to increase (over the portion BC). The vertical portion of the Keynesian AS curve is the same as the classical AS curve. The horizontal/Keynesian portion and the vertical/classical portion of the aggregate supply curve combine to form an L-shaped supply curve.

3 Basic Keynesian models

Specific objectives

You should have an understanding of:

autonomous and induced consumption concepts of:

- income = consumption plus saving
- marginal propensity to consume and save
- average propensity to consume and save

simple multiplier 1/1 – mpc

the relationship between changes in investments and national income

government expenditure and its effects on national income

concept of injections and withdrawals in an economy

the effect of injections and withdrawals on national income

small multipliers in the Caribbean context due to leakages

the relationship between net exports (x – m) and national income

exports as an injection and imports as a withdrawal

the determination of equilibrium income using:

- 45° line or E = Y
- withdrawals and injections approach
- the Keynesian aggregate demand and supply curves (long run and short run)

The notion of the consumption function

Consumption expenditure refers to the amount of money households spend on goods and services to satisfy their consumption requirements.

Factors influencing consumption

Income: the main factor influencing consumption is the household's income. However, whether the appropriate income is current income, life cycle income or permanent income, is the subject of much theoretical debate.

Activity 3.1

Using the data in Table 3.1, compare the trends in consumption as a percentage of Gross Domestic Product (GDP) for Jamaica and Trinidad and Tobago for the period 1995–2006.

Table 3.1 *GDP and consumption (current US$ billion) for Jamaica and Trinidad and Tobago, 1995–2006*

	Jamaica		Trinidad and Tobago	
	GDP	**Consumption**	**GDP**	**Consumption**
1995	5.8	4.7	5.3	3.4
1996	6.5	5.4	5.8	3.8
1997	7.5	6.2	5.7	4.2
1998	7.8	6.5	6.0	4.3
1999	7.8	6.5	6.8	5.0
2000	8.0	6.7	8.2	5.5
2001	8.2	7.1	8.8	6.5
2002	8.6	7.5	9.0	6.8
2003	8.3	7.2	11.2	8.5
2004	8.9	7.7	12.7	8.8
2005	9.7	8.6	15.1	9.6
2006	10.0	9.3	18.1	12.2

Source: World Development Indicators (2008)

Feedback

The data in Table 3.1 illustrates the trends in GDP and consumption for Jamaica and Trinidad and Tobago. As a percentage of GDP, consumption accounted

Specific objectives

the full employment level of output

the actual level of output

the equilibrium level of national income, which could be either below, at or above potential level of output.

for an average of 85.5% of GDP in Jamaica compared with 70.1% of GDP in Trinidad and Tobago. Consider Figure 3.1 which illustrates the specific trends.

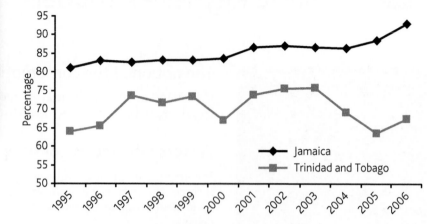

Figure 3.1 *Consumption as a percentage of GDP*

- **Availability of credit and cost of borrowing:** In general, if it is easy and cheap to borrow then people will borrow and consume more. If people spend more money than they are earning then they are dissaving.
- **Age distributions:** Middle-aged consumers tend to save more of their income than young people.

Example

Age distribution and savings: middle-aged consumers tend to save more than young people

The empirical experiences of many countries have shown that the age distribution of the population significantly affects savings, and, more importantly, the structure of savings. Ageing populations in many developed and industrial countries means that understanding the impact of these changes on the macroeconomic variables, such as consumption and the dynamics of consumption, and hence savings, is critical. The economic literature points to the fact that one of the factors affecting the structure of consumption and savings is the structure of the population.

Table 3.2 shows the age distribution of the population of Trinidad and Tobago at three points: 1980, 1990 and 2000. Notice that the number of persons in the 35–65 age group has increased from 28% of the population in 1980 to over 42% in 2000. This would no doubt have implications for the marginal and average propensity to save in the Trinidad and Tobago economy.

Table 3.2 *Age structure of the Trinidad and Tobago population, 1980, 1990 and 2000 censuses*

	1980	1990	2000
0–4	128 199	131 832	86 026
5–9	120 448	146 885	104 507
10–14	121 064	127 438	129 404
15–19	133 833	114 377	138 477
20–24	112 473	104 107	11 980

25–29	88 805	111 181	96 605
30–34	72 324	96 359	92 193
35–39	57 206	79 552	102 573
40–44	48 386	66 053	90 371
45–49	40 323	52 447	74 822
50–54	37 111	43 313	82 433
55–59	32 157	34 348	46 498
60–64	27 286	30 100	37 109
65–69	25 252	27 573	30 421
70–74	16 204	20 354	23 399
75–79	10 261	14 291	17 000
80 and over	8 459	13 523	18 548
Total	1 079 791	1 213 733	1 262 366

Source: CSO Census (various years)

- **Inflation:** The effect of inflation on consumption is uncertain. Some people spend more money if they expect prices to increase. Other consumers tend to spend less in the presence of higher prices so that they can maintain the real value of their savings.
- **Indirect taxes:** As indirect taxes increase, the prices of goods and services also increase and people tend to buy less.
- **Range of goods and services:** People spend more if goods of a high quality are available.

The basic Keynesian consumption function

In his publication *The General Theory of Employment, Interest and Money*, Keynes made two assumptions regarding the behaviour of consumption (spending):

1 People's decisions on their consumption are a function of current income.
2 Increments to income are partly spent and partly saved.

The consumption function: autonomous and induced spending

The consumption function describes the relationship between consumption expenditure and the variables that influence it. A representative form of the consumption function is:

$$C = f(Y, \text{other variables})$$

where

C = aggregate consumption

Y = aggregate income (current)

Other variables include such factors as wealth.

Activity 3.2
Write a paper advising the Trinidad and Tobago government of the programmes and policies they need to put in place to ensure economic sustainability, in light of the evidence in Table 3.2.

Feedback

Your essay should include consideration of the following concerns:

- Age structure and the short and long run productive capacity of the economy
- Age structure of the population and the education structure
- Age structure of the population and the health sector capacity
- Age structure and the social security network
- Age structure and the tax regime

A simplified consumption function proposed by John Maynard Keynes in *The General Theory of Employment, Interest and Money* can be expressed as:

$$C = C_0 + c_1 Y^d$$

where

C = aggregate consumption

C_0 = autonomous consumption

$c_1 Y^d$ = endogenous consumption

c_1 = marginal propensity to consume

y^d = current disposable income

Autonomous consumption C_0 occurs when a household's income is zero. Consumption still occurs when income is zero because such a household can borrow, beg, or use their savings.

Endogenous consumption is consumption that varies as income varies.

Two important concepts associated with the consumption function are the average and the marginal propensity to consume. The average propensity to consume (apc) is simply the ratio of aggregate consumption to national income and can be represented as:

$$apc = \frac{C}{Y}$$

The marginal propensity to consume (mpc) is given as the ratio of the change in consumption to the change in income:

$$mpc = \frac{\Delta \text{ consumption}}{\Delta \text{ in national income}}$$

The consumption function has a slope given by its mpc. Other properties of the consumption function are that:

1 there is some point at which the apc = 1. Let us call this point apc*. Below apc* the apc is greater than 1 and above apc* the apc is less than one (shown in the calculation below)

2 0 < mpc < 1 for all levels of income

If $Y = C + S$

Then $1 = \dfrac{C}{Y} + \dfrac{S}{Y}$

– that is, apc + aps = 1

Also $\Delta Y = \Delta C + \Delta S$

Then $1 = \dfrac{\Delta C}{\Delta Y} + \dfrac{\Delta S}{\Delta Y}$

– that is, mpc + mps = 1

The 45° line

Before proceeding further to explain the Keynesian consumption function we need to outline and discuss the concept of the 45° line in more detail.

A 45° line is equidistant from both the vertical and the horizontal axis. In Figure 3.2, the distance $x_0 = y_0$. The 45° line therefore shows the line of perfect equality between income and expenditure.

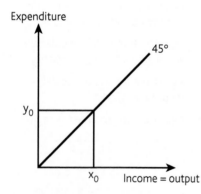

Figure 3.2 *The 45° line*

The simple Keynesian consumption function may be sketched as illustrated in Figure 3.3.

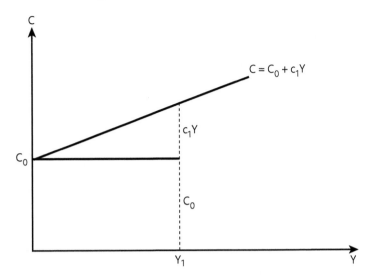

Figure 3.3 *The Keynesian consumption function*

In Figure 3.3, C_0 is autonomous or fixed consumption while c_1Y is induced consumption. We can generalise the plot of the consumption function shown in Figure 3.3 to show the ranges of values that the apc can take (Figure 3.4).

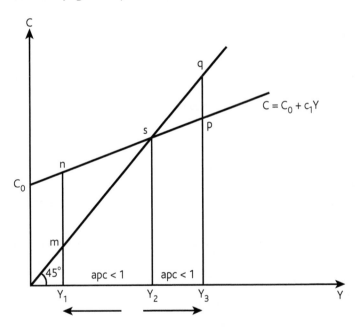

Figure 3.4 *Range of values that the apc can take*

Assuming a constant mpc, $C = Y$ at the point s with an income level of Y_2. At Y_2 the apc is equal to 1. At income levels less than Y_2, consumption is above income and the apc is in excess of unity – that is, the consumer is dissaving. At the income levels above Y_2 such as Y_3, the apc is less than unity and the consumer accumulates a saving (see Figure 3.4).

Table 3.3 provides data that can be used to analyse a simple Keynesian consumption function.

Table 3.3 *Analysis of the simple Keynesian consumption function*

Y ($)	C ($)	S ($)	apc	mpc
3 000	3 400	−400	1.13	−
4 000	4 200	−200	1.05	0.8
5 000	5 000	0	1.00	0.8
6 000	5 800	200	0.97	0.8
7 000	6 600	400	0.94	0.8
8 000	7 400	600	0.93	0.8
9 000	8 200	800	0.91	0.8
1 000	9 000	1 000	0.90	0.8

Note in Table 3.3 that as income increases, consumption also increases. The apc fluctuates in value from being greater than 1 to less than 1 and the mpc is constant at 0.8 (800/1000) (Figure 3.5).

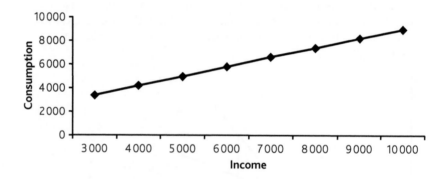

Figure 3.5 *Consumption function*

Activity 3.3

Copy the table below and fill in the blanks. Plot the consumption and savings function.

Year	Income ($)	Consumption ($)	Saving ($)	apc	aps	mpc	mps
1	1 000	500		0.50		−	−
2	2 000		1 000				
3	3 000	1 500					
4	4 000		2 000				
5	5 000	2 500					

Feedback

Year	Income ($)	Consumption ($)	Saving ($)	apc	aps	mpc	mps
1	1000	500	500	0.50	0.50	–	–
2	2000	1000	1000	0.50	0.50	0.5	0.50
3	3000	1500	1500	0.50	0.50	0.5	0.50
4	4000	2000	2000	0.50	0.50	0.5	0.50
5	5000	2500	2500	0.50	0.50	0.5	0.50

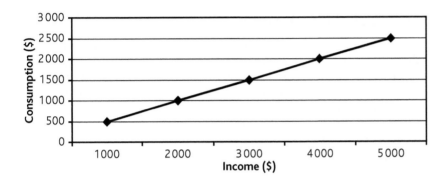

Figure 3.6 *Consumption function*

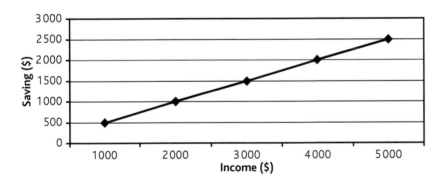

Figure 3.7 *Saving function*

The simple multiplier

An economic multiplier exists when a change in one variable triggers
multiple changes in another variable. With economic multipliers each
successive ripple of the initial change (or shock) is smaller than the
first. In macroeconomic theory there are two important multipliers: the
national income multiplier and the money multiplier. This section is
concerned with the national income multiplier.

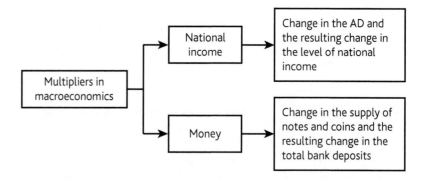

Figure 3.8 *Multipliers in macroeconomics*

The national income multiplier

The multiplier was introduced into the economic literature by Lord R.F. Kahn in 1931. Kahn was a former student of John Maynard Keynes at the University of Cambridge. In its early conceptualisation, the multiplier was mainly used to explain the implications for employment and so was considered an employment multiplier. Keynes subsequently deployed the multiplier in 1933 to show the impact on national income of a change in government expenditure.

Keynes wrote:

> If the new expenditure is additional and not merely in substitution for other expenditure the increase in employment does not stop there. The additional wages and other incomes paid out are spent on additional purchases which in turn lead to further employment … the newly employed who supply the increased purchases of those employed on the new capital works will, in their turn, spend more, thus adding to the employment of others and so on.
>
> *The General Theory of Employment, Interest and Money* (1935)

After Keynes's use of the multiplier it became understood that any of the factors influencing aggregate demand can lead to a multiplicative effect on national income. The most common multipliers identified in the literature are the:

- autonomous consumption multiplier
- investment multiplier
- government multiplier
- taxation multiplier
- net export multiplier.

In practice, the government spending multiplier and investment multiplier are the most frequently encountered.

The multiplier as a dynamic process

The multiplier process occurs over a period of time – it is a dynamic process. To illustrate the multiplier process, let us assume that the government of Jamaica spends US$1 billion on the commercialisation of its ackee plants to facilitate the penetration of foreign markets. Assume that the mpc is 0.9 and that all of the other components of aggregate demand are constant. Note that if mpc = 0.9, the mps = 0.1 (where 1 – mpc = mps); that is, mpc + mps = 1, so 0.9 + 0.1 = 1.

Table 3.4 *The multiplier process illustrated assuming mpc = 0.9 and 0.6*

Period	Injection of US$1 bn into ackee industry (mpc = 0.9)	Amount spent (mpc = 0.9)	Injection of US$1 bn into ackee industry (mpc = 0.6)	Amount spent (mpc = 0.6)
1	1000	900	1000	600
2	900	810	600	360
3	810	729	360	216
4	729	656.1	216	129.6
5	656.1	590.5	129.6	77.8
6	590.5	531.4	77.8	46.7
7	531.4	478.3	46.7	28.0

Table 3.4 shows that an initial investment shock of US$1 billion would result in US$900 million being spent (given an mpc = 0.9). When this US$900 million is received by workers and agricultural hardware dealers and so on, 90% of it is spent and 0.1 is saved so that US$810 million is passed back into the system with this second round of spending. The process will go on and on until the ripple dies out. The eventual addition to incomes from the initial government injection of US$1000 million is can be represented as the sum of US$1 billion + US$810 million + US$729 million. This represents the sum of a **geometric progression** with first term US$1 billion and the common ratio of 0.9. Algebraically the sum of a geometric progression can be found as:

$$\text{Sum} = \frac{a}{1-r} = \frac{US\$1 \text{ billion}}{1-0.9}$$

where

a = initial sum

r = common ratio

Substituting into our formulation $\dfrac{US\$1 \text{ billion}}{0.1}$ = US$10 billion.

In this simple setting the multiplier is 10 and an initial increase of US$1 billion leads to a US$10 billion increase in income. Note that because the multiplier process takes time to work itself through and because there may be a variety of shocks at work in the economy at the same time, the economy is more likely to be in a continuous state of disequilibrium but always tending towards equilibrium.

Calculating the multiplier

The simple multiplier can be easily calculated using the following basic steps.

Step 1: Define parameters

Keynesian consumption function C: $C_0 + c_1 Y$, where C_0 is autonomous consumption and c1 is the marginal propensity to consume.

Investment function $I = \bar{I}$

Government expenditure function $G = \bar{G}$

Taxation function $T = \bar{T}$

Export function $X = \overline{X}$

Import function $M = \overline{M}$

Aggregate national income $= Y$

The national income equilibrium is given by the identity:

$$Y = C + I + G + X - M$$

Step 2: Substitution

Using the national income identity, the equilibrium level of national income can be evaluated as:

$$Y = c_0 + c_1 Y + \overline{I} + \overline{G} - \overline{T} + \overline{X} - \overline{M}$$

Step 3: Gather terms

This step involves pulling all the like terms in Y together on the left-hand side:

$$Y - c_1 Y = c_0 + \overline{I} + \overline{G} - \overline{T} + \overline{X} - \overline{M}$$

Step 4: Factorising and simplifying

$$Y = (C_0 + \overline{I} + \overline{G} - \overline{T} + \overline{X} - \overline{M}) / 1 - c_1$$

$$Y = \left(\frac{1}{1 - c}\right) \times (c_0 + \overline{I} + \overline{G} - + \overline{X} - \overline{M})$$

where $\dfrac{1}{1 - c} = k$

Note that:

1 $\Delta Y / \Delta G$ = government expenditure multiplier

This is a number that indicates how national income will change if government expenditure changes. In general there is a positive relationship between changes in government expenditure and changes in national income. That is, if a government increases its level of expenditure then national income will rise, and vice versa.

2 $\Delta Y / \Delta I$ = investment multiplier

This is a number that indicates how national income will change if investment expenditure changes. In general there is a positive relationship between changes in investment expenditure and changes in national income. That is, if investment expenditure rises then national income will also rise, and vice versa.

3 $\Delta Y / \Delta X$ = foreign export multiplier

This is a number that indicates how national income will change if the level of exports changes. In general there is a positive relationship between changes in the level of exports and changes in national income. That is, if the level of exports increases, national income will also increase, and vice versa.

Activity 3.4

1 Copy and complete the following table.

Real income (Y) $ millions	Consumption (C) $ millions	Savings (s) $ millions
0	800	
2 500	2 800	

5 000	4 800	
7 500	6 800	
10 000	8 800	

2   What is the marginal propensity to consume?

3   Calculate the multiplier.

4   What is the equilibrium level of real income if investment spending is $500 million and government spending is $200 million?

5   State whether this economy is open or closed. Give one reason for your answer.

Feedback

1

Real income (Y) $ millions	Consumption (C) $ millions	Savings (S) $ millions
0	800	−800
2 500	2 800	−300
5 000	4 800	200
7 500	6 800	700
10 000	8 800	1200

2   The marginal propensity to consume is 0.8 (MPC = $\Delta C/\Delta Y$)

3   Multiplier (k) $= \dfrac{\Delta Y}{\Delta C} = \dfrac{1}{1 - mpc}$

Where z is the marginal propensity to spend out of national income

$= \dfrac{1}{1 - 0.8} = 5$

4   Equilibrium level of real income is where withdrawal from the circular flow of income equals injection.

Given that investment spending is $500 million and government spending is $200 million, injections equal 700 (500 + 200). Referring to the table derived above, the level of income in which withdrawal equals 700 is $7 500 million (withdrawal = savings). Therefore the equilibrium level of national income is $7 500 million.

5   This economy is a closed economy because there is no international trade transaction by the country.

National income equilibrium

Injections and withdrawals approach to national income equilibrium

In Chapter 1 of this Study Guide, three injections were introduced – investment, government spending, and exports – each of which were shown to be independent of the level of national income. Injections essentially increase the level of national income in the economy, via the

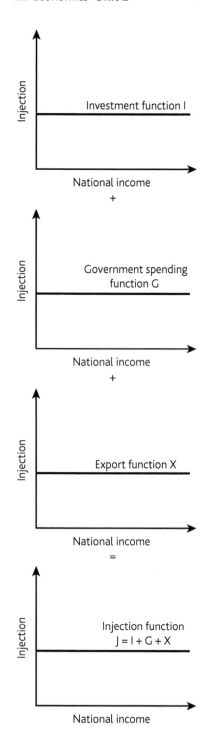

Figure 3.9 *Deriving the injections function*

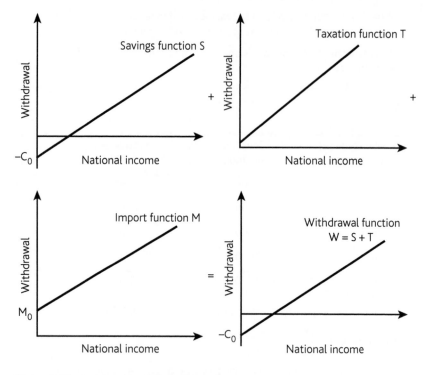

Figure 3.10 *Deriving the withdrawals function*

associated multiplier effects. Graphically the injections function (J) is therefore a summation of I, G and X, as shown in Figure 3.9.

Additionally there were three withdrawals: savings, taxes and imports. Each of these withdrawals functions were shown to have a negative impact on the level of national income. As with the total injection function, the total withdrawal function (W) is simply the summation of each of the three withdrawal functions. This is illustrated in Figure 3.10.

The withdrawals and injections approach to national income equilibrium shows that equilibrium occurs where the level of withdrawals is exactly equal to the level of injections. As indicated above, injections have a positive effect on national income while withdrawals have a negative effect on national income. If the level of injections exceeds the level of withdrawals, then there is a tendency for national income to rise, while if the level of withdrawals exceeds injections there is a tendency for national income to fall. There is no tendency for the level of national income to change when injections are exactly equal to withdrawals. The income level that corresponds to this situation is known as equilibrium national income (Figure 3.11, opposite).

Note that if the level of injections increases on account of an increase in investment spending, government spending or exports, then this will cause an upward shift (parallel) of the injections function, and as a consequence the equilibrium level of national income increases from Y_0 to Y_1, as shown in Figure 3.12. On the other hand, if the level of injections were to decrease, then the equilibrium level of national income would fall, to Y_1^*, also shown in Figure 3.12 (opposite).

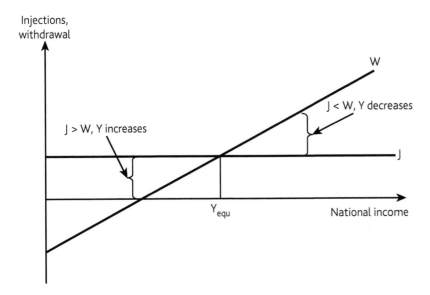

Figure 3.11 *Equilibrium – withdrawals injections approach*

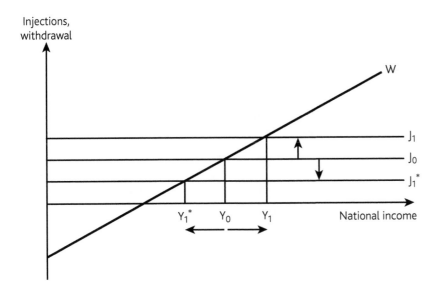

Figure 3.12 *The impact of changes in the level of injections on national income*

Net exports and national income

You will recall that the national income equilibrium level is given by the identity $Y = C + I + G + X - M$. Note that in the context of the above discussion, exports is defined as an injection and imports as a withdrawal from the circular flow of income system. The term x – m, or exports net of imports, can also be evaluated as net exports. Note that all else held constant, as net exports increase (implying that either exports is increasing or imports is falling), national income increases, and as net exports decrease (implying that either exports is falling or imports is rising), national income falls.

Feedback

Activity 3.5
Why is the value of the multiplier greater than 1?

Consider the following illustration.

In the country of Euphoria, assume that the conditions as per the applied example above, hold. The government of Euphoria has increased its level of expenditure by $100 million. The government spends directly on the public service by increasing wages and indirectly by expanding the number of grants and subsidies awarded.

The result of this increase in autonomous spending is that people's income would rise. As people's incomes rise, so too does their expenditure. Specifically, for every $1 increase in income received, consumption expenditure would increase by $0.75.

From the previous chapters, recall that expenditure is equal to income and is equal to output. In which case, as the level of expenditure of individuals increases, the income of the local merchants also increases. This process continues in rounds where for each round as income increases expenditure increases by 75% of the increase in income.

The cumulative effect of an initial increase is autonomous and is therefore greater than the initial increase. The following table illustrates this.

Round of spending	Increase in expenditure (millions)	Cumulative effect
Initial increase	100	100
2	75	175
3	56.25	231.25
4	42.19	373.44
5	31.64	305.08
6	23.73	328.81
7	17.80	346.61
8	13.35	359.95
9	10.01	369.97
10	7.51	377.47
All other rounds combined	22.53	400

From the above example, it can be seen that at every consecutive round of spending the increase in expenditure is 75% less than the previous round. The above illustration is shown diagrammatically in Figure 3.13 (opposite). This is because 25% of every increase in income earned at every round is saved or withdrawn from the economic system.

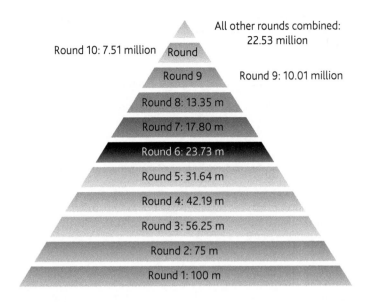

Figure 3.13 *Increase in expenditure at every round*

Alternatively, the effects of the multiplier can be explained as follows:

With the initial increase in spending, income immediately increases by the total of the increase – $100 million. Given that the mpc is 0.75, the second round of spending increases only by [(0.75) (100)] 75 million; in the third round [(100 x 0.75) (0.75)] 56.25 million. This process will continue indefinitely as shown below, where the cumulative effect of the initial investment would be:

$$(100 \text{ m} + (100 \text{ m} \times 0.75) + (100 \text{ m} \times 0.75)(0.75) \dots \dots \dots)$$

the totality of which is $400 million. This shows that an initial increase in government spending of $100 million with an mpc of 0.75 causes an increase in national income of the magnitude $400 million.

Multipliers in the Caribbean

The multiplier as defined above refers to a number that shows the extent to which national income changes if autonomous spending changes. In the Caribbean, the extent of the impact of changes in autonomous spending, given the amount of leakages from the economic system tends to be relatively small. One of the most significant leakages is that of imports. Table 3.5 shows the trend in the imports as a proportion of GDP for the period 1990–2006. Notice that throughout the data set, this ratio has been increasing and even exceeding 100% as in the case of Guyana.

Table 3.5 *Imports of goods and services as a percentage of GDP*

	Trinidad and Tobago	Barbados	Guyana	Jamaica	Suriname
1990	28.59	51.73	79.86	51.88	44.45
1991	32.93	50.14	128.03	51.39	44.95
1992	33.03	46.24	152.81	63.22	33.77
1993	39.09	51.56	137.23	55.63	22.24
1994	32.66	49.73	117.93	57.48	26.40

	Trinidad and Tobago	Barbados	Guyana	Jamaica	Suriname
1995	39.22	56.25	112.12	60.78	27.21
1996	41.28	56.67	108.72	55.28	30.76
1997	57.34	58.84	109.48	51.88	34.79
1998	53.82	55.09	107.91	49.73	52.49
1999	44.18	56.86	104.55	48.99	33.63
2000	45.49	57.04	110.69	53.92	33.20
2001	44.59	53.67	111.42	54.36	54.43
2002	44.74	55.33	105.46	55.24	39.59
2003	37.91	56.47	99.79	57.81	45.55
2004	41.36	60.98	105.66	59.89	47.83
2005	43.47	63.47	123.89	60.86	45.57
2006	–	–	–	63.04	–

Source: World Bank Development indicators (2008)

The income and expenditure approach: the Keynesian cross explanation

Earlier in this chapter the concept of the 45° line was developed. This line shows all the equilibrium points where expenditure is exactly equal to income. This concept will now be used to illustrate and evaluate national income equilibrium using the aggregate demand function.

The Keynesian aggregate demand function, Y, as shown above, is also known as the national income identity and refers to the sum of consumer spending, investment spending, government spending and net exports. Using the Keynesian cross diagram it can be shown that national income equilibrium corresponds to the income level where aggregate demand intersects the 45° line, as shown in Figure 3.14.

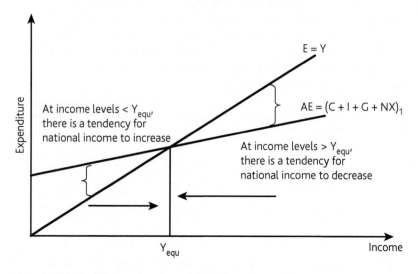

Figure 3.14 *Equilibrium – income and expenditure approach*

Y_{equ} is the equilibrium level of national income. At income levels below this level, the level of expenditure in the economy exceeds income (this is the zone where the apc is greater than 1), the result of which is that, through the multiplier effect, national income would increase. On the other hand, at income levels less than Y_{equ} the level of expenditure is less than income, the result of which is there would be a tendency for national income to decrease.

In Chapter 2 an overview of the Keynesian assumptions of the macroeconomy was presented. One of these assumptions highlighted Keynes's view that national income equilibrium can occur at income levels that are different from the full employment level of national income (output). The full employment level of output corresponds to that level of output produced when the economy is fully employed. Keynes therefore argued that national income equilibrium can occur at levels below or above the full employment level.

When national income equilibrium is less than full employment equilibrium, the difference between the actual level of aggregate demand and the level of aggregate demand required to achieve full employment equilibrium is known as a deflationary gap. Alternatively, when the actual national income equilibrium is greater than the full employment level, the difference between the actual level of aggregate demand and that required to restore full employment equilibrium is known as an inflationary gap. The deflationary and inflationary gaps are illustrated in Figure 3.15.

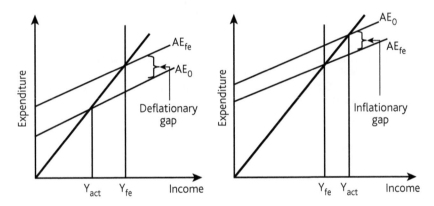

Figure 3.15 *Deflationary and inflationary gap*

Activity 3.6

1 Name the type of GDP gap illustrated in Figure 3.16 (overleaf).

2 Calculate the size of the GDP gap in Figure 3.16.

3 What is the equilibrium level of income?

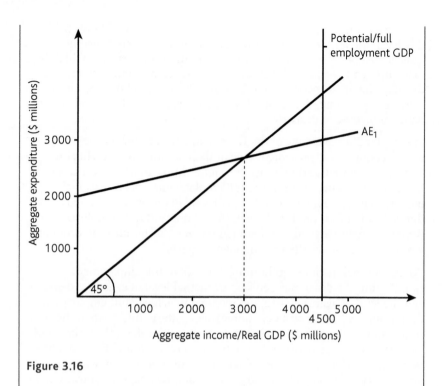

Figure 3.16

Feedback

1 Inflationary gap

2 $1500 million

3 $3000 million

Activity 3.7

The data in the following table refer to the GDP of country X.

Year	National GDP ($ bn)	Real GDP 1997 ($ bn)	Real potential GDP 1997 ($ bn)	Output gap	Growth in nominal GDP (%)	Growth in real GDP (%)
1990	2708.0	3776.3	3912.9			
1992	3149.6	3760.3	4090.9			
1994	3777.2	4148.3	4267.9			
1996	4268.6	4404.5	4499.8			
1998	4900.4	4718.6	4658.4			
2000	5513.8	4884.9	4966.0			
2002	5672.6	4848.8	5092.7			

1 Make a copy of the table. What was the percentage increase, to one decimal place, in each of the following for the period 1990–2002?
   a Nominal GDP
   b Real GDP
2 a Calculate the size of the output gap for each year stated and record your answer in the respective column in the table you have drawn.
   b State the years in which **a recessionary gap** and **an inflationary gap** existed.

Feedback

Year	National GDP ($ bn)	Real GDP 1997 ($ bn)	Real potential GDP 1997 ($ bn)	Output gap	Growth in nominal GDP (%)	Growth in real GDP (%)
1990	2708.0	3776.3	3912.9	136.6	–	–
1992	3149.6	3760.3	4090.9	330.6	16.3	–0.4
1994	3777.2	4148.3	4267.9	119.6	19.9	10.3
1996	4268.6	4404.5	4499.8	95.3	13.0	6.2
1998	4900.4	4718.6	4658.4	–60.2	14.8	7.1
2000	5513.8	4884.9	4966.0	81.1	12.5	3.5
2002	5672.6	4848.8	5092.7	243.9	2.9	–0.7

A recessionary gap existed in the years 1990, 1992, 1994, 1996, 2000 and 2002. An inflationary gap existed in the year 1998.

The aggregate demand and aggregate supply approach

A last approach that can be used to determine national income equilibrium is that of the aggregate demand and supply approach. This approach was dealt with in detail in the previous chapter and illustrated that national income equilibrium levels occur at the point of intersection of aggregate demand, short run aggregate supply and long run aggregate supply curves.

End test

1   What are the factors that affect consumption?

2   What is a consumption function?

3   Describe the Keynesian consumption function.

4   Illustrate the Keynesian consumption function.

5   Copy the following table and complete it with the missing values.

Analysis of the simple Keynesian consumption function

Y	C	S	apc	mpc
3000		–1000	1.33	
	4500	–500		0.50
5000		0	1.00	
6000	5500			0.50
7000		1000	0.86	
	6500	1500		0.50
9000		2000	0.78	
10000	7500			0.50

6   What is an economic multiplier?

7   Give three examples of economic multipliers.

8   How is national income equilibrium determined?

End test feedback

1   There are several factors that affect consumption. Some of these factors include the following:

   a   Income

   b   Age distribution of consumers

   c   Access to credit

   d   Inflation

   e   Taxes

2   The consumption function describes the relationship between consumption expenditure and the variables that influence it. A representative form of the consumption function is:

$$C = f(Y, \text{other variables})$$

   where

   C = aggregate consumption

   Y = aggregate income (current)

   Other variables include such factors as wealth.

3   A simplified consumption function proposed by John Maynard Keynes in *The General Theory of Employment, Interest and Money* can be expressed as:

$$C = C_0 + c_1 Y^d$$

   where C = aggregate consumption

   C_0 = autonomous consumption

   $c_1 Y^d$ = endogenous consumption

   c_1 = marginal propensity to consume

   y^d = current disposable income

4   The Keynesian consumption function should be illustrated as Figure 3.3 on page 43.

5   Analysis of the simple Keynesian consumption function:

Y	C	S	apc	mpc
3 000	4 000	−1 000	1.33	−
4 000	4 500	−500	1.13	0.50
5 000	5 000	0	1.00	0.50
6 000	5 500	500	0.92	0.50
7 000	6 000	1 000	0.86	0.50
8 000	6 500	1 500	0.81	0.50
9 000	7 000	2 000	0.78	0.50
10 000	7 500	2 500	0.75	0.50

6   An economic multiplier exists when a change in one variable triggers multiple changes in another variable. With economic multipliers each successive ripple of the initial change (or shock) is smaller than the first.

7   a   Government expenditure multiplier

   b   Investment multiplier

   c   Foreign export multiplier

8   National income equilibrium can be determined using various methods, including the injections withdrawals approach, the Keynesian cross approach and the savings investment approach.

4 Investment

Specific objectives

You should have an understanding of:

investment: autonomous and induced

marginal efficiency of capital (investment demand as a function of expected rate of return)

marginal efficiency of investment (non-interest rates as determinants of investment demand, taxes, costs, stock of capital goods on hand expectations

accelerator theory of investment

determinants of investment:

- the accelerator
- durability
- irregularity of innovation
- variability of profits, expectations and interest rates.

Investment: autonomous and induced

Investment spending refers to spending that increases the productive capacity of an economy – to the purchase of real resources. A firm's investment may comprise two types of spending: spending on expanding in fixed capital such as buildings, fixtures and fittings; and spending on inventory or stocks or raw materials. At the economy level, investment spending is undertaken to replace worn-out or depreciated capital, known as replacement investment, and to expand the capital stock, known as net investment.

Investment spending can also be regarded as being autonomous or induced. Autonomous investment refers to investment spending that is independent of the level of national income. In Chapter 1 of this Study Guide, investment was tackled briefly and shown to be independent of the level of national income. Autonomous investment in this regard is dependent on other factors such as the rate of interest and future expectations. This is addressed later in this chapter.

Induced investment, on the other hand, responds to changes in the level of national income. Increases in national income result in increases in the level of investment undertaken, while a fall in the level of national income results in a fall in the level of investment undertaken.

Induced investment is addressed later in this chapter.

The marginal efficiency of capital

At any point in time there are many potential investment projects that an economy can undertake. The internal rate of return is the discount rate that equates the initial cost of an investment with present value of the stream of returns generated by the investment. Let us assume that these projects could be stacked up in terms of their internal rates of return, starting with those projects with the highest internal rate of return (This is the discount rate that equates the initial cost of an investment with present value of the stream of returns generated by the investment. See http://www.commonfund.org.). If these investments are plotted on a graph, the resultant curve is the marginal efficiency of capital (MEC), also known as the marginal efficiency of investment (MEI) function.

The theory of the MEI was first introduced into economics discourse by John Maynard Keynes. With this theory, the rate of interest is determined by the monetary authorities. Given the MEI function the equilibrium level of investment is I_0. If there was a change in money market conditions such that the internal rate of return were to increase from i_0 to i_1, then the equilibrium level of investment would decrease from I_0 to I_1. Note that with the increase in the rate of interest, all of the investment projects between I_1 and I_2 become unprofitable.

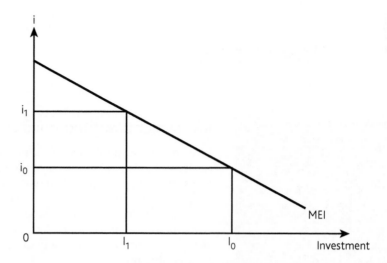

Figure 4.1 *The marginal efficiency of investment*

In terms of the responsiveness of investment to the rate of interest, consider Figure 4.2. Keynes defined the rate of interest as the cost of borrowing. Assuming that the rate of interest is r_0, which is equivalent to the internal rate of return (i), the level of investment is I_0. As the rate of interest falls the level of investment increases to I_1.

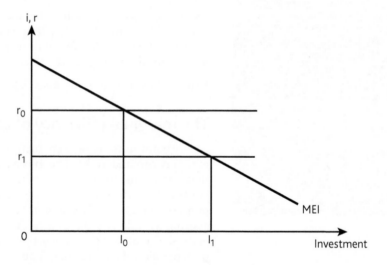

Figure 4.2 *The marginal efficiency of investment and the interest rate*

In terms of total aggregate demand, investment is a much more unstable component than consumption. This may be explained using the MEI theory as follows. When expected profits are high, business people will invest (this means that the MEI function shifts outwards). In contrast, when the expectation of profits is low, the MEI shifts inwards (Figure 4.3 (opposite)).

Observe that if the MEI falls to MEI_4 then the general economic climate will prevent investments altogether. This is what occurred in the Great Depression.

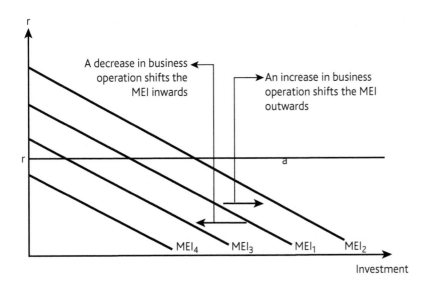

Figure 4.3 *Shifts of the MEI curve*

The Great Depression (1929–39)

The Great Depression refers to the period of severe economic contraction first experienced in the US, which then spread to the rest of the world. To date it is the longest economic depression experienced by western industrial economies.

Although the economic literature pointed to the fact that the US economy began to decline some 9–12 months previously, the event that marked the start of the 'depression' was the collapse of the New York Stock Exchange in October 1929. Over the next few years stock prices continued to fall so that by 1932 the average stock price was valued at a mere 20% of its 1929 value.

The decline in stock prices had a negative ripple effect throughout the American economy and in particular the financial sector. Commercial banks were hardest hit, especially those banks that held stocks in their portfolio. Of the 25 000 banks existing during that time, 11 000 filed for bankruptcy as a result. As the financial sector declined, the capital markets also declined along with the much-needed levels of spending in the economy. The result was a continuous downward spiral which crippled the economy. Unemployment increased to about 30% while output, especially from the manufacturing sector, also decreased (estimated fall in manufacturing output is 50%).

The decline in the US economy very quickly began to affect other economies which had developed trade and investment relationships with the US, in particular Germany and the UK. Unemployment began to rise in Europe, reaching as high as 25% in Germany, where it had a crippling effect on some of the industrial and export sectors.

Consequently the level of exports began to decline globally; countries began to impose heavy trade restrictions in an effort to protect their own domestic markets, which further exacerbated the decline in the already depressed global economy.

With the outbreak of the Second World War in 1939, the US and the rest of the global economy started to recover as the level of international demand began to increase.

The Great Depression marked a significant turn in the macroeconomic management literature:

> Prior to the Great Depression, governments traditionally took little or no action in times of business downturn, relying instead on impersonal market forces to achieve the necessary economic correction. But market forces alone proved unable to achieve the desired recovery in the early years of the Great Depression, and this painful discovery eventually inspired some fundamental changes in the United States' economic structure. After the Great Depression, government action, whether in the form of taxation, industrial regulation, public works, social insurance, social-welfare services, or deficit spending, came to assume a principal role in ensuring economic stability in most industrial nations with market economies.

Source: The Encyclopaedia Britannica

Accelerator theory of investment

The economics literature presents two predominant theories regarding the determination of the level of investment in the economy: the accelerator theory and the marginal efficiency of investment (MEI) theory.

The accelerator principle was first introduced into the economics literature by John Maurice Clark in 1923 in his publication *Studies in the Economics of Overhead Costs*. Clark showed that investment demand is closely correlated with consumer demand fluctuations under conditions of full employment. Keynes later developed these ideas further to explain the existence of investment and business cycles.

The accelerator theory is founded on the notion that investment in an economy is a function of the change in the level of income:

$$I_t = v \, (\Delta Y) = v \, (Y_t - Y_{t-1})$$

where v is the capital to output ratio (alternatively v is called the accelerator coefficient).

The change in income between two successive years (year t and year t-1) is given by $Y_t - Y_{t-1}$. Y_t is the level of national income in year t and Y_{t-1} is income in year t-1.

Gross investment may be defined as follows:

$$GI_t = NI_t + RI_t$$

where

GI = gross investment

N = net investment

RI = replacement investment

Note that the accelerator principle focuses on net investment. The accelerator principle may be illustrated using the data in Table 4.1 (opposite).

Table 4.1 *The accelerator principle*

Year	Current year income ($)	Last year income ($)	V	Net investment ($)
T = 2008	200	180	4	80
T = 2009	220	200	4	80
T = 2010	260	220	4	160
T = 2011	270	260	4	40

Let us assume that the income of an economy in 2008 was US$200 million and in 2007 it was US$180 billion. Assuming a capital to output ratio of 4, the increase in income of US$20 billion would require US$80 billion worth of capital to facilitate it. If in 2009 income increased to US$220 billion – again an increase of US$20 billion – then this would also lead to an increase in net investment of US$80 billion. If, however, in the year 2010 current income increased to US$260 billion then net investment would have to increase by US$160 billion. If in the last year, 2011, income increased by US$10 billion, this would lead to an increase in net investment by US$40 billion.

Feedback

The amount of net investment is conditioned by the growth rate of income and as income increases, the amount of net investment required increases as well.

Observe further that:

- a change in income each year by the same amount will lead to a constant amount of net investment

- an increase in the size of the change in income will result in an increase in net investment

- a decrease in the growth of income will see a decline in the size of net investment.

Activity 4.1

Interpret the results shown in Table 4.1.

Weaknesses of the accelerator theory

The accelerator theory has a number of limitations and these may be cited as follows:

1 **The theory is too mechanical:** The accelerator theory assumes that all firms react in a similar manner to an expansion in demand. In practice this is not true as some firms are more reserved while others may react overzealously by ordering in excess of the required amount of plant and machinery.

2 **No spare capacity:** The accelerator theory presumes that firms do not have any spare capacity. However, it is possible that some firms may actually be carrying spare capacity prior to any increase in demand and so may not need to engage any additional investments to increase productive capacity.

3 **Full capacity in capital good industries:** Even if there is an increase in demand for capital goods, the full-capacity operation of the capital good industry may limit its ability to meet a greater level of demand for capital goods.

Other determinants of investment

To illustrate the relationship between durability and the level of new investment, consider the following example. A particular household needs to replace its washing machine. The previous machine that the family owned lasted some five years. Now that it is worn and has depreciated, the washing machine needs to be replaced. The family makes the decision to purchase a new washing machine, perhaps with new features, with the expectation that it will last some years before it has to be replaced. It can, therefore, be concluded that the more durable an investment is, the longer it will be before it is necessary to replace or upgrade it.

The rate of innovation is another important determining factor of investment. Innovation often makes certain goods, processes or commodities obsolete. With a high rate of innovation, it is expected that the level of investment would be higher than if the rate of investment was irregular.

Determinants of investment also include the variability of profits and future expectation. Generally, a firm with a high degree of variability in its profitability levels is less likely to engage investment opportunities than a firm with a lower degree of variability in its profitability levels. Lower degrees of variability enable easier planning and forecasting.

Future expectations are a key factor in determining whether or not firms undertake investment opportunities. If firms are optimistic about the market and economic environment then they are more likely to engage in investment projects than if future expectations are dismal.

End test

1   What is investment spending?

2   Distinguish between autonomous and induced investment.

3   What are the two main theories associated with investment determination?

4   Define gross investment.

5   List three determinants of investment other than interest rate.

End test feedback

1   Investment spending refers to spending that increases the productive capacity of an economy. It refers to the purchase of real resources.

2   Autonomous investment refers to investment spending that is independent of the level of national income. Induced investment, on the other hand, responds to changes in the level of national income.

3   The economics literature has two predominant theories regarding the determination of the level of investment in the economy: the accelerator theory and the marginal efficiency of investment (MEI) theory.

4   Gross investment may be defined as:

$$GI_t = NI_t + RI_t$$

where

GI = gross investment

NI = net investment

RI = replacement investment

5   a Durability of the asset

b Profitability of the firm

c Future expectations

5 Unemployment and inflation

Specific objectives

You should have an understanding of:

the terms 'employed' and 'unemployed'

the unemployment rate

unemployment and underemployment

the effect on output, income and growth: additional financial burden on the state, social costs

labour immobility, other market imperfections, structural changes in the economy, inadequate aggregate demand, increase in labour force participation rate, seasonality, intervention

fiscal policy, monetary policy, wage subsidies, retraining programmes, investment tax credit, employment tax credit, government employment programmes, reducing market imperfections

inflation: general price level

real and money wages: real and nominal GDP, real and nominal interest rate

the GDP deflator, the retail price index, the producer price index, calculations and limitations of the indices

demand shocks, supply shocks, increase in the money supply growth rate

Unemployment

Employed and unemployed

The Central Statistical Office (CSO) of Trinidad and Tobago defines the labour force as the total of all persons aged 15 years and over 'engaged in or willing and able to engage in the production of goods and services', while persons who were actively seeking work within a three-month period and who at the time of the survey of the labour force were still 'looking for work', are defined as being unemployed. The minimum age of the labour force will vary from country to country. For example, the Education Act of Barbados CAP requires that children aged 16 years and under should be in educational institutions, not in the labour force.

The proportion of the labour force defined as being employed includes all persons who have 'worked for pay for any length of time (up to the time of the labour force survey), persons who were temporarily absent from work (due to vacation or sick leave) and persons who worked on a family firm or business or as an apprentice.'

One of the central variables of interest in macroeconomics is the unemployment rate (U) and this is defined as the proportion of the labour force that is unemployed and is actually seeking employment. It is calculated as:

$$U = \left(\frac{\text{number of persons unemployed}}{\text{labour force}} \right) \times 100$$

The unemployment rate is one of the most important macroeconomic variables as it provides an indication of the economic health of an economy in terms of its ability to provide jobs for people. Table 5.1 (overleaf) shows the trends in the unemployment rate for selected CARICOM economies 1995–2005.

Notice that for the period 1995–2005 the unemployment rate decreased for all of the listed economies except St Lucia, for which the unemployment rate marginally increased by 0.7 percentage points. In Barbados the unemployment rate fell by 10.5 percentage points, in Trinidad and Tobago by 9.2 percentage points and in Jamaica by 4.9 percentage points.

Unemployment and underemployment

While some workers may be actively unemployed, others may be underemployed. An underemployed worker is one who is working in a position that requires capacity less than his or her skill level, compensation or experience level. In other words, underemployment refers to a situation where an individual accepts a job for which they are overqualified so they are effectively working on a part-time basis.

The costs of unemployment

The implications, or costs, of unemployment extend far beyond the loss in income suffered by the unemployed individual. Society and the economy as a whole are losers when resources are unemployed or underemployed. Because unemployed resources produce no output, the economy as a whole produces at a level lower than that associated with its optimal potential. In this situation the economy operates within its production possibility frontier rather than along the curve itself. The loss in economic activity as a result of unemployed resources can be measured as the Gross Domestic Product (GDP) gap:

$$\text{GDP gap} = \text{potential real GDP} - \text{actual real GDP}$$

where the potential real GDP level can be defined as the level of output that corresponds to the point where all non-labour factors of production are fully employed and where unemployment is at its natural rate. The natural rate of unemployment is that level of unemployment which would exist in the absence of demand deficient unemployment – that is, the natural rate of unemployment includes those workers who are seasonally unemployed, frictionally unemployed and structurally unemployed. It should be noted however that the natural rate of unemployment is not fixed at a particular rate but rather varies as conditions in the economy change over time. The natural rate of unemployment is also known as the non-accelerating inflation rate of unemployment (NAIRU).

Table 5.1 *Unemployment rate for selected CARICOM economies, 1995–2005*

	1995	1996	1997	1998	1999	2000	2001	2002	2003	2004	2005
St Lucia	16.3	16.3	20.5	21.6	18.1	16.5	13.5	20.4	21.0	22.3	17.0
Barbados	19.6	15.8	14.5	12.3	10.4	9.3	9.9	10.3	11.0	9.8	9.1
Trinidad and Tobago	17.2	16.2	15.0	14.2	13.1	12.1	10.8	10.4	10.5	8.3	8.0
Jamaica	16.2	16.0	16.5	15.5	15.7	15.5	15.0	14.2	11.4	11.7	11.3

Source: Caribbean Development Bank and CSSP

A high unemployment rate can significantly reduce the growth potential of an economy. Consider for example the Great Depression: because of the high levels of unemployment in the US economy (statistics quoted that up to 30% of the labour force was unemployed), the level of spending required to reverse the effects of the depression was not forthcoming from the population, and this in turn exacerbated the depression.

Unemployment in this regard also presents an additional financial burden to the state as a whole, especially in those economies with social security facilities and unemployment benefits, as these transfers would increase as the rate of unemployment increases. Some of the addditional social costs associated with unemployment include poverty and crime.

Okun's Law

Okun's Law refers to the relationship between changes in the level of unemployment and a country's GDP. The American economist Arthur Okun in 1962 was the first to recognise that for every 1% increase in the rate of unemployment above the natural level, an economy's GDP would fall by an average of 2–4% from its potential level.

Causes and types of unemployment

The cause of unemployment has traditionally been a contentious issue, in that in each school of economic thought has proposed a different cause of unemployment. For example, the Keynesian school of thought defines unemployment as being involuntary and caused by the downturns in economic activity. Some types of unemployment are defined by their cause (Figure 5.1).

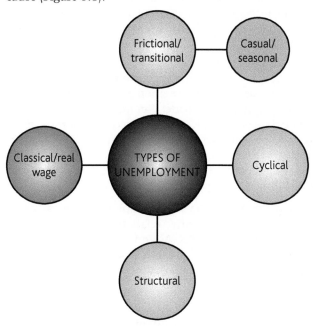

Figure 5.1 *Types of unemployment*

- **Frictional unemployment/transitional unemployment:** Frictional unemployment is defined as unemployment that arises as a result of the time lag associated with moving from one job to another. In other words, frictional unemployment may be defined as the result of the short-term movement of workers. Frictional unemployment may also arise as a result of geographical or occupational immobility, for example, unemployment may exist if unemployed labour and the demand for labour occur in two different geographical regions or if the skills of the labour force do not match the labour needs of the market.

- **Casual/seasonal unemployment:** This is one type of frictional unemployment. Specifically, this type arises as a result of the changes in the employment needs of certain industries. For example, casual unemployment occurs in the agricultural and tourism sectors, both of which experience peak and off-peak seasons.

- **Structural unemployment:** Structural unemployment results from the mismatch between the existing skills base of the labour force and the needs of the labour market. Specifically, structural unemployment arises when the capital stock of an economy cannot efficiently absorb the existing labour force. Structural unemployment can occur as a result of technological change or shifts in demand.

- **Classical/real wage unemployment:** The classical school of thought advocated that unemployment existed due to the excessively high real wage level, which rendered the market mechanism unable to clear. The backdrop against which the classical economists were writing, however, was the Great Depression. A more detailed discussion of classical unemployment is presented later in this chapter.

- **Keynesian/demand deficient/cyclical unemployment:** Keynes, also writing during the time of the Great Depression, highlighted that the major cause of unemployment was an insufficient level of aggregate demand. It was in this context that Keynes suggested that increased government intervention would stimulate aggregate demand and hence alleviate the problem of unemployment. Keynesian/demand deficient unemployment is, therefore, associated with economic downturns of the business cycle; it is also known as cyclical unemployment.

Labour market imperfections may also contribute to unemployment. Examples include imperfect knowledge and barriers to entry. Unemployed labour simply may not have access to information about available jobs and so remain unemployed. Another imperfection may relate to barriers to entry into a certain field. For example, many Caricom economies are characterised by high vacancy rates among nursing positions, but it takes an average of three years to become qualified as a nurse. Unemployment persists in these economies because the 'unemployed' may not posses the required skills base to fill the vacant positions.

The labour force participation rate refers to the fraction of the population that is in the labour force. There is a positive relationship between the participation and unemployment rates. Assuming a fixed or given number of positions, a higher participation rate would result in a larger proportion of the labour force being unemployed.

Policies to address unemployment

Governments are often faced with the challenge of reducing unemployment rates. The appropriate policy chosen will obviously depend on the nature and cause of unemployment. The various tools that policymakers have at their disposal to address the issue of unemployment include the following:

- **Fiscal policy:** Governments can use fiscal tools to manipulate aggregate demand. For example, an increase in government spending or a reduction in the rate of taxation has a positive effect on national income. The multiplier effect associated with such expansionary fiscal policy would increase the level of output income and employment in an economy.

- **Monetary policy:** Expansionary monetary policy has a similar effect on the economy as expansionary fiscal policy. Expansionary monetary policy includes the reduction in interest rates, reserve requirement rates, discount rates and the purchase of securities from the general public. Expansionary monetary policy is intended to increase the amount of spending in the economy and thereby generate economic activity to increase output, income and employment.

- **Wage subsidies:** Wage subsidies could either be targeted to a particular industry or to all industries. Wage subsidies is an employment generation programme in which the government (or other national labour organisation) provides funding to employers to encourage them to increase the level of employment.

- **Retraining programmes:** Retraining programmes can be used to augment the skills base of the labour force, and thereby reduce the level of structural unemployment. Retraining programmes enable the labour force to be dynamic and responsive to changes in the economic environment.

- **Investment tax credit:** An investment tax credit refers to a facility by which firms can reduce their tax burden by investing in physical capital formation, such as buildings and fixtures. The investment tax credit is designed to reduce the overall cost of production of the firm.

The reduction in the cost of production coupled with the increase in physical capital would increase the willingness of firms to hire more labour.

- **Employment tax credit:** An employment tax credit is another fiscal facility that governments can use to increase the level of employment in an economy. In particular, firms benefiting from an employment tax credit receive a tax credit and a reduction in their tax burden, which is an incentive to increase the number of persons employed.

- **Government employment programmes:** The government may also undertake employment programmes. These are specifically aimed at providing the unemployed with the various tools necessary to obtain employment. They can either be compulsory, being linked to unemployment benefits, or voluntary. Some of these programmes include teaching interview skills, resumé writing, work-based learning / on-the-job training, and work trials or 'temp' jobs. Governments may also set up centres or workshops that bring employers and the unemployed together. Additionally, the government may provide support in the form of information through the creation of a labour market database that members of the labour force and employers can access either to lodge or obtain information about job applications and job vacancies.

- **Reducing market imperfections:** Reducing the extent of labour market imperfections is another mechanism used to address the unemployment problem. As noted above, market imperfections may exist in the form of imperfect knowledge and barriers to entry. Through timely and accurate information dissemination the unemployed can obtain information about vacancies and opportunities that may arise in the labour market. The creation of a labour market database can help to reduce the imperfections associated with information access and dissemination. There may also be direct government intervention (see above) through specific programmes designed to improve the skills base of the labour force, enabling the unemployed to be more marketable and hence more likely to obtain employment.

Inflation

Inflation refers to the persistent rise in the general price level. Note the term 'persistent', which implies that the increase in prices is sustained over a prolonged period of time. Generally inflation is quoted in percentage points annually; so, for example, Trinidad and Tobago experienced an inflation rate of 8.6% in 2006 – that is, the general price level in 2006 increased by 8.6%. Table 5.2 shows the trends in the inflation rates of several CARICOM countries over the period 2000–05.

Table 5.2 *Inflation trends in select CARICOM countries, 2000–05*

	2000	2001	2002	2003	2004	2005
Trinidad & Tobago	3.56	5.54	4.14	3.81	3.72	6.89
Barbados	2.44	2.58	0.15	1.58	1.43	6.08
Guyana	6.15	2.63	5.34	5.98	4.67	6.93
Jamaica	8.17	6.99	7.08	10.32	13.63	15.30

Source: World Bank Data for CARICOM Countries (1960–2004)

The difference between absolute and relative price changes

In calculating the changes in the general price level, economists must consider the fact that in any economy some prices change faster than others. To this end understanding the difference between absolute and relative prices is key. Consider the following example which illustrates that a given basket consists of two goods, mangoes and oranges. The price level per pound is also given for two consecutive years, 2010 and 2011.

	2010	2011
1 lb mangoes	$2	$6
1 lb oranges	$4	$12

In 2010, the price per pound of oranges was twice that of the price of mangoes. This represents the relative price of oranges to mangoes in 2010. In 2011, the prices of both goods tripled. Consider the price per pound of mangoes whose price increased from $2 to $6. This represents an absolute increase in the price level of mangoes. The absolute price per pound of oranges has also increased.

Note, however, that although the absolute prices of mangoes and oranges increased, the prices of either good increased by the same proportion. This implies that the relative price relationship between the prices of mangoes and oranges has remained the same. Specifically, in 2011, the price per pound of oranges was twice that of the price per pound of mangoes, the same as in 2010.

Given that prices in any economy do not change by the same proportion in any given year, both the absolute prices as well as the relative prices change. In analysing the inflation rate, however, economists use the average of absolute price changes.

Types and causes of inflation

Each type of inflation can be defined by the factors that cause it. Specifically, there are two types of inflation: demand-pull inflation and cost-push inflation.

Demand-pull inflation: demand shocks

This type of inflation is generally associated with increased levels of spending. In other words, demand-pull inflation occurs when the supply capacity of the economy cannot effectively meet the increase in demand generated by an increase in spending. This type of inflation occurs when an economy is at or nearing full employment and aggregate demand increases.

Consider Figure 5.2 (opposite), which assumes that the economy is operating at full employment output level Y_{fe}, at a price level represented by P_0. Assume that the government initiates an expansionary fiscal policy, the evidence of which is that AD shifts from AD_0 to AD_1. In the short run, although the national output level increases to Y_1, the domestic price level also increases. This type of inflation is known as demand-pull inflation.

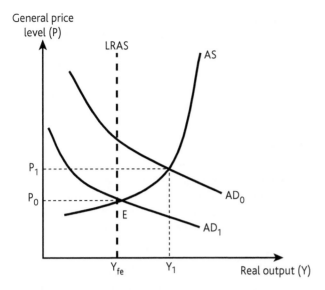

Figure 5.2 *Demand-pull inflation*

Inflation associated with the increase in money supply

This type of inflation is demand driven and often associated with the phrase '*too* much money chasing too few goods', implying that this type of inflation stems from changes in the money supply. During the 1950s Milton Friedman showed that as the money supply in the economy increased, assuming that the quantity of output and the velocity of circulation remained constant, prices would have to increase in order to maintain equilibrium in the market. This is the Quantity Theory of Money, which is evaluated in Chapter 6 of this Study Guide.

Cost-push/supply-side inflation: supply shocks

This type of inflation occurs as increases in production costs are passed on to consumers in the form of higher prices. Cost-pull inflation is, therefore, also attributed to profit-push and wage-push pressures. Specifically, the increases in the cost of production are passed on to consumers in order to maintain firms' profitability.

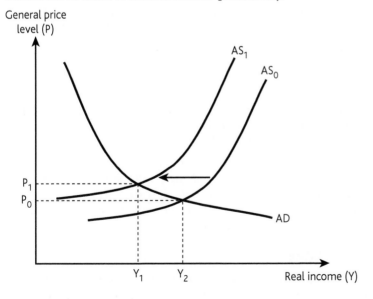

Figure 5.3 *Cost-push inflation*

Consider Figure 5.3, which assumes that the economy is operating at an output level of Y_{fe} and a price level of P_0. Assume now that the cost of labour increases. The evidence of this supply-side shock on the system is a leftward shift of the AS curve, which implies that firms become less willing to supply as their cost of production increases. The overall national output falls to Y_1 with domestic prices increasing to P_1. This type of inflation is known as cost-push inflation.

Real and money wages

Money wages or nominal wages refer to the actual wage earned. For example, if the wage rate per day is $100 and a labourer works for 20 days per month then his nominal or money wage is equal to $2 000. The labourer's real wage however refers to the purchasing power of wages. In particular, real wage is determined using the following formula:

$$\text{Real wage} = \frac{\text{nominal wage}}{\text{price level}}$$

To evaluate the labourer's real wage consider the following simplified example. Assume that the labourer purchases 20 items with his wages, each at a price of $10. In this case the purchasing power of his wage is 20 units. If the price per unit were to increase, say to $20 each, then the labourer would only be able to obtain 10 items. In this regard his real wage fell as a result of a rise in prices.

Inflation and interest rates

To explain the relationship between inflation and interest rates, consider the following example.

Inflation is assumed to be 10% per annum. With $1 000, Amartya can buy 10 books each costing $100 each today. In one year's time, however, to purchase the same number of books, he will need $1100.

The going interest rate – that is, the nominal or actual interest rate in the economy – is 20% per annum. If Amartya opts to save the $1 000 today, at the end of the year he would have $1 200 in hand with which he can now purchase the 10 books needed at a total cost of $1 100. Amartya would have earned $100 extra for postponing his purchases. In this case it can be shown that 10% is the real interest rate, or the net increase in purchasing power gained as a result of postponing consumption.

Specifically the real interest rate can be calculated as:

$$\text{Real interest rate} = \text{nominal interest rate} - \text{inflation rate}$$

In the example, the nominal interest rate is greater than the inflation rate. However, if the opposite occurred – that is, if the inflation rate outstripped the nominal interest rate – then Amartya would have lost purchasing power as a result of postponing his decision to purchase the books.

Using the above example, if the nominal interest rate was 5% then at the end of the year Amartya would have only earned $1 050, but the cost of the purchases would be $1 100. If this were the case, then Amartya would lose $50 purchasing power (or 5%, calculated as $5 - 10 = -5$) as a result of his decision to postpone his purchases.

Measuring inflation

As defined above, inflation refers to the persistent increase in the general price level. In this regard, changes in indices that represent the general price level can be used as a measure of inflation.

The retail price index

The retail price index (RPI) is the most common index used to measure and evaluate the inflation rate. It is a composite index which measures the changes in the average price level of a given basket of goods. Each of the commodities in this basket is assigned a particular weighting, implying that changes in the prices of those goods that carry a heavier weighting have a greater influence on the changes of the overall index. Consider Table 5.3 which gives the various components of the basket of goods and its associated weight used to calculate the RPI for the Trinidad and Tobago economy.

Table 5.3 *Basket of goods for the index of retail prices*

	Weight
Food	217
Meals out	14
Drink and tobacco	24
Clothing and footwear	104

Housing: total
    (Housing: ownership 196)
    (Housing: rent 20)
	216

Household operations	66
Household supplies and services	77
Health and personal care	62
Transportation	152
Recreation and reading	68
All items	1000

Source: Central Statistical Office for Trinidad & Tobago

There are several limitations associated with the use of the RPI. Not all expenditure patterns may be captured by the RPI, so the basket of goods used in rural communities, for example, may be different from that in cities and suburban areas. Black market activities and other expenditures arising out of the informal sector are also not considered.

The GDP deflator

Another index that can be used to evaluate the inflation rate is the implicit GDP deflator. This is a measure of the change in the price level of all domestically produced goods and services. The GDP deflator is calculated as:

$$\text{GPD deflator} = \left(\frac{\text{nominal GDP}}{\text{real GDP}} \right) \times 100$$

The producer price index

The producer price index (PPI) is also used to evaluate the inflation rate, though less frequently than the RPI. The PPI is used to measure the changes in the price received by producers for their output. This index can be defined as a weighted price index of wholesale prices. It is helpful because it offers analysts several benefits:

- The PPI is an accurate indicator of the expected changes in the consumer or RPI.
- Data for its calculation is generally easily and widely available.
- The PPI offers analysts a disaggregated view of the economy, so different industries show different trends.

Some of the weaknesses associated with the use of the PPI relate to the fact that producer markets are subject to a high degree of volatility, especially given the volatility of factor input markets. Additionally, the PPI does not always cover all industries in the economy.

The effects of inflation

With the persistent rise in the general price level, it is expected that some economic agents will benefit while others will lose. When inflation occurs, households living on a fixed income are faced with the problem of reduced purchasing power – as the domestic price level rises the amount of goods and services that a fixed level of income can command falls. Pensioners tend to fall into this category of fixed-income earners.

Savers or lenders also tend to lose when inflation occurs. Consider the following illustration. Over a period of one year Ava has saved $1 000, which she lends to her friend Jayelle. Assume that Jayelle uses this money to purchase 1 000 items costing $1. Assume now that inflation has occurred and that prices in the economy have doubled. Upon repayment of the loan, Ava can command only 500 items. It can, therefore, be concluded that lenders and savers lose because inflation reduces the purchasing power of money. Borrowers on the other hand gain: Jayelle was able to command 500 more items than Ava.

The economy as a whole also suffers as a result of inflation. Investment into productive sectors may be forgone for 'safer', less productive options: both individuals and firms may tend to opt for more stable investment options such as real estate in order to hedge against the loss in purchasing power associated with an inflationary economic environment.

Inflation and the impact on the balance of payments

Inflation, as defined above, refers to a rise in the general price level in an economy. As prices increase, the cost of producing all goods and services also increases. These increases in cost are often passed on to consumers in the form of higher prices, and some of these consumers include foreigners (through exports). As the price of exports becomes more expensive, other things being equal, the demand for exports will fall, thus worsening the balance of payments position.

Additionally, as domestic prices increase, local consumers may switch their demand to relatively cheaper foreign goods, thereby increasing the level of imports which, other things being equal, will result in a worsening on the balance of payments account.

Policies to address inflation

A government has a variety of tools that can be used to address the inflation:

- **Income policy:** This refers to the deliberate manipulation of the wage determination process in order to control unjustified wage increases and hence the inflation rate. As highlighted above, excess demand can fuel inflation by controlling the main determinant of demand: income. Governments can indirectly control the inflation rate.

- **Monetary policy:** Changes in the money supply can significantly affect price level in an economy, by augmenting the level of aggregate demand. Monetary authorities can manipulate monetary variables, including the interest rate, the money supply, the reserve requirement or the discount rate, in order to curb the rate of increase in prices in an economy.

- **Fiscal policy:** Government spending and taxation can be manipulated to reduce the level of aggregate demand, and hence the inflation rate in an economy. In particular, this can be achieved by a reduction in government spending complemented by an increase in taxation.

- **Supply-side measures:** Supply-side-oriented policies are geared towards expansion of the productive capacity in an economy. Supply-side policies are implemented to reduce the amount of production (supply-side) bottlenecks that contribute to rising prices. Some of these measures include investment in tertiary education, investment in capital formation and investment in infrastructural development.

> **Activity 5.1**
> **Class discussion:** Food price inflation in Trinidad and Tobago, in the context of rising global food prices.

Over the last few years, the national inflation rate has increased and the average for the period 2000–07 is some 1.5 times higher than that for the period 1990–09. In particular, the food inflation rate has skyrocketed. Notice in Figure 5.4 that food prices are subject to a greater degree of variability from month to month over the identified period. Notice also that the food inflation rate is above that of the national inflation rate, indicating that food prices exert significant pressure on domestic inflation rate.

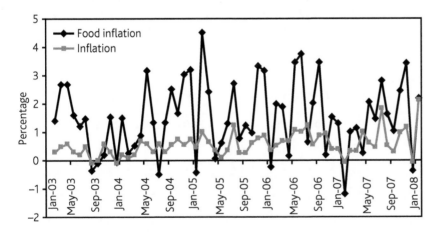

Figure 5.4 *Food inflation and national inflation rate, 2003–08*

This increase in domestic food prices is not peculiar to the Trinidad and Tobago economy. This phenomenon, coined 'agflation', has now become an international concern, rivalling even global warming.

According to the Food and Agriculture Organization (Growing demand on agriculture and rising prices of commodities, 2008) the prices of most agricultural commodities have risen internationally. This has been due to several reasons including diminished levels of world stocks for stable products such as wheat and corn (maize). Consequently over the period March 2005 to March 2007, the price of wheat in the US increased by some 34%, corn by 47.4%, and barley by 59.4%.

As a result the price of flour increased, a problem that was compounded by below average harvests in Europe in 2006 and 2007. Additionally, major agricultural producers experienced below average production levels due to severe changes in the weather patterns. In Australia, for example, severe frosts resulted in wheat output being less than anticipated. On the other side of the world, heatwaves during the summer of 2006 scorched orchard harvests, pushing the prices of sugar and juices upward.

Exacerbating these trends is the growing demand for agricultural land for the production of biofuels necessitated by an increase in the price of energy from fossil fuels. The green movement has significantly increased the demand for grain for the production of ethanol as an alternative fuel. The IMF (World Economic Outlook, Chapter 3, 2008) noted that this has resulted in an increase in the price of corn and soybean and reports have shown that these commodity prices are closely related to the trends in oil prices. These trends have also significantly and positively affected the price of edible oils, meat, dairy products and chicken.

With the changing policy orientation of the developed countries of the OECD, agricultural subsidies have been decreased, with the result that agricultural production in these countries has also declined. There has also been an increasing demand for food from the developing world, in particular from China and India.

For Trinidad and Tobago, however, these international influences, though significant, compound the effects of the Dutch Disease. On the commodity side, the influence of the growing dominance of the petroleum sector has essentially crowded out and crippled the agricultural sector in terms of production and export and hence the relative size of the cocoa, coffee, citrus and sugar sectors has declined in economic importance. On the other hand, there has been some expansion in the domestic agricultural sector, and agricultural prices have soared (Table 5.4). Notice from the data in the table that prices for many of the basic agricultural commodities in a typical household basket have increased by over 100% over the defined period.

Table 5.4 *Trinidad and Tobago: annual average food crop prices (TT$) received by farmers for traditional food crops, 1995–2005*

	1995	1996	1997	1998	1999	2000	2001	2002	2003	2004	2005	% change
Cabbage (kg)	2.61	2.80	2.23	4.01	4.32	2.53	3.89	4.01	3.76	4.82	4.50	72.4
Cucumber (kg)	1.08	1.14	1.43	1.48	1.44	1.45	1.35	1.51	2.12	3.06	1.40	29.6
Melongene (kg)	1.46	1.75	1.89	2.05	1.91	2.23	1.90	3.13	1.99	3.12	3.55	143.2
Bodi (bundles)	1.24	1.25	1.31	1.47	1.46	1.61	1.56	1.48	1.73	2.21	3.90	214.5
Ochro (singles)	0.04	0.06	0.07	0.07	0.06	0.07	0.06	0.09	0.21	0.25	0.26	550.0
Lettuce (heads)	1.24	1.36	1.06	1.24	1.52	1.48	1.53	1.48	2.14	2.24	4.39	254.0
Pumpkin (kg)	1.39	1.14	1.24	1.49	1.24	1.44	1.01	2.19	0.83	1.77	1.49	7.2
Pachoi (bundles)	1.12	1.44	1.11	1.54	1.49	1.55	1.42	1.53	1.40	1.88	3.39	202.7
Watermelon (kg)	1.49	1.25	1.34	1.99	1.93	2.24	2.15	4.79	2.14	2.13	1.15	−22.8
Celery (bundles)	0.32	0.29	0.29	0.31	0.32	0.32	0.32	0.54	0.31	0.30	1.04	225.0

Cauliflower (kg)	3.73	3.71	3.46	5.66	7.38	4.63	6.14	6.02	7.16	7.23	5.32	42.6
Chive (bundles)	0.56	0.43	0.36	0.40	0.37	0.48	0.47	0.47	1.16	2.04	7.71	1276.8
Hot pepper (singles)	0.06	0.07	0.05	0.10	0.06	0.11	0.06	0.13	0.09	0.17	0.24	300.0
Dasheen bush (bundles)	0.87	0.86	0.87	0.93	1.11	1.03	1.17	1.34	1.62	2.05	3.54	306.9
Sorrel (kg)	1.34	1.98	1.54	3.81	2.56	4.03	3.41	6.01	3.66	3.85	5.72	326.9
Cassava (kg)	1.82	1.62	1.80	2.51	2.12	1.94	2.41	2.34	2.37	2.18	1.88	3.3
Dasheen (kg)	1.69	1.45	1.42	2.22	1.68	1.79	2.62	2.60	1.88	1.87	1.78	5.3
Eddoes (kg)	1.63	1.85	1.85	2.77	1.94	2.65	3.23	2.85	3.76	3.28	2.71	66.3
Ginger (kg)	5.08	5.38	5.35	4.49	8.80	8.53	6.43	4.98	5.55	9.42	19.70	287.6
Sweet potato (kg)	2.62	1.70	1.69	3.14	2.18	2.90	3.41	4.11	5.02	4.34	2.74	4.6
Green corn (ears)	0.60	0.55	0.59	0.74	0.67	0.75	0.70	0.92	0.76	0.67	2.84	373.3
Beans (kg)	2.65	2.25	2.54	4.22	5.32	3.53	5.01	6.05	5.39	5.03	5.43	104.9
Pigeon peas (kg)	2.69	2.65	2.57	5.09	5.52	4.90	5.89	5.98	6.61	6.99	4.96	84.4

Source: Central Statistical Office for Trinidad & Tobago

If left unchecked these trends can lead to unrest not unlike that experienced in 1990.

Trade-off between inflation and the rate of unemployment: Phillips curve

Professor A.W. Phillips (1958), in *The Relationship Between Unemployment and the Rate of Change in Money Wage Rates in the United Kingdom*, established a close negative relationship between the rate of unemployment and the rate of money changes. He found this result using data for the period 1861–1956. This empirical relationship became known in the literature as the Phillips curve. Phillips began his theorising by noting that if labour demand was greater than labour supply, then the wage rate would increase. As the demand for labour increased further, the wage rate would rise and the supply of labour to the market would extend so that unemployment would tend to zero (or to the natural or full employment level).

In his actual empirical work, Phillips found that:

1 the relation was negative between money wage rate growth and unemployment (Figure 5.5, overleaf)
2 the zero rate of monetary increase was associated with an unemployment level of u_{fe}, or the non-accelerating inflationary rate of unemployment.

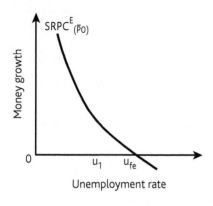

Figure 5.5 *The short run Phillips curve*

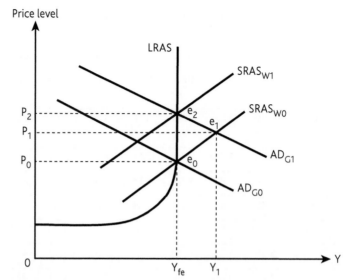

Figure 5.6 *The expectations-augmented Phillips curve*

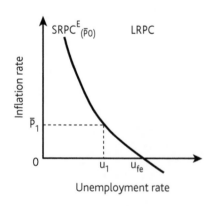

Figure 5.7 *Reconciling the fooling model*

Consider Figures 5.6 and 5.7. In Figure 5.6, let initial conditions be specified by AD_{G0}, LRAS and $SRAS_{W0}$. Let us assume that the economy is initially in full employment equilibrium so that we start off at the point e_0. In this initial scenario, the price level in the macroeconomy is P_0. Assume now that the government wishes to push the unemployment rate down by expanding the level of real national income from Y_{fe} to Y_1. At the prevailing wage rate, w_0, the government increases its expenditure from G_0 to G_1, forcing a shift in the AD curve from AD_{G0} to AD_{G1}. This encourages a movement from point e_0 to e_1. Thus, employment and hence output increases, alongside an increase in the price level from P_0 to P_1. Let this increase in the price level represent an inflation rate of $\bar{P}_1$. At $\bar{P}_1$; unemployment has now fallen from u_{fe} to u_1 (Figure 5.7). Note carefully that we are operating on a Phillips curve on which the expected rate of inflation is $\bar{P}^e_0$ while the actual rate of inflation has now risen to $\bar{P}_1$.

This is the proposed inverse relationship between inflation and unemployment: for any given expected rate of inflation, a rise in actual inflation above the expected rate leads to a fall in unemployment in the short run. It is at this point, though, that Professor Milton Friedman points out that this trade-off between inflation and unemployment is merely a short run phenomenon.

However, when expectations are brought into the discussion, using aggregate demand will not lead to a decline in unemployment, but will instead result in a higher rate of inflation. To see this consider Figure 5.6 again. At the point e_1 the actual inflation rate is P_1 and the expected rate of inflation is $\bar{P}_0^e$; $P_1 > P_0^e$.

With $P_1 > P_0^e$ firms enjoy an increase in profitability and increased output so that unemployment falls from U_{fe} to U_1 on the short run Phillips curve drawn on the assumption that the expected rate of inflation is 4%. Workers, however, will eventually realise that their money wages have fallen (because money wages are growing at 4% and the actual inflation rate has increased to 6%) and consequently ask for a 6% increase in money wages so that they can improve their real wage back to its original level. The growth in money wages increases the firms' cost of production and the short run aggregate supply curve shifts leftward. The increase in the expectation of inflation to 6% means that the Phillips curve shifts to SRPC 6%.

In the long run, the unemployment level remains at the full employment level. This is the natural rate of unemployment. In the long run, the Phillips curve is a vertical straight line.

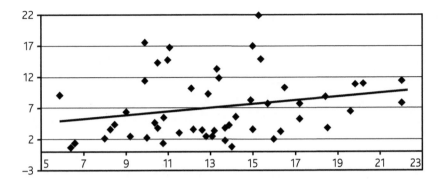

Figure 5.8 *The long run relationship between unemployment and inflation in Trinidad and Tobago, 1955–2006*

Figure 5.8 shows the scatter plot of the relationship between unemployment and inflation in the long run in the Trinidad and Tobago economy. The correlation between these two variables is 66%. The correlation score indicates that there is no long run relationship between the inflation rate and the unemployment rate in the Trinidad and Tobago economy.

In the short run, however, the scatter plot of the inflation rate and the unemployment rate shows a negative correlation of 84%, providing some degree of empirical support for the existence of an inverse relationship between unemployment and inflation in the Trinidad and Tobago economy.

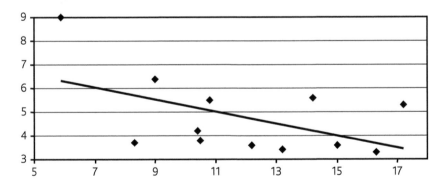

Figure 5.9 *The short run relationship between unemployment and inflation in Trinidad and Tobago, 1995–2006*

Stagflation

Before the 1960s the Phillips curve held. In the 1970s, however, both the unemployment rate and the inflation rate increased, a situation known as stagflation (Figure 5.10).

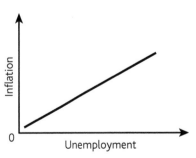

Figure 5.10 *Stagflation*

End test

1 How is the unemployment rate calculated?

2 How is unemployment associated with the GDP gap?

3 List the various types/causes of unemployment.

4 What types of policy can the government use to reduce unemployment?

5 What is inflation?

6 What are the types or causes of inflation?

7 How is inflation measured?

8 What is the relationship between inflation and unemployment in the short run?

End test feedback

1 The unemployment rate (U) (the proportion of the labour force that is unemployed, and is actually seeking employment) is calculated as:

$$U = \left(\frac{\text{number of persons unemployed}}{\text{labour force}} \right) \times 100$$

2 The loss in economic activity by virtue of unemployed resources can be measured as the GDP gap.

3 • Frictional unemployment
   • Structural unemployment
   • Causal/seasonal unemployment
   • Classical unemployment
   • Keynesian unemployment

4 • Fiscal policy
   • Monetary policy
   • Retraining policy
   • Investment and employment tax credits

   • Government employment programmes
   • Reduced market imperfections

5 Inflation refers to the persistent rise in the general price level. The term 'persistent' implies that the increase in prices is sustained over a prolonged period of time.

6 • Cost-push inflation
   • Demand-pull inflation
   • Increase in money supply

7 Changes in indices that represent the general price level can be used as a measure of inflation. The most common index used to measure and evaluate the inflation rate is the retail price index (RPI).

8 In the short run there is a negative relationship between inflation and unemployment. In the long run there is no relationship between inflation and unemployment. This relationship is illustrated using the short run Phillips curve. Look back to Figures 5.6 and 5.7 on page 78 and the explanatory text.

6 Monetary theory and policy

Specific objectives

You should have an understanding of:

the meaning of money

types of money: token and commodity

functions of money

Liquidity Preference Theory

motives for holding money (transactions, precautionary, speculative)

the money supply (M1, M2)

monetary policy – expansionary and contractionary policies

the role of the central bank in creating high-powered money (monetary base)

instruments of monetary control: open market operations, discount rates, financing fiscal deficits, reserve requirements, moral suasion, interest rates

excess reserves, credit creation, the money multiplier

the nature of currency substitution and hoarding

the Quantity Theory of Money

tight monetary policy (inflation), easy monetary policy (unemployment), balance of payments

how monetary policy affects national income

The nature of money and its functions

Before money came into existence, exchange was based on barter. This involved the exchange of one type of goods for another. It is founded on the principle of mutual desire.

Bartering as a system of exchange was discontinued for three substantive reasons:

1 It was difficult to satisfy the double coincidence of wants which is an important base criterion for exchange to take place in a system of barter.

2 It was difficult to determine exchange rates, for example, how many kidney beans per calf.

3 Some commodities were not easily divisible.

The use of a monetary unit helped to override these problems:

1 There was no longer a need for a double coincidence of wants as money could now be used to pay for goods.

2 Money was now the medium through which exchange took place.

3 Money could be used to facilitate any size of transaction.

Types of money: token and commodity

There are essentially two types of money: token money and commodity money.

- **Token money** was the term used to describe the counters or tokens originally issued by traders and bankers as a record of monies deposited by the public. Today it is used to describe the currency in circulation and includes notes and coins.

- **Simply commodity money** refers to a medium of exchange that has value both as a commodity and as money. In particular, furs, shells and tobacco, which have been used as a medium of exchange in the past, are examples of commodity money. Other examples include gold, silver, copper, salt and alcohol.

The functions of money

Money has to perform the following functions:

- It must serve as a **medium of exchange:** Money facilitates the exchange of goods and services within an economy. Workers in various segments of the economy accept money as a form of payment for goods and services because money can be exchanged for goods and services within the economy.

- **Unit of account:** This means that the price of goods and services can be quoted in monetary terms. Money, therefore, provides us with the flexibility to value the vast miscellany of things that make up the economy.

■ **Store of value:** Money allows wealth from one period to be available in another time period. It provides the most convenient means to set aside part of current income for savings. For example, instead of putting aside sea shells or corn cobs under a non-monetised economic system, one can now set aside money to meet expenses later on.

■ It must act as a **standard of deferred payment:** Money allows economic agents to draw up hire purchase arrangements and mortgage agreements. Money makes these types of payment at a future date possible.

To perform these functions, money must possess the following seven attributes:

1 **Acceptability:** Money must be acceptable as a means for the settlement of debt.

2 **Durability:** Money should not wear out quickly, so that wealth can be transferred from one time period to another.

3 **Homogeneity:** Monetary units should be identical so, for example, each dollar bill should be same as the previous one.

4 **Divisibility:** Money should be divisible so that both expensive and low-priced commodities can be easily valued.

5 **Portability:** Money should be easy to transport, for example, in one's wallet or purse, without being excessively bulky or heavy.

6 **Stability of value:** Over time money should maintain its value.

7 **Difficult to forge:** Money should not be easy to duplicate, as this could erode its worth as a medium of exchange.

Feedback

1 Store of value

2 Medium of exchange

Activity 6.1

Indicate which function of money is demonstrated in *each* of the following activities.

1 Farmer Brown puts his cash in his mattress.

2 Mr Lee, a salesman, buys $100 worth of gasoline per week.

Liquidity Preference Theory

The Liquidity Preference Theory was introduced by John Maynard Keynes, in his book *The General Theory of Employment, Interest and Money*, published in 1936.

The theory shows that the demand for money is determined by the transactionary motive (T^m), the precautionary motive (P^m) and the speculative motive (S^m). These three motives can be combined to give a single demand curve by adding onto the demand for active balances ($T^m + P^m$), which is not influenced by the rate of interest, to S^m, which is influenced by the rate of interest.

Motives for holding money

Transaction demand for money

This refers to money held for the explicit purpose of meeting everyday or expected economic expenses. These might include money demanded for the purpose of purchasing food, travelling to and from work, and so on. The amount of money held for transactionary purposes is a function of the level of income of the household. Consequently, and as Figure 6.1

shows, an increase in income from Y_0 to Y_1 leads to an increase in the amount of income held for transactionary purposes from T_0 to T_1.

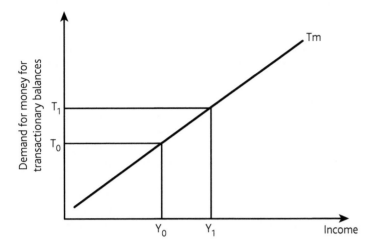

Figure 6.1 *Transaction demand for money*

Precautionary demand for money

Precautionary demand for money refers to the demand for money to meet unforeseen contingencies. For example, a person may carry a transactionary amount of money with him or her when going somewhere unfamiliar, in case there isn't an ATM available. Like the transactionary demand for holding money, one's precautionary balance is a positive function of income. If this argument is extended it would mean that a low-income household will hold a lower precautionary balance (say P_0) than a higher-income household (P_1).

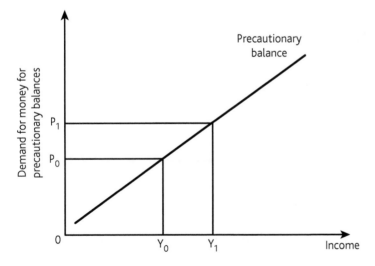

Figure 6.2 *Precautionary demand for money*

Speculative motive

Holding money balances is often preferred when the market value of other assets is volatile. Keynes suggested that if people expected bond prices to fall, they would respond by selling bonds and building up their money balances.

If money is put into assets it provides utility; for example, from furniture we get pleasure. If we put money in a bond we get a dividend. Thus holding money in pure liquid form carries some type of opportunity cost which may be labelled as the rate of interest, and so before people hold money in a liquid form they have to consider this cost. As the rate of interest increases, the greater will be the cost of holding money. Building on this logic, Keynes argued that people hold idle balances to take advantage of changes in the price of bonds. He called this motive for holding money the speculative motive (S^m).

To simplify the discussion for this section, the analysis focuses on undated bonds but it is assumed that all security prices move in the same direction. At any one point the price of some bonds may increase and some may decrease. At other times, however, bond prices may be moving in the same direction together. If economic agents expect that the price of bonds will increase, by virtue of falling interest rates, then they will buy bonds now and sell them in the future to make a capital gain. If they think the price of bonds will decrease, by virtue of rising interest rates, they will sell bonds and keep money, as money will now represent a better store of value.

Given that bond prices and the rate of interest are inversely related, it follows that one can relate the demand for money to the demand for speculative balances, as shown in Figure 6.3. The graph curve shows that when interest rate is at a level such as r_0, the speculative demand for money balances is lower than if the interest rate was at r_1.

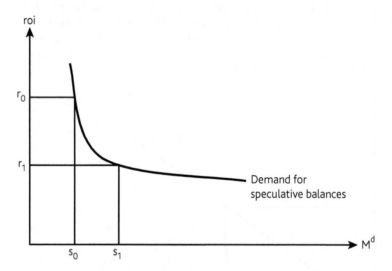

Figure 6.3 *Speculative demand for money*

Figure 6.4 (opposite) illustrates the demand curve for money balances. It is simply a horizontal summation of the transaction motive, precaution motive and the speculative motive for holding money.

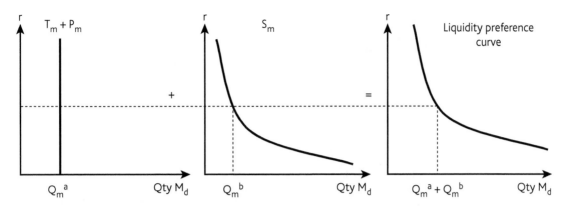

The demand for active balances, i.e. transactionary and precautionary demand for money – unresponsive to interest rate changes.

Speculative demand for money is inversely related to the demand for money balances.

The total demand for money curve, the liquidity preference curve, is the horizontal summation of T_m, P_m and S_m at each interest rate.

Figure 6.4 *Deriving the liquidity preference curve*

The money supply (M1, M2)

The money supply refers to the quantity of currency in circulation in an economy at a particular time. The money supply also includes demand deposits.

In trying to distinguish monetary assets in terms of their liquidity, economists have produced several definitions of the money supply, including M1 and M2.

M1: Defined as narrow money and refers to the total of all currency, travellers' cheques demand deposits and other checkable deposits. Currency includes both coin and paper money in circulation. (M0 refers to the currency and is included in M1 which is the narrow monetary base.)

M2: The M2 money supply includes assets in less liquid form than M1. The M2 money supply consists of M1 together with savings deposits and small denomination time deposits. (Savings deposits include all ordinary savings accounts, also known as 'passbook'-type savings accounts, held at commercial banks, as well as money market deposit accounts. A time deposit, also referred to as a term deposit, refers to monies deposited into any account held at a commercial banking institution that cannot be withdrawn for a specified period of time. A small denomination time deposit is therefore a deposit under a certain defined threshold; in the US, for example, the threshold is $100 000.) In some countries a third component of M2 is retail money market mutual fund balances.

Table 6.1 (overleaf) shows the trends in some of the different types of deposit at commercial banks. Note that between 1995 and 2007 the balances in demand deposits, savings deposits and time deposits increased significantly.

Table 6.1 *Trinidad and Tobago commercial bank sector*

	Total deposits (TT$ million)	Demand deposits (TT$ million)	Savings deposits (TT$ million)	Time deposits (TT$ million)
1995	12 349.91	2 827.98	4 827.47	4 694.46
1996	12 888.06	3 052.71	5 320.55	4 514.80
1997	14 168.09	3 567.10	6 066.09	4 534.90
1998	16 202.42	3 757.41	6 754.50	5 690.52
1999	16 463.18	3 993.36	7 132.31	5 337.52
2000	18 516.71	4 959.39	7 561.28	5 996.04
2001	21 430.05	6 510.28	8 509.48	6 410.29
2002	22 503.98	8 075.68	8 843.06	5 585.24
2003	23 817.70	8 262.93	10 575.79	4 978.98
2004	27 647.57	10 563.44	11 525.77	5 558.36
2005	34 306.11	13 277.05	13 001.10	8 027.96
2006	42 282.73	14 563.09	15 677.23	12 042.41
2007	47 705.71	15 521.95	17 629.66	14 554.10

Source: Central Bank of Trinidad and Tobago

Table 6.2 shows trends in the money supply aggregates for the Trinidad and Tobago economy. Note that each component of the money supply increased, implying that the overall money supply also increased over the period 2003–07.

Table 6.2 *Trinidad and Tobago money supply aggregates*

Date	Currency in active circulation	Base money M_0	Narrow money M_{1A}	Money supply M_2
2003	1 708.60	4 663.80	7 309.40	18 593.30
2004	1 957.40	4 739.90	8 377.60	20 841.20
2005	2 425.40	7 097.90	12 316.10	28 012.40
2006	2 654.40	8 342.40	13 507.90	32 859.90
2007	3 182.80	9 269.30	15 122.10	37 323.10

Source: Central Bank of Trinidad and Tobago

Monetary policy

Monetary policy gained ascendancy in the economics literature during the 1980s when monetarism as an arm of macroeconomic theory became more popular. Monetary policy refers to the deliberate actions of the monetary institutions to manipulate monetary instruments to achieve macroeconomic objectives. Some of these objectives include:

- full employment
- stable prices

Activity 6.2

Indicate whether *each* of the following could be included in the M_1 (narrow money) or M_2 (broad money) definition of the money supply.

1   A demand deposit in First Nation Bank

2   A savings account in Northern Savings Bank

Feedback

1   M_1

2   M_2

- a consistent but satisfactory level of economic growth
- equilibrium in the balance of payments account.

Some of the monetary instruments include the interest rate, the reserve requirement, the discount rate and open market operations. Manipulation of these variables affects the money supply, and hence the level of aggregate demand. Monetary policy can be manipulated to increase the money supply and thereby increase the level of aggregate demand, which is known as expansionary monetary policy. Expansionary monetary policy can involve lowering the interest rates, the reserve requirement and the discount rate, or the purchase of securities from the public. Additionally, monetary policy can be used to lower the level of aggregate demand, in which case contractionary monetary policy would involve an increase of the interest rate, reserve requirement and discount rate as well as the sale of securities to the public.

The main target variables of monetary policy are the rate of interest and the M^S. These are not independent variables – it is not possible to fix both the supply of money and the price of money. In Figure 6.5 the monetary authorities can choose a target level of money supply, say M^S_0, and given the liquidity preference in the economy will then need to accept a rate of interest of r_0. In turn if the monetary authority wanted a rate of interest of r^1 they would have to accept a money supply of M^S_1.

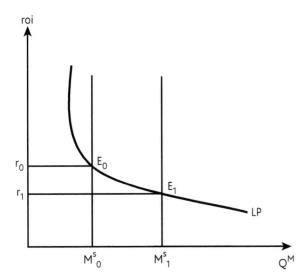

Figure 6.5 *The targets of monetary policy*

The role of the central bank in creating high-powered money

Professor Milton Friedman noted that to control the money supply it was necessary to control the size of the monetary base, where the monetary base is defined as monetary assets that are highly liquid, such as cash, demand deposits and checkable accounts. To control the issuing of loans, the government could proceed as follows. The significant part of the monetary loans is the supply of high-powered money. The monetary authorities can reduce the amount of cash that is available to the banking system, say through open market operations or increasing the legal reserve requirement.

In order for a strategy of control to have a predictable effect on the money supply and hence the economy, the money multiplier in the economy must be stable. The commercial banks must not simply adjust their cash-to-reserve ratio in response to a cash squeeze.

For a system of monetary base control to be effective, the central bank must relinquish its role as a lender of last resort – otherwise money squeezed out of the system can re-enter through the discount market.

Instruments of monetary control

There are seven principal instruments of monetary control:

- Open market operations
- Legal reserve requirement
- Discount rate
- Financing fiscal deficits
- Moral suasion
- Selective credit control
- Interest rates

Open market operations

Open market operations (OMO) are the sale or purchase of securities on the money market by the government. Governments use OMO when they want to influence the money supply in an economy. OMO can either give the bank more reserves or take away reserves from them and in so doing this can expand or contract the money supply. When the government thinks the money supply is too low, it can issue instructions that lead to an increase in the purchase of securities and treasury bills, thereby pumping money into the banking system. Similarly, but from the opposite position, if the government wants to decrease the money supply it can sell securities on the open market and as economic agents purchase these securities, money flows out of the system, promoting a contraction in the supply of money.

Legal reserve requirement

Commercial banks are required by law to keep a proportion of their deposits with the central bank. This is referred to as the legal minimum reserve requirement. Suppose that the government of, say, Guyana decides its money supply is too low, then it can decrease the reserve requirement of commercial banks so that there is an expansion in the proportion of money banks have for lending. The reverse is also true: if the central bank wishes to decrease the money supply, it can simply increase the reserve requirement and take money out of the system.

Example

The reserve requirement as a tool of monetary control

Caribbean

The reserve requirement is one of the only direct tools of monetary control that central banks in the Caribbean use. The reserve required, as defined above, is that proportion of deposits that commercial banks must 'keep on hand' in order to facilitate the daily transactions of their customers. The reserve requirement therefore imposes stipulations on the credit facilities that commercial banks can extend to the public and, by extension, it can be used manipulate the money supply.

Trinidad and Tobago

There has been a conscious policy direction on the part of the central bank to reduce the reserve requirement for commercial banks. In 2003 the central bank undertook the first of three phases to implement this strategy:

- Phase 1: Reduction in the reserve requirement from 18% to 14% of deposits – implemented October 2003.

- Phase 2: Reduction in the reserve requirement from 14% to 11% of deposits – implemented September 2004.

- Phase 3: Reduction in the reserve requirement from 11% to 9% – yet to be implemented.

According to the Central Bank of Trinidad and Tobago, the statutory reserve requirement as at 30th November 2010 is 17%.

Jamaica

The following is a chronological list of the changes in the reserve requirements imposed by the Bank of Jamaica on commercial banks:

- 01/08/2002: The liquid asset ratio for commercial banks was reduced from 27% to 23%.

- 10/01/2003: Each commercial bank was required to lodge 5% of all deposits at the Bank of Jamaica.

According to the Bank of Jamaica, effective from the 1st July 2010, the reserve requirement is 12%.

Guyana

The Bank of Guyana, the foremost monetary institution in Guyana, publishes its required reserves on a weekly basis. The following table provides a summary of this information and also shows that the actual amount of reserves lodged with the Bank of Guyana for the first two quarters of 2007 were always greater than the stipulated amount.

According to the Bank of Guyana, the effective reserve requirement for commercial banks in 2009 stood at 12%.

Table 6.3 *Required reserve for the Bank of Guyana, 2007 (G$ million)*

Date		Required reserves	Actual reserves
January	5	18 882.2	25 488.2
	12	18 991.8	27 146.2
	19	19 304.0	25 806.0
	26	19 444.6	25 956.1
April	6	19 528.7	22 215.7
	13	19 721.5	23 857.8
	20	19 990.6	27 355.7
	27	20 133.0	25 175.8

Source: Bank of Guyana

Discount rate

The discount rate refers to the interest rate at which commercial banks can borrow from the central bank. By varying the discount rate – the cost of borrowing loans from the central bank – the government can regulate how much money is at the disposal of the commercial banks and so can influence the money supply. If the central bank decreases the discount rate, commercial banks will borrow more and the money supply will increase. If the central bank increases the discount rate, it can decrease the amount of money at the disposal of the central bank and so doing increase the money supply.

Financing fiscal deficits

The government may use the tools of monetary financing to cover fiscal deficits. These may include increasing the money supply or actually printing more money (this practice is known as seigniorage). However, financing deficits in this way can exert inflationary pressures on the entire economy, and may also result in the crowding out of the private sector. According to the World Bank (Global Development Finance, 2006): 'Monetary policy needs to be insulated from the pressures created by the government's need to finance its fiscal deficit. The authorities need to curtail monetary financing of the fiscal deficit, and the government should pay market rates of interest on its debt and refrain from pressuring the central bank to keep interest rates low'. Efforts should, therefore, be made to maintain the political independence of the monetary authorities.

Example

Applied monetary policy in Trinidad and Tobago: anti-inflationary strategy

The inflation rate reached 10% by the third quarter of 2006. Consequently the central bank of Trinidad and Tobago shifted its 'anti-inflation' strategies towards mopping up the excess liquidity in the system. The existence of excess liquidity in the system reduced the level of effectiveness of interest rate policy. The central bank opted for a more directed approach, through the auctioning of securities, designed to lower the rate of spending and to encourage longer-term investment.

Over the period November 2006 to November 2007, government bonds sold amounted to $3 103 million, the total of which central bank sterilised. These bonds are estimated to mature at periods between 5½ and 10 years' time. Other anti-inflationary strategies used by the central bank included:

- the imposition of a secondary reserve requirement
- a special insurance of government securities at the bank
- an intensified programme of ONOs.

Through these measures the central bank of Trinidad and Tobago was able to reduce the level of liquidity in the system.

Activity 6.3

1 List *two* of the *major* monetary policy instruments available to a central bank.

2 State how *each* of the policy instruments you listed in (1) could be used to increase the money supply.

3 How will an increase in the interest rate affect the demand for money?

Feedback

---

1 Two major monetary policy instruments available to a central bank are open market operation and the reserve requirement.

2 The *open market operation* can be used to increase the money supply by issuing instructions that the money supply be expanded through the purchase of securities like treasury bills from private individuals and banks that wish to sell.

   The *reserve requirement* can be used to increase the money supply by lowering the required minimum reserves so that the excess reserves and, therefore, the money supply will increase.

3 An increase in the interest rate will cause the quantity demand for money to fall. This is so because at higher interest rates it becomes more attractive to hold non-liquid assets such as bonds.

Moral suasion

Moral suasion is persuasion in the form of letters and verbal statements which the central bank uses to encourage commercial banks to take a particular line of action that they consider necessary.

Selective credit control

Selective credit control refers to a non-traditional technique that the central bank can use to discourage particular types of investment. A central bank may wish to limit spending on, say, consumer durables and may offer preferential treatment (in terms of favourable discount rates) to those commercial banks that adhere to its directive.

Excess reserves

This refers to the reserves held by commercial banks in excess of the stipulated reserve requirement.

Credit creation

Credit creation refers to the process by which commercial banks, through a system of fractional reserve banking, creates money by issuing loans.

The money multiplier

The money multiplier is simply a number that indicates the amount by which the money supply would increase if commercial banks' reserves or deposits increased by $1. The money multiplier is calculated as:

$$\text{money multiplier} = \frac{1}{\text{reserve requirement}}$$

The role of commercial banks in creating money

For the purpose of this section a commercial bank may be defined as an institution that can accept deposits from the general public and creates deposits for the general public when it makes loans to the general public. The following is a demonstration of how a commercial bank can create money; for simplicity, this illustration assumes that there is only one commercial bank in existence.

Let us assume that the bank receives a cash deposit and that it has historically deduced that a customer would not, at any point in time, demand all of its cash deposits. This means that a prudent banker would only need to keep a certain proportion of the initial deposit to meet customer demands for cash. The remaining balance can be loaned to borrowers. (If the bank does not lend out any of the $1 000 then it is simply a safe deposit institution. While banks do perform safety deposit activities, they also lend money out to customers.)

Assume here that an individual deposits $1 000 cash into the bank.

After the initial deposit, the commercial bank's balance sheet may be presented as:

Liabilities		Assets	
Customers' deposits	1000	Cash	1000

Presuming a reserve requirement of 10%, the bank can lend the extra $900. After the first loan is issued, and an additional account is created for the first borrower, the bank's balance sheet would be represented as:

Liabilities		Assets	
Initial deposits	1000	Cash	1000
Created deposits (first borrower)	900	Loans	900
Total liabilities	1900	Total assets	1900

Recall that the reserve requirement is 10%, which implies that the bank is only obliged to hold $90 for the first borrower, so the bank can issue another loan up to $810. If this is done, the bank creates another account for the second borrower, to whom was issued a loan on $810. After the second loan is issued the bank's balance sheet can be represented as:

Liabilities		Assets	
Initial deposits	1000	Cash	1000
Created deposits (first borrower)	900	Loans	900
Created deposits (second borrower)	810	Loans	810
Total liabilities	2710	Total assets	2710

Again, the bank is only obliged to hold 10% of the deposit as reserves, which implies that a third loan can be issued for up to $729 (810 − (10% × 810)). This process, by which the bank continues to issue loans and create deposits, continues. Through this continuous reiterative process the commercial bank would create an additional $9000 in deposits, equivalent to the amount of loans that were issued. At the end of this process, the bank's balance sheets will read as follows:

Liabilities		Assets	
Initial deposits	1000	Cash	1000
Created deposits	9000	Loans	9000
Total liabilities	10000	Total assets	10000

Thus we see that the bank has expanded the amount of money by $9000 given an initial deposit of $1000. In a multibank system, the same type of credit creation process can work, providing all the banks are prepared to expand credit fully. This principle of credit creation in our example may be represented in a simple form as follows:

$$\frac{1}{10}\% = \text{money multiplier} = 10$$

The money multiplier shows that with a $1000 deposit, total bank deposits can increase to 10000 of which

$$\text{new deposits} = \text{total deposits} = \text{initial deposits}$$

$$9000 = 10000 − 1000$$

The nature of currency substitutions and money hoarding

The usefulness of money as a store of value is compromised by high rates of inflation. In economies in which the inflation rate is high and rising money loses value quickly, inflation rates quickly erode the purchasing power of money, and some economic agents look for other means of storing wealth. In many cases people use another currency to store their wealth; this is known as currency substitution.

Table 6.4 (opposite) shows the trends in the amount of foreign currency assets and foreign currency deposits held by commercial banks in Trinidad and Tobago. The table also provides information on the exchange rate with the US. Notice that as the exchange rate increased, implying that the Trinidad and Tobago dollar depreciated in value relative to the US dollar, the amount of foreign currency assets and foreign currency deposits increased: the amount of foreign currency assets held at commercial banks increased by over 450%, while the amount of foreign currency deposits increased by over 350%.

Table 6.4 *Nominal exchange rate, foreign currency assets and foreign currency deposits at commercial banks in Trinidad and Tobago, 1995–2006*

	Exchange rate with the US	Foreign currency assets (US$ million)	Foreign currency deposits (US$ million)
1995	5.95	545.26	414.85
1996	6.04	764.33	496.21
1997	6.28	914.94	549.28
1998	6.30	910.04	654.51
1999	6.30	1079.70	687.80
2000	6.30	1214.23	866.95
2001	6.23	1480.53	854.70
2002	6.25	1575.00	987.13
2003	6.30	1583.87	976.38
2004	6.30	2262.46	1265.38
2005	6.30	2498.35	1296.80
2006	6.31	2974.08	1798.51
2007	6.32	3071.19	2025.91

Source: Central Bank of Trinidad and Tobago

Money hoarding refers to the tendency to hoard money as it increases in value. This is Gresham's Law, named after Thomas Gresham, a successful British businessman who was an advisor to Queen Elizabeth I. Gresham argued that if we have two coins worth the same extrinsic amount, say $1, but one is made from brass and the other silver – that is, they have different intrinsic values – then the cheaper coin will be used for exchange, while the tendency will be to hoard the more expensive one. Gresham, therefore, speculated that 'bad money drives out good money'. What Gresham's Law infers is that economic agents will use the low commodity value for the purpose of exchange, while the money that has high commodity exchange will be hoarded.

The Quantity Theory of Money

The first equation of exchange which identified the relationship between the money supply and the monetary value of transactions was addressed by John Stuart Mill who expanded on the work of David Hume in 1848. Later the Quantity Theory of Money was explicitly developed and refined by Simon Newcomb, Alfred de Foville, Irvin Fisher and Ludwig von Mises during the 19th and 20th centuries. Additionally, the Quantity Theory of Money was later restated by Milton Friedman in 1956 in the post-Keynesian era.

The Quantity Theory of Money was challenged in the 1930s by Keynes as part of the Keynesian counter-revolution and subsequently fell out of fashion until it was revived in the 1950s by Milton Friedman.

In its simplest format, the Quantity Theory of Money can be explored through the equation of exchange. The equation of exchange can be presented as:

$$VM = PT$$

where

M = money supply

P = price level

T = total number of transactions

V = velocity of circulation of money

The term V shows the amount of times a given amount of money has to change hands to facilitate this level of transaction. Thus V = 4 means that the available money supply changes hands four times to facilitate the value of the total number of transactions (PT) in the economy.

Types of monetary policy

Tight monetary policy: Tight monetary policy refers to a deliberate course of action taken by the central monetary authority to restrict the amount of spending in an economy. Tight monetary policy is implemented to control the rate of inflation, and includes raising interest rates which effectively reduces the attractiveness of borrowing and reduces interest sensitive expenditure.

Easy monetary policy: Easy monetary policy is designed to stimulate economic activity in an economy and increase the level of employment by making borrowing more attractive.

Balance of payments: Monetary policy also affects the balance of payments account. For example, expansionary monetary policy (easy monetary policy) would tend to exert downward pressure on the exchange rate (assuming flexible or managed float), which would weaken the capital account but improve the current account. On the other hand, contractionary monetary policy would tend to exert upward pressure on the exchange rate, thereby resulting in an improvement on the capital account but worsening the current account.

Monetary policy and national income

Monetary policy affects the level of national income by influencing aggregate demand. As noted above, monetary policy is targeted towards controlling either the interest rate or the money supply. Recall that the Liquidity Preference Theory evaluates the demand for money balances against the money supply to determine equilibrium interest rate. And consider the effect of expansionary monetary policy which will effectively increase the money supply, as shown in Figure 6.6 (opposite). With an increase in the money supply (step 1), domestic interest rate falls (step 2), the consequence of which is that aggregate demand increases as investment (step 3) and consumption increase (step 4). National income also increases (step 5).

Limitations of monetary policy

Monetary policy has several limitations. Given that monetary policy is indirect in its approach to the macroeconomic fundamentals, policymakers must be careful to consider all possible effects of the implementation of a particular policy. Monetary policy has been criticised as being permissive and not compelling because of its 'hands-off' approach to macroeconomic management.

Additionally, monetary policy cannot be manipulated to set the priorities for government fiscal operations, nor does it have any control of either labour or product markets. The effectiveness of monetary policy has also been questioned in situations where foreign-owned commercial banks, whose policies and actions are exogenously determined, operate in the economy.

Lags in monetary policy

A variety of reasons are offered in the literature to explain why monetary policy does not have an immediate effect on the economy:

1 Deposits take time to be created. Suppose the central bank engages in ONOs and changes the amount of reserves at the disposal of the central bank. This occurs very quickly, but it takes a lot more time for the commercial banking system to properly expand to the full amount, given the prevailing reserve ratios in the banking system.

2 It takes time to expand the capital stock. If the central bank were to increase the money supply and promote a lower market rate of interest, this would increase the level of investment. However, it takes time for investments to be made and so a fall in the rate of interest, while expanding the level of investment, will do so only with a time lag.

3 An increase in the level of investment in an economy working through the multiplier expands the size of the national income. However, this process takes time to work through the system. Again we see that there is a time lag between the implementation of monetary policy and its effect on national income.

Weakening by fiscal indiscipline

Monetary policy may not be as effective as is planned if the government's fiscal policy strategies do not have the same objective. For example, tight monetary policy that is aimed at curbing the inflation rate can be negated by an increase in government spending. On the one hand, tight monetary policy would restrict consumer spending but the increase in government spending can swamp the fall in consumer demand and actually worsen macroeconomic conditions. Conversely, early monetary policy may attempt to stimulate aggregate demand. But faced with balance of payments crises and high levels of national debt the government will be forced to increase taxes and reduce government spending. These problems would have arisen because of fiscal indiscipline.

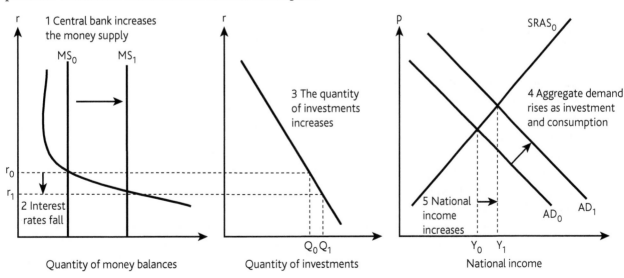

Figure 6.6 *Monetary policy and national income*

End test

1   What does bartering involve?

2   What are the two types of money?

3   What are the functions of money?

4   What are the attributes of money?

5   According to the Liquidity Preference Theory, why do people demand money balances?

6   What is the money supply?

7   What is monetary policy? What are the objectives of monetary policy?

8   What are the tools of monetary policy?

End test feedback

1   Bartering involves the exchange of goods for other goods. It is founded on the principle of mutual desire.

2   There are essentially two types of money: token money and commodity money.

3   Money has to perform the following functions:
   - Medium of exchange
   - Unit of account
   - Store of value
   - Standard for deferred payment

4   - Acceptability: Money must be acceptable as a means for the settlement of debt.
   - Durability: Money should not wear out quickly so that wealth can be transferred from one time period to another.
   - Homogeneity: Monetary units should be identical so that each dollar bill should be same as the previous one.
   - Divisibility: Money should be divisible so that both expensive and low-price commodities can be easily valued.
   - Portability: Money should be easy to transport around (e.g. in one's wallet or purse), without being excessively bulky or heavy.
   - Stability of value: Over time money should maintain its value.
   - Difficult to forge: Money should not be easy to duplicate as this could erode its worth as a medium of exchange.

5   According to the Liquidity Preference Theory there are three motives for demanding money balances:
   - Transactionary motive
   - Precautionary motive
   - Speculative motive

6   The money supply refers to the quantity of currency in circulation in an economy at a particular time.

7   Monetary policy refers to the deliberate actions of the monetary institutions to manipulate monetary instruments to achieve macroeconomic objectives. Some of these objectives include:
   - full employment
   - stable prices
   - a consistent but satisfactory level of economic growth
   - equilibrium in the balance of payments account

8   Some of the monetary instruments include:
   - open market operations
   - legal reserve requirement
   - discount rate
   - financing fiscal deficits
   - moral suasion
   - selective credit control
   - interest rates

7 Fiscal policy

Specific objectives

You should have an understanding of:

the meaning of fiscal policy

fiscal policy as a means of addressing: aggregate demand, unemployment, inflation, balance of payments

the nature of the budget:
- taxation, revenue, transfer, expenditure
- budget surplus and budget deficit
- balanced budget

explanation of the balanced budget multiplier

methods of financing budget deficits including external and domestic borrowing

lags and potency of fiscal policy

the meaning of expansionary and contractionary

automatic stabilisers.

Fiscal policy

Fiscal policy involves the deliberate intervention by government to manage government expenditure and government income to achieve particular economic and social outcomes. The instruments of fiscal policy are taxation (T) and government expenditure (G). These changes in T and G can be made in terms of:

- the level
- the timing of changes in T and G
- the structure of T and G.

Government/public expenditure

Public expenditure refers to the expenditure by government which is fed from taxation revenues or from government borrowing. Government expenditure can take two principal forms, current and capital, and may be undertaken by the central government, local government and/or by national industries.

Table 7.1 shows the trends in government spending as a percentage of Gross Domestic Product (GDP). Note that for Jamaica this proportion increased from 22.2% in 1992 to 38.7% in 2006, while for Trinidad and Tobago the proportion fell from 26.9% in 1991 to 22.4% in 2006.

Table 7.1 *Government expenditure as a percentage of GDP*

	Jamaica	Trinidad and Tobago
1991	–	26.9
1992	22.2	27.2
1993	30.4	26.5
1994	29.4	24.2
1995	33.3	24.7
1996	39.4	26.4
1997	33.6	24.4
1998	34.4	24.6
1999	35.8	24.6
2000	35.4	22.2
2001	35.0	22.9
2002	38.0	24.1
2003	39.1	21.3
2004	37.9	22.3

	Jamaica	Trinidad and Tobago
2005	33.9	23.5
2006	38.7	22.4

Source: World Development Indicators

Public expenditure is made in two distinct areas: spending on goods and services, and by transfer payments.

Spending on goods and services

The government is a huge employer and also purchases a vast amount of goods and services from a wide variety of sources. Figure 7.1 shows the trends in government expenditure of goods and services for the period 1991–2007. The average for the entire period is 11%, with the proportion in 2007 being 14.9%.

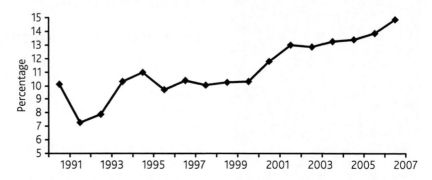

Figure 7.1 *Central government expenditure on goods and services, percentage of total*

Government employment

In many developing countries, government is one of the major employers of the labour force. In Trinidad and Tobago government employment is categorised as shown in Table 7.2, into public service and statutory board and government enterprises. Collectively, for the given period, employment in these sectors accounted for an average of 26% of total employment. Additionally, whereas the total number of persons employed increased by some 14% between 2000 and 2005, employment in the public service increased by 32% but employment in government enterprises declined by 19%.

Table 7.2 *Employment in the government sector (thousands)*

	Total employed	Government/public service statutory board	Government enterprise
2000	5 029	993	253
2001	5 139	1059	273
2002	5 251	1115	286
2003	5 341	1148	252
2004	5 623	1244	198
2005	5 740	1309	204

Source: Central Statistical Office for Trinidad & Tobago

In terms of government expenditure on wages and salaries, consider information in Table 7.3. The total expenditure on wages and salaries increased by over 100% between 2000 and 2007, but as a proportion of total spending it fell by 4.49 percentage points.

Table 7.3 *Government expenditure on wages and salaries*

	Central government expenditure on wages and salaries (TT$ 000s)	Central government expenditure on wages and salaries share of total (%)
2000	3 190 098	27.96
2001	4 091 262	32.48
2002	4 176 512	31.25
2003	4 627 866	30.49
2004	4 998 280	27.11
2005	5 304 481	23.63
2006	5 492 650	20.38
2007	6 576 093	23.47

Source: Central Bank of Trinidad and Tobago

Transfer payments

Transfer payments are disbursements made by the government that represent a redistribution of income. Figure 7.2 maps the trends of transfers and subsidies as a percentage of total government expenditure. Note that in 1991, this proportion was 21% and by 2007 transfers and subsidies accounted for 35% of government expenditure. In 2006, though, this ratio stood at 40%.

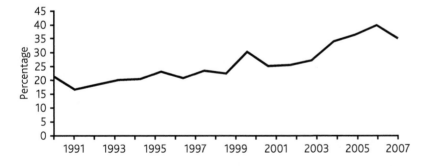

Figure 7.2 *Central government expenditure on transfers and subsidies as a percentage of total government expenditure*

Financing public expenditure

Government expenditure is financed in a variety of ways, by:

- taxes levied by central government
- taxes by local authorities, for example, land taxes
- borrowing
- sale of assets.

The functions of government expenditure

The functions of government expenditure depend on the philosophy of the government by the day: a command-type government will spend much more than a government with market-based ideals.

The major functions of government generally involve the following:

- **Providing public and merit goods:** Public and merit goods are goods that the free market would not provide in adequate amounts, for example, primary health care or primary education. The state typically provides public goods and provides some merit goods.

- **Social security:** Social security refers to a framework of social protection against the recognised social ills associated with poverty, unemployment, disability and aging. In some economies, such as the UK, the state also has to make transfer payments. Social security is one of the largest claims on government expenditure. A list of social security facilities offered in Trinidad and Tobago includes:

  - old age benefits: minimum old age pension $1 000 per month
  - disability benefits: average between $1 050 and $1 150 per month
  - survivors' pensions: widow(er) receives up to 40% of the deceased average weekly earnings
  - sickness benefit: up to 60% of average weekly earning, payable for a maximum of 52 weeks
  - maternity benefit: up to 60% of average weekly earnings, payable for a maximum of 13 weeks
  - work injury, temporary disability benefits: up to 66.6% of average weekly earnings, payable for a maximum of 52 weeks
  - work injury, permanent disability pension: pension is dependent on the degree of disability.

- **Regulation of economic activities:** The state also provides a number of services that can help to ensure that the activities of the private sector are properly regulated. In many economies the state also allocates a part of its resources to guide the resource allocation and industrial development process. In this regard, the work or Sir Arthur Lewis, who in 1955 published *The Theory of Economic Growth*, is still relevant today. Lewis advocated that the state was not only to create the preconditions necessary for development but to oversee the allocation process, thereby ensuring that the actions of the government are complementary to and facilitative of the private sector entrepreneurs.

Fiscal policy and macroeconomic management

Fiscal policy and aggregate demand

Fiscal policy can be used to manipulate aggregate demand. A government can increase its own spending or reduce taxes in order to increase the level of aggregate demand, or reduce its spending and increase taxes in order to reduce the level of aggregate demand. Figure 7.3 (opposite) shows how an expansion in aggregate demand can achieve an increase in economic activity and a consequent reduction in the rate of unemployment.

Fiscal policy and unemployment

In an economy in which there is a high level of unemployment, the government can use fiscal policy in a variety of ways to improve the employment situation. This can include two main types of response:

increasing G or decreasing t. In Figure 7.3 an increase in government expenditure from G_0 to G_1 shifts the aggregate demand curve from AD_0 to AD_1 and leads to an increase in the level of economic activity from Y_0 to Y_1. Similarly a fall in the level of taxation will lead to an increase in consumption.

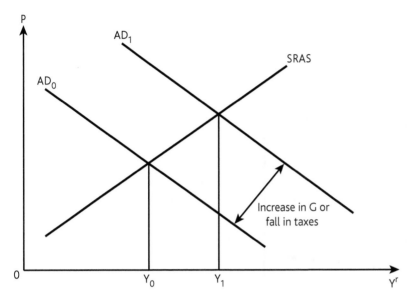

Figure 7.3 *Fiscal policy and unemployment*

Feedback

The government can use fiscal policies to increase the equilibrium level of output from $900 billion to $1100 billion by increasing spending by the appropriate amount (it is assumed that taxes remain at the present level). Government spending, which is an injection into the economy, will cause aggregate output to increase via the multiplier principles.

$$\text{Multiplier} = \frac{1}{1 - \text{mpc}}$$

The following facts are given:

MPC = 0.75

The desired increase in income is $200 billion (1100 – 900)

Therefore the increase in government spending must be sufficient to induce an increase in aggregate output by $200 billion.

$$\text{Multiplier} = \frac{1}{1 - 0.75} = \frac{1}{0.25} = 4$$

Increase in government spending

$$= \frac{\$200}{4} \text{ billion} = \$50 \text{ billion}$$

Therefore the government must increase spending by $50 billion to achieve the desired increase in aggregate output to $1100 billion.

Fiscal policy and inflation

In order to reduce demand-led inflation the government of an economy may deploy a deflationary fiscal strategy. Thus if a government increases

---

Activity 7.1

Suppose that as Chief Economic Adviser, the Minister of Finance calls you into his office and says the following:

Unemployment is too high. We need to lower it by increasing both output and income. Right now the equilibrium level of income/ output is $900 billion, but perhaps an acceptable unemployment rate can be achieved if aggregate output increases to some $1100 billion. Note however that the marginal propensity to consume is 0.75, and taxes must remain at the present level – so adjusting taxes (t) is out of the question.

Under the circumstances outlined above, explain how the government can use fiscal policy – taxes and spending – to increase the equilibrium level of output from $900 billion to $1100 billion.

income taxes this will lead to a decrease in consumption. A reduction in investment may also follow if the government increases fiscal taxes and this reduces the attractiveness of investment options. When a government implements these types of change it leads to a negative multiplier effect on the economy and can close the inflationary gap. This is shown on Figure 7.4, where an increase in T or a decrease in G leads to a leftward shift of the AD curve from AD_0 to AD_1 and a decline in the price level from P_1 to P_0.

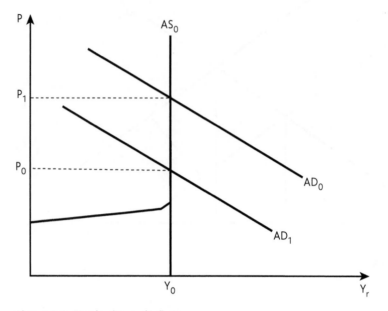

Figure 7.4 *Fiscal policy and inflation*

Inflation and balance of payments

Inflation, as defined above, refers to the persistent rise in the domestic price level. As prices rise, domestic consumers begin to substitute the more expensive domestically produced goods and services for the relatively cheaper imports. This can cause a worsening of the balance of payments position.

Additionally, as the price of exports increases, foreign consumers will also begin to substitute towards cheaper alternatives and, consequently, the level of exports falls and the balance of payments worsens.

The budget: taxation, revenue, expenditure and transfers

Budgets can either be in surplus, deficit or in balance. A budget deficit occurs when government expenditure (GE) is greater than government revenue (GR). A budgetary surplus occurs when GE less than GR. Governments may run two main types of budgetary surplus and two main types of budgetary deficit. A deflationary budgetary surplus occurs when government slashes government expenditure to prevent the economy from overheating. By reducing government expenditure and hence aggregate demand, government runs a budgetary surplus. This type of budgetary surplus is also called a deflationary surplus. A cyclical surplus occurs when buoyant economic activity allows government to collect much more tax revenue than it catered for in its budgetary planning process.

A reflationary deficit occurs when an economy wishes to stimulate aggregate demand and in so doing reduce the level of unemployment and promote the level of economic activity. The money to finance the budget comes from taxes in general.

Figure 7.5 shows the budgetary position of an economy with three alternative budgetary positions, B_1, B_2 and B_3.

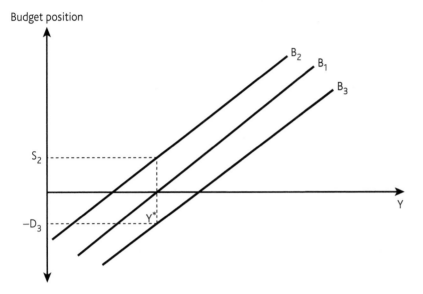

Budget position

Figure 7.5 *Alternative budgetary positions*

In Figure 7.5 Y^* represents the full employment level of income. With a budgetary position of B_1 the economy is in full employment with a balanced budget. If the government is running a budgetary surplus, then at the full employment level of income Y^*, if the government were to run a deflationary budget then it would have a budgetary surplus of S_2. If the government runs a budgetary deficit, then the government with a full employment position of Y^* engages a deflationary budgetary stance, with a deficit of $-\$D3$ at Y^*.

Symbolically, this can be represented as:

$G - T > 0$ budget surplus

$G - T < 0$ budget deficit

$G - T = 0$ balanced budget

The balanced budget multiplier

It is interesting to understand the implication of running a balanced budget in terms of its effect on the multiplier. A balanced budget occurs when:

$G - T = 0$

or $\Delta G = \Delta t$

Assuming that consumption expenditure is determined by the level of disposable income, then with an increase in G equal to an equivalent change in T or $\Delta G = \Delta t$, then:

$$\Delta Y = \left(\frac{1}{1-c}\right)\Delta G + \left(\frac{-c}{1-c}\right)\Delta t$$

Example

If the Jamaican government were to spend US$10 million on reflating its economy by a public infrastructure development programme and its government spending multiplier is $k = 5$ then:

$\Delta Y + (5)(10)$

$= US \$50$ million

But with a balanced budget and $K = 1$, equilibrium income increases by the increase in government spending.

Activity 7.2

1 Define the term *fiscal policy*.

2 State briefly what is meant by *each* of the following:

   a A budget deficit
   b A balanced budget

3 State TWO ways by which a country can reduce its budget deficit.

Feedback

1 Fiscal policy is the use of the government's tax and spending policies in an effort to regulate the economy.

2 a A budget deficit is a situation where current expenditure exceeds current revenue.

   b A balanced budget is a situation where current expenditure equals current revenue.

3 A country can reduce it budget deficit by:

   a increasing its tax rate and/or increasing the taxable income in the country

   b reducing government spending.

In a balance budget fiscal stance, $\Delta G = \Delta t$, so:

$$\Delta Y = \left[\left(\frac{1}{1-c} \right) + \left(\frac{c}{1-c} \right) \right] \Delta G$$

$$\Delta Y = \Delta G$$

This means the balance budget multiplier is equal to 1 and a change in government expenditure equivalent to ΔG will change Y only by ΔG.

This is an important derivation because it means that governments trying to reflate an economy will be much better off by running a budgetary deficit or by borrowing.

Alternative financing mechanism of a budget deficit

Monetarists have argued that it is critical to understand the monetary effect of expansionary fiscal policy. There are two main options available to a government to finance a budgetary deficit:

1 Increase the money supply

2 Increase interest rates

If the budget deficit is financed by borrowing from the local banking sector then this expansion in the money supply can cause inflation. When a government borrows this money and spends it, it is re-circulated to the general public. When the general public spends this money it pulls the domestic price level upwards, thus borrowing from local banks, which effectively increases the domestic inflation rate.

If instead the government finances the budget by selling government bonds, then in order to encourage the public to finance the deficit, it would have to increase the attractiveness of these government bonds. The consequence of this, however, is an increase in the general interest rate. When the general interest rate increases this will crowd out domestic private sector investment and make it more difficult for private sector firms to increase private sector investment. Consequently, government's use of a deficit financing strategy, financed by a strategy that raises domestic interest rates, will be ineffective to stimulate levels of economic activity.

Budget deficits can also be financed by external borrowing from institutions outside of the domestic economy.

Lags and potency of fiscal policy

Fiscal policy, whether it is expansionary or contractionary in nature, takes time to be effected in an economy on account of lags in the deliberation and the execution processes. First the government will take time to be aware of the problem because data collection takes time. Hence there is a recognition lag. Fiscal policy changes in the level of taxation and in certain types of government expenditure have to be debated in parliament and approved by cabinet. However, because taxes and government expenses have an impact on the basic well-being of most economic agents, politicians will be careful and deliberate for considerable periods of time in determining the exact nature of an intervention. This lag is known as a decision lag or implementation lag.

Even when a policy agreement, to cut the tax rate, for example, is eventually agreed, the system still has to deal with the execution, or operational lag. The execution lag is the time period between the making of a decision and the time it takes to be effective. It is likely that by the time a policy change has been implemented, the situation has changed so much that the policy itself is redundant.

Automatic stabilisers

It is difficult for government to slash government expenditure when an economy is in a recession. Expenditure slashing by government, especially on social programmes, can lead to social unrest.

Some economists have suggested using automatic stabilisers to regulate economic activity during periods of booms and slumps.

With a fall in aggregate income, the unemployment rate in an economy increases and in states with welfare programmes there is a rise in welfare payments. With taxation systems founded on progressive taxation, the fall in Y leads to a rapid fall in tax revenues at a pace faster than national income. These two automatic stabilisers tend to help to reflate the economy.

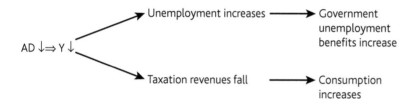

Figure 7.6

Automatic stabilisers also help to dampen economic activity where the economy is in a buoyant state. When income increases and unemployment decreases there is a reduction in payments of welfare benefits, and with a progressive taxation system a greater amount of income is paid in tax so the rate of expansion of consumption expenditure is kept in check. The consequence is a reduction in the size of the multiplier.

The general effect of automatic stabilisers is to dampen fluctuations in business cycles.

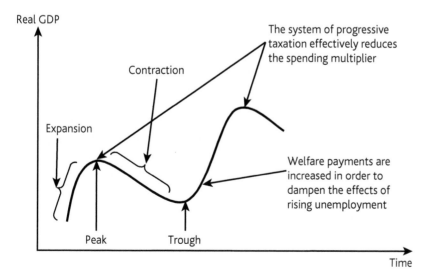

Figure 7.7 *Business cycles with built-in automatic stabilisers*

Example
Coup d'état, Trinidad and Tobago, 1990

Friday 27 July 1990 was one of the darkest days in the history of Trinidad and Tobago. On this day some 114 members of the Jamaat al Muslineen, led by Yasin Abu Bakr, attempted to overthrow the then National Alliance for Reconstruction (NAR) government. Forty-two members of this insurgent group stormed the Red House, the seat of Parliament, and held the Prime Minister, the honorable A.N.R. Robinson, and his cabinet hostage. The other 72 insurgents attacked the offices of the Trinidad and Tobago TV station (TTT), the country's only TV station, and the Trinidad Broadcasting Company, one of only two radio stations existing at the time. At approximately 6pm on the evening of the 27 July, Yasin Abu Bakr announced through the media that the government had been overthrown.

The Trinidad and Tobago protective services were quickly mobilised, sealing off the areas surrounding the Red House. A state of national emergency was declared and martial law imposed by the acting president Emmanuel Carter. The army worked quickly to seize control of the TTT transmitter, thereby blocking feeds for the TTT station. TTT was effectively taken off the air.

After six days of nationwide turmoil and through extensive negotiations with the Islamic faction, on 1 August 1990 the Muslineen surrendered. Although the group was tried for treason, they were given amnesty as promised in exchange for their surrender. The privy council later revoked the amnesty but no member of the Muslineen was re-arrested on the charge.

In total, approximately 24 persons died during the attempted coup of 1990, including a member of parliament Diego Martin, Central Leo Des Vignes. Financial losses amounted to millions of dollars.

Source: Wikipedia

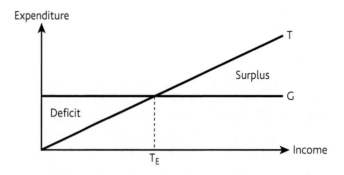

Figure 7.8 *Business cycles and government budget*

Government expenditure is fixed, since it is independent of the level of national income; in periods of high income and growth the government will automatically run a budget surplus (above income level Y_E).

End test

1 Define the term *fiscal policy*.

2 What are the instruments of fiscal policy?

3 What is public expenditure?

4 How is government expenditure financed?

5 What is the role of automatic stabilisers in an economic system?

End test feedback

1 Fiscal policy involves the deliberate intervention by government to manage government expenditure and government income to achieve particular economic and social outcomes.

2 The instruments of fiscal policy are taxation (t) and government expenditure (G). These changes in T and G can be made in terms of:

- the level

- the timing of changes in T and G

- the structure of T and G.

3 Public expenditure refers to the expenditure by government that is fed from taxation revenues or from government borrowing.

4 Government expenditure is financed in a variety of ways:

- Taxes levied by central government

- Taxes by local authorities (e.g. land taxes)

- Borrowing

- Sale of assets

5 Automatic stabilisers help to dampen economic activity where the economy is in a buoyant state. When income increases and unemployment decreases there is a reduction in payments of welfare benefits, and with a progression taxation system a greater amount of income is paid in tax so that the rate of expansion of consumption expenditure is kept in check.

8 Public debt

Specific objectives

You should have an understanding of:

the national debt: stock/flow, fiscal indiscipline, domestic and foreign debt

the causes of the national debt

the effects of the national debt on the economy: output and investment decisions, exchange rate pressures, inflation, crowding out and crowding in

the responsibility for debt repayment

management of the national debt: internal and external borrowing, taxation, debt rescheduling, debt forgiveness

interpretation of the debt service ratio

calculation of the debt service ratio (principal plus interest as a percentage of export).

National debt

Stock/flow

The national debt refers to the debt of the central government. Let DB represent the government's budgetary deficit in year 1. Thus for years 1, 2 and 3 we have:

$$BD_1 = GR_1 - GE_1 \quad \Rightarrow \quad ND_1 = BD_1$$
$$BD_2 = GR_2 - GE_2 \quad \Rightarrow \quad ND_2 = BD_1 + BD_2$$
$$BD_3 = GR_3 - GE_3 \quad \Rightarrow \quad ND_3 = BD_1 + BD_2 + BD_3$$

Each of BD_1, BD_2, and BD_3 has to be financed. If initially the national debt is zero (0) then with the first budget deficit of BD_1, if the government finances it by borrowing, the national debt increases to BD_1. Suppose in the very next year the government runs a budgetary deficit again of size BD_2, if financed by borrowing there is another flow that increases the stock of the national debt to ND_2, and so on.

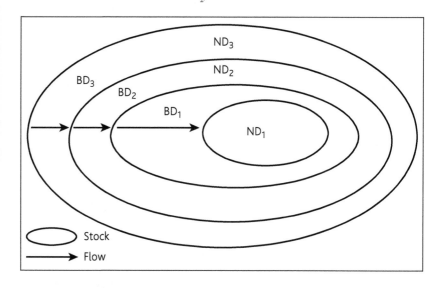

Figure 8.1 *National debt*

In the absence of sufficient savings, governments tend to borrow both locally and abroad. Borrowed resources are sometimes wasted but even when they are used to expand the country's infrastructure the returns are not immediately forthcoming.

Complementary investments by private investors are also sometimes necessary to make full use of infrastructural developments. In the absence of proper debt management, debt servicing can become a major problem, worsening fiscal deficits. Current fiscal deficits are a notable feature of most CARICOM economies. In 1990 the deficit as a percentage of Gross Domestic Product (GDP) ranged from minus 25% for Guyana to a surplus of 4.8% in Jamaica. By 2000, the country with the largest fiscal deficit as a percentage of GDP was St Kitts (–14.2%) with Trinidad and Tobago having the largest surplus of 1.6% (see Table 8.1). On average per annum for the period 1990–2000, Guyana had the largest fiscal deficit as a proportion of GDP, while Trinidad and Tobago had the smallest. In 2000, the average fiscal deficit as a percentage of GDP across all CARICOM countries had worsened to –5.15%. For Guyana, economic reforms in the 1990s have helped to improve the fiscal balance to a deficit of 8.3% in 2000. The fiscal balance in Jamaica continues to be a cause for concern.

Table 8.1 *Fiscal balance as a percentage of GDP in CARICOM member states, 1990–2001*

	1990	1991	1992	1993	1994	1995	1996	1997	1998	1999	2000	2001
Antigua	1.2	–1.9	–0.5	–1.4	–2.8	–2.9	–3.1	–4.3	–4.4	–2.5	–2.2	n.a.
Bahamas	n.a.	n.a.	n.a.	n.a.	n.a.	–1.2	–0.9	–3.2	–1.1	–0.3	0.4	–0.8
Barbados	–8.4	–1.8	–1.9	–2.5	–1.2	–0.9	–3.8	–1.4	–1.0	–2.3	–1.5	–3.5
Belize	0.3	–5.0	–7.5	–9.1	–7.6	–4.3	–0.4	–2.2	–2.3	–2.1	–9.0	–11.0
Dominica	–10.0	–3.3	–5.7	–0.3	–4.8	–5.7	–1.9	–2.3	–1.2	–9.9	–5.5	n.a.
Grenada	–15.0	–4.8	–0.6	–0.9	–1.9	0.3	–2.7	–2.2	–3.2	–2.8	–3.4	n.a.
Guyana	–25.0	–27.0	–20.0	–8.1	–1.8	0.1	–1.6	–7.0	–7.4	–5.7	–6.6	–8.3
Jamaica	4.8	–5.6	–6.6	–2.7	–11.0	–5.4	–24.6	–8.3	–8.1	–6.1	–0.3	–6.9
St Kitts	–0.3	–2.3	–1.2	–1.4	–3.0	–6.6	–3.8	–3.1	–6.2	–11	–14.2	n.a.
St Lucia	1.0	0.7	–1.8	–0.7	–0.8	–1.2	–2.2	n.a.	n.a.	n.a.	n.a.	n.a.
St Vincent	–0.8	–0.2	–4.3	–4.8	–0.3	–2.4	0.6	–4.0	–3.0	–1.5	–5.8	n.a.
Suriname	n.a.	n.a.	–8.7	–9.4	5.1	4.3	0.8	n.a.	n.a.	n.a.	n.a.	n.a.
Trinidad	–1.2	–0.2	–2.7	–0.2	0.0	0.2	0.5	0.1	–2.0	–3.2	1.6	–0.4

Source: UNELAC (2002)

Fiscal indiscipline

As explained above, it is the excess of government expenditure over government revenue that leads to an increase in the flows to the national debt. When government expenditure is greater than government revenue economists say that the government was not fiscally prudent or, alternatively, they were fiscally indisciplined.

Domestic and foreign debt

The composition of the national debt is important. If one segment of the economy is in debt to another segment of the economy then the wealth of the economy as a whole is not changed and any interest payment on the debt is an internal matter and is made within the economy. However, when the debt is externally owned it means that the interest payments and repayment on the capital have to be made in foreign currencies so the debtor nation will have to export goods and services to earn this foreign currency. This servicing and repayment of the foreign debt represents a loss of real output from the debtor nation that could be used to help repay the debt.

Causes of national debt

In understanding the causes of the national debt it is critical to understand the causes of persistent fiscal deficits.

One of the main reasons for borrowing in many developing countries, including those of the CARICOM sphere, is to counter the adverse effects of external economic shocks and natural disasters. As shown in Cape Economics 1 Study Guide, in the aftermath of a hurricane or another such natural disaster, the rebuilding of these economies requires substantial resources, some of which are borrowed from the international community. Adverse movement in the terms of trade also makes borrowing necessary to meet various fiscal needs.

Another causative factor of the accumulation of debt in the region is the need to maintain the level of public sector consumption even in the presence of stagnant or declining fiscal revenues. The debt problem in the CARICOM sphere is partly because of fiscal mismanagement. As can be seen in Table 8.1, nearly all CARICOM economies are in a position of fiscal deficit.

Another reason for the build-up of debt in the CARICOM region is to speed up the economic growth and development process. A good case in point is the Trinidad and Tobago economy. Trinidad and Tobago's national debt increased from US$42.6 million in 1955 to US$2 790.3 million in 1999, with the external debt obligation in 1999 representing just over 53% or US$1 482.9 million. However, it should be noted that during the period 1955–73 the central government debt increased by a mere US$261.4 million. However, from US$304 million in 1973 the central government debt would escalate to US$712.1 million in 1980 although the sums of the surpluses on the fiscal and external current account balances during this time period were US$552.5 million and US$1,434 million respectively. This emphasises the important point that Trinidad and Tobago borrowed freely to speed up the economic growth and development process.

The effects of the national debt on the economy

Fiscal burden of interest payments and its effect on output and investment decisions

Interest payments deprive indebted nations of resources to finance education (creating human capital) and health (preserving human capital). Resources targeted at interest payments could also have helped to encourage the growth of non-traditional dynamic comparative advantage in export commodities on the upswing of the international product cycle or in the creation of an even better infrastructural base to attract foreign direct investment inflow in export-oriented sectors.

National debt and exchange rate pressures

National debt can hamper a country's ability to finance current account deficits as debt servicing essentially reduces the amount of foreign reserves that a country possesses. Additionally, debt servicing can exhaust export revenues thus worsening the overall balance of payments position which consequently results in a depreciation of the domestic currency.

National debt and inflation

When measuring national debt it is important to look at it in real terms as compared with nominal terms. Consider the following illustration. Let the real and nominal debt in 2005 be US$100 million (the price deflator to deflate the nominal debt had a base year of 2005). Let the nominal debt in 2006 income be US$8 million million to give a total nominal national debt of US$108 million million at the end of 2006. If the inflation rate in 2006 was 5% it means that the real national debt at the end of 2006 was:

$$\left(\text{US\$ } \frac{106}{105}\right) \times 100 = \text{US\$101 million}$$

What we see here is that although government nominal debt increased, its real debt actually fell. The analysis above assumed no interest payment on the nominal debt. If we assume that in 2006 the budget was balanced but interest payments on the debt caused it to accumulate to US\$108 million then with an inflation rate of 10% the government gains and debt holders lose. In other words, inflation led to a redistribution of wealth from lenders (debt holders to the government). In this type of situation economists say that the real burden of the debt has fallen.

Crowding out and crowding in

Unsustainable levels of national debt can have an adverse effect on the economic growth process in developing economies. Suppose, for example, a heavily indebted government cannot lower its consumption levels in order to free up resources to make debt service payments, then they may borrow resources from the domestic commercial banking system. The consequence of this could be an increase in demand for investible resources, a rise in the domestic interest rates and a crowding out of private sector investments.

A crowding-in effect would take place in the reverse situation if an increase in national debt is successfully used to stimulate economic growth and development in the borrowing economy. Specifically, if the domestic economy is expanding and economic activity is growing so that business expectations are buoyant, then domestic investors would invest more.

The responsibility of debt repayment

The responsibility of debt repayment really refers to the burden of the public debt. Three principal issues arise when discussing the burden of the public debt:

1 The size of the debt in relation to the ability to repay
2 Who pays the debt – that is, whether one government borrows and another government pays
3 Interest payments

Size of debt

In assessing the burden of the national debt, one has to make an assessment in terms of supporting the debt. Many people argue that when economic agents borrow they are actually imposing a burden on future generations to repay. In particular it is said that borrowing and increasing present spending has to be carried by future generations who will need to make interest payments and take responsibility for repaying the debt. However, this is not entirely correct.

Specifically, if a government borrows US\$x million today then the government in which the borrowing takes place carries the burden. How so? This is because it is this generation that has to go without consumer goods so that capital goods can be purchased (in moving economies, when governments borrow to finance war, real resources are directed away from consumer goods to war materials).

When money is borrowed by governments and used to finance corrupt and fiscally irresponsible activities then the whole economy suffers. If the national debt is held locally then the wealth of the economy remains the same, although equity considerations can arise if the money borrowed is from a small segment of the national community. When the money is borrowed externally and resources, therefore, leave the economy to service and repay the debt in foreign currency, then exports are made without any exchange for imports.

Management of the national debt

Internal and external borrowing

When a government has to borrow resources to cover its fiscal deficit it can turn to either foreign or national sources. The benefit of turning to national sources is that it keeps the wealth level of the economy intact as it represents a redistribution of resources. In contrast, when money is borrowed from abroad it means that the repayment of this money would represent a net leakage of resources from the system.

In addition, when a government borrows from abroad it usually comes with conditions, some of which may create problems of their own. For example, one of the conditions attached to borrowing financial resources from the International Monetary Fund (IMF) or the World Bank is that the state has to play a smaller part in the running of the economy. However, because the state is a large employer in many developing economies, a downsizing of the state's participation is typically associated with a rise in unemployment and this has social implications.

Taxation

In managing the national debt a critical part of this whole process is boosting domestic revenues. This can be done by reforming the tax machinery in the relevant economy.

Debt rescheduling

The external debt crisis of most developing economies is a profound challenge into the 21st century. Eatwell and Taylor (Global Finance at Risk, 2000) have argued that 'international debt crisis has become a defining feature of the contemporary world economy'. Since the end of the 1980s many developing economies that are heavily indebted have been unable to meet their debt servicing requirements and this has prompted some economists to promote the case for a greater degree of debt rescheduling. As one economist noted, rescheduling is:

> a mechanism which not only allows debtors not to default on their loans and remain in the international financial system but also prevents creditors from facing the whole consequences of a financial crisis.
>
> Marchesi, Adoption of an IMF programme
> and debt restructuring: An econometric analysis, 2000

There are a number of factors, both international and domestic, that influence whether an indebted nation may require debt rescheduling. The international factors are:

- import expenditures that cannot be reduced even if the capacity of the economy to import has fallen because of, say, falling export revenues – this may be goods like capital equipment needed to build bridges and medicine for hospitals and so on
- deterioration in the terms of trade so that the major export items from the indebted nation now bring in less export revenues – this may be viewed as a fall in exports as capacity to import

Example

Guyana: a heavily indebted poor country

Guyana is one of the most heavily indebted developing countries. The issue of the level of national debt has been one of the most pressing for the present government. In 1999 through effects of the Paris Club and the Heavily Indebted Poor Countries (HIPC) initiative, Guyana was able to successfully negotiate up to $256 million in debt forgiveness.

Approximately 50% of the Guyanese national debt is owed to the international multilateral development banks (IMF and World Bank), and about 20% to its CARICOM counterpart Trinidad and Tobago. Guyana's debt burden has seriously hampered the development of the economy to the extent that a high debt burden to foreign creditors has meant limited availability of foreign exchange and reduced capacity to import necessary raw materials, spare parts and equipment, thereby further reducing production. The increase in global fuel costs also contributed to the country's decline in production and growing trade deficit. The decline of production has increased unemployment. Although no reliable statistics exist, combined unemployment and underemployment are estimated at about 30%.

- a recession in the destination market for exports from the heavily indebted economies which, in turn, lowers their demand for the export goods and in so doing compromises the export revenue earnings of the indebted economy. (You should bear in mind that the heavy focus on export revenue earnings is critical because it conditions the ability of the developing economy to repay its external debt.)

Internal factors that affect the ability of developing economies to repay their debt include:

- a disruption to the productive capacity of the indebted economy for economic or non-economic reason; for example, the *coup d'état* that occurred in the Trinidad and Tobago economy in 1990 brought virtually all productive activity to a standstill while the defence force sought to restore order
- poor economic management by the indebted nation which can quickly use up valuable foreign exchange in the pursuit of pet projects, some of which may be economically unfeasible
- an increased amount of investible resources leave the indebted economy to go to other economies that offer more stable economic conditions.

The list of distortions in the domestic economy has an adverse effect on production and hence export revenues and these, in turn, can potentially hamper the ability of the indebted economy to repay their debt.

Debt forgiveness

As the debt of the developing economies in the world increases, some economists believe that it may never be repayable. It is argued in some circles that it may be in the interest of both lenders and borrowers to forgive the debt of these economies. Economists such as Jeffery Sachs have argued that partial forgiveness could allow heavily indebted nations with developing economies to use their debt servicing monies to build capacity to finance investment and to increase future levels of output. The problem here is that where do we strike the balance, as the creditors would always want less debt forgiveness and the debtor nations would always want more debt forgiveness.

Debt service ratio

The cost of servicing the national debt is represented by interest payments to the holders of the national debt. Caribbean economies are among some of the most indebted economies in the world. National debt to GDP ratios in excess of 50% are typically considered high and so, in accordance with the data in Table 8.2, either by total national debt or the proportion held externally, have high debt ratios.

Table 8.2 *Debt as a percentage of GDP*

Country	Total national debt as % of GDP, 2004	External debt as % of GDP, 2004
Antigua and Barbuda	99	64
Barbados	46	10
Bahamas	86	24
Belize	102	74
Dominica	115	73

Grenada	129	77
Guyana	166	137
Jamaica	139	58
St Kitts	179	82
St Lucia	70	43
St Vincent	79	54
Trinidad and Tobago	45	13

Source: World Bank Development Indicators

The debt service ratio is calculated as the ratio of interest payments as a proportion of the key exports of goods and services and the current revenue receipts of government.

Table 8.3 *Interest payments as a percentage of current revenues in CARICOM member states, 1990–2001*

	1990	1991	1992	1993	1994	1995	1996	1997	1998	1999	2000	2001
Antigua	19.90	19.86	17.47	8.82	9.72	8.91	11.92	11.81	11.77	9.16	11.97	n.a
Bahamas	n.a	n.a	n.a	12.80	12.26	12.81	13.58	12.80	n.a	n.a	n.a	n.a
Barbados	13.92	16.51	16.38	14.29	15.42	16.28	16.28	13.84	14.17	13.95	13.04	14.92
Dominica	5.61	6.23	7.77	9.97	9.81	10.76	10.18	8.77	9.23	9.78	19.56	n.a
Grenada	9.53	12.27	10.89	10.22	9.65	8.75	6.69	9.40	6.43	9.16	8.14	n.a
Guyana	78.24	73.39	64.14	45.12	51.56	29.30	24.61	30.35	27.92	27.94	26.20	n.a
Jamaica	35.16	33.76	33.92	32.39	37.54	33.37	46.63	39.41	49.37	51.44	45.99	49.05
St Kitts	12.55	14.59	10.33	10.53	9.84	9.29	12.83	11.05	10.43	12.68	16.75	n.a
St Lucia	3.27	2.76	3.06	3.06	2.92	3.36	4.32	5.40	4.69	5.59	5.52	n.a
St Vincent	4.07	3.31	3.93	4.21	4.43	6.10	5.49	5.44	5.38	7.87	9.01	n.a
Suriname	n.a	n.a	12.97	11.91	6.12	1.92	2.09	n.a	n.a	n.a	n.a	n.a
Trinidad	17.53	15.97	20.24	21.52	20.98	18.65	15.73	18.52	18.13	19.87	20.77	16.67

Source: Economist Intelligence Unit; Country Reports (various years)

For small states, interest payments on debt can have a serious impact on the growth potential of their economy. In terms of interest payments as a percentage of current revenues, the average value of this ratio for the entire CARICOM body was 19.9% with a range of 3.27% in St Lucia to 78.24% in Guyana in 1990. By 2000, the average value of this variable across all CARICOM member states would have increased to 16.7% with a range from 5.52% in St Lucia to 45.9% in Jamaica. Between 1990 and 2000, interest payments as a percentage of current revenues increased in all the member states for which consistent data is available except for Antigua and Barbuda, Barbados, Grenada and Guyana. Both Dominica and Jamaica realised an increase in the share of interest payments as a proportion of current revenues by more than 10 percentage points.

As a percentage of the exports of goods and services, the debt service ratio increased between 1997 and 2004 for most of the listed CARICOM economies (Table 8.4, overleaf).

Table 8.4 *Debt service as a percentage of the exports of goods and services*

Country	1997	2004
Antigua and Barbuda	2.7	9.4
Barbados	5.2	3.4
Bahamas	5.6	5.5
Belize	9.0	50.9
Dominica	6.7	11.4
Grenada	6.0	11.3
Guyana	10.5	7.7
Jamaica	15.3	20.4
St Kitts	4.7	22.0
St Lucia	3.5	7.8
St Vincent	3.5	11.5
Trinidad and Tobago	15.4	4.6

Source: World Bank Indicators

End test

1 Define the term *national debt*.

2 Explain the term *fiscal indiscipline*.

3 What are THREE factors to consider when determining who carries the burden of public debt?

4 What are some of the internal factors that affect the ability of developing economies to repay their debts?

5 How is the debt service ratio calculated?

End test feedback

1 The national debt refers to the debt of the central government.

2 When government expenditure is greater than government revenue, national debt levels increase. When government expenditure is greater than government revenue economists say that the government was not fiscally prudent or, alternatively, they were fiscally indisciplined.

3 The responsibility of debt repayment really refers to the burden of the public debt. Three principal issues arise when discussing the burden of the public debt:

   • The size of the debt in relation to the ability to repay

   • Who pays the debt – whether one government borrows and another government pays

   • Interest payments

4 Internal factors that affect the ability of developing economies to repay their debt include:

   • a disruption to the productive capacity of the indebted economy for economic or non-economic reasons

   • poor economic management by the indebted nation which can quickly use up valuable foreign exchange in the pursuit of pet projects, some of which may be economically unfeasible

   • an increased amount of investible resources leaving the indebted economy to go to other economies that offer more stable economic conditions.

5 The debt service ratio is calculated as the ratio of interest payments as a proportion of the key exports of goods and services and the current revenue receipts of government.

9 Growth and sustainable development

Specific objectives

You should have an understanding of:

differences between growth and development

current growth versus the well-being of future generations

differences between exogenous (technical change) and endogenous growth (capital accumulation, human capital)

economic, social and environmental factors

indices of human development including mortality rates, literacy, per capita income, life expectancy

structural characteristics of Caribbean economies including: small size, openness, composition of exports, resource base, poverty, economic dependence

implications for regional economies:

- dependence on aid

- preferential trade agreements

- foreign direct investment (FDI)

- vulnerability to natural and man-made change

- changes in world prices.

Economic growth and economic development

Economic development is much more than economic growth. While economic growth is focused on the changes in real Gross Domestic Product (GDP), economic development takes into account other variables, including social sector variables.

Some important variables that need to be considered when looking at the differences between growth and development are:

- health status
- literacy
- crime situation
- environmental pollution.

Thus an economy may be experiencing rapid economic growth but with an attendant high level of stress, so that workers are more at risk of suffering stress-related medical problems including heart attack and stroke. In other economies, economic growth may be progressing rapidly but with intolerably high levels of crime. In the Trinidad and Tobago economy, for example, there was an increase in the level of real GDP from TT\$53 539.6 million in 2001 to TT\$89 444.8 million in 2007, an increase of over 140%. However, in the same interval of time, there was an increase in the level of kidnappings, from 135 in 2001 to 162 in 2007. Finally, some economies may be experiencing economic growth but at the cost of a high level of environmental pollution. Again in Trinidad and Tobago, while real GDP increased there was an increase in the amount of carbon dioxide emissions from 28560.41 kt in 2001 to 32527.44 kt in 2004.

When considering issues of economic growth the literature also emphasises the need to balance the current level of economic growth with that of the well-being of future generations. This is an intergenerational issue and raises the whole notion of sustainable economic development. Sustainable economic development refers to development today that does not compromise the level of development tomorrow.

The concepts of economic growth and economic development

Economic growth refers to the expansion in a country's national income, output and employment. It is the quantitative increase in national income and results from an increase in either the quantity or quality of factors of production, and the efficiency with which it is utilised.

Some of the factors that influence the rate of economic growth include the following:

- Human capital formation – that is, augmenting the skills base and educational level of the population
- Investment to increase the productive capacity of the economy

- Implementation of technology
- Reallocation of resources in order to minimise wastage

Economic development, on the other hand, refers to the more qualitative changes associated with growth. Note though that economic growth is a prerequisite condition for development as development essentially implies an improvement in the standard of living of the population.

Exogenous and endogenous growth

The traditional theories of economic growth assumed that persistent economic growth emanates from technical change. However, these models do not provide an explanation of technical change but merely assume that it occurs. A new body of economic literature – endogenous growth theory – attempts to take growth theory beyond these traditional models and develop models that explain how technological progress occurs. These growth theories that attempt to explain how technological progress occurs have been collectively referred to as endogenous growth models and include the work of Paul Romer and Robert Lucas. Endogenous growth theorists emphasise the importance of physical capital accumulation, research and development and human capital development in driving the economic growth process in modern economies.

Social and environmental factors

The economic growth of an economy is partly dependent on the level of economic activity in that economy. In low-income economies, for example, the state has to play a major part in the economic development process because the private sector simply does not have enough resources to initiate change. In contrast, in more developed, wealthier economies, much of the stimulus for, say, research and development can come from the private sector. Less developed economies, because of where they are starting on the ladder of economic development, have the prospect of having high rates of economic growth conditioned by their ability to absorb and utilise foreign technology and methods of protection.

Sport, as one form of social activity, helps to boost the economic development process as it helps to strengthen community involvement, engagement, identity and pride. Sporting activities and events contribute to the development of stronger social networks and more cohesive communities. They provide opportunities for social engagement, often with alternative peer groups, which can create awareness of differences and break down barriers for individuals and communities. Sports can be used to build relationships with hard-to-reach individuals. Building and maintaining trust in a sporting environment can open up the opportunity to seek views on a wider range of issues, and where appropriate to provide information and support on other community issues.

Sport can also contribute to building the capacity of a community. The involvement of local people as volunteers in decision-making and management of local sporting activities, events, teams and facilities, can make local sporting opportunities more relevant to local needs, and more sustainable. Through participation in activities as a sport volunteer, individuals can develop greater self-esteem and transferable skills, and communities may develop a sense of empowerment or ownership. This can often give individuals or communities the confidence to then tackle wider local issues.

Measuring economic development

Activity 9.1

1 Outline TWO differences between 'growth' and 'development'.

2 List THREE factors that can allow economic growth to take place. Give an example for each.

3 Discuss the benefits and costs of growth.

Feedback

1 Growth is associated with an increase in income and in many regards refers to a quantitative improvement while development is associated with a qualitative improvement in standard of living. Additionally, growth can occur without development.

2 Three factors that can allow economic growth to take place are:

- Implementation of technology

- Human capital formation, for example, the introduction of free tertiary education in Trinidad and Tobago

- Investment to increase productive capacity of the economy, for example, purchase of machinery

3 Two benefits of growth are:

- The government will be able to spend more money on developmental infrastructures, for example building of roads and bridges. This will enable people to commute faster and as a result spend more time on productive activities.

- The government will also be able to spend more money on education, health and other factors that can induce human development. The end result is sustainable development.

Two costs of growth are:

- As a country becomes more affluent, people tend to adopt an unhealthy lifestyle. Their diet will mainly be sourced from fast food outlets.

- Individuals will be busy generating an income and the basic procedure of exercising will be left out. Therefore such people tend to develop the 'rich man's diseases', for example, diabetes, hypertension.

Indices of human development

The Human Development Index (HDI), developed in 1990 by Mabhub ul Haq and used by the United Nations Development Programme since 1993, is a composite index that is used to compare the standard of living across countries. This index averages the performance of economies based on three basic criteria or dimensions of economic development:

- Life expectancy at birth
- The quality of the education system as measured by adult literacy, the enrolment rate for primary, secondary and tertiary education
- Level of GDP per capita

The HDI is calculated simply as the average of each of these individually calculated indices. The HDI is published in UNDP's *Human Development Report*.

Table 9.1 gives an indication of the development progress of several CARICOM countries since 1975.

Table 9.1 *HDI trends for selected CARICOM economies*

	1975	1980	1985	1990	1995	2000	2005
Barbados	0.804	0.827	0.837	0.851	n.a.	0.888	0.892
Trinidad and Tobago	0.756	0.784	0.782	0.784	0.785	0.796	0.814
Jamaica	0.686	0.689	0.690	0.713	0.728	0.744	0.736
Guyana	0.682	0.684	0.675	0.679	0.699	0.722	0.750
St Lucia	n.a.	n.a.	n.a.	n.a.	n.a.	n.a.	0.795
St Kitts	n.a.	n.a.	n.a.	n.a.	n.a.	n.a.	0.821
St Vincent	n.a.	n.a.	n.a.	n.a.	n.a.	n.a.	0.761
Suriname	n.a.	n.a.	n.a.	n.a.	n.a.	n.a.	0.774

Source: Human Development Report (various years)

Table 9.2 *Human Development Index (HDI) ranking for select CARICOM countries*

Country	Rank
Trinidad and Tobago	59
Barbados	31
Jamaica	101
Guyana	97
St Lucia	72
St Kitts	54
St Vincent	93
Suriname	85

Source: Human Development Report (2007)

The UNDP also calculates a Gender Development Index which essentially readjusts the HDI to reflect each of the developmental dimensions highlighted above for each of the respective sexes, in order to gauge the degree of equity. Table 9.2 gives the 2005 HDI rank for selected CARICOM economies.

The rest of this section provides a brief focus on several other relevant development-related variables.

Per capita income

The per capita income of an economy is obtained as follows:

$$\text{per capita income} = \frac{\text{real (GDP) income}}{\text{population}}$$

Table 9.3 provides an indication of how the per capita GDP of Trinidad and Tobago is calculated.

Table 9.3 *Real per capita GDP in Trinidad and Tobago*

	GDP (constant 2000 US$ million)	Population, total	GDP per capita (constant 2000 US$)
1995	6 397.1	1 270 008	5 037.1
1996	6 649.6	1 277 422	5 205.5
1997	6 829.5	1 284 015	5 318.8
1998	7 360.0	1 289 925	5 705.8
1999	7 683.0	1 295 374	5 931.1
2000	8 154.3	1 300 545	6 269.9

2001	8 488.2	1 305 464	6 502.1
2002	9 168.4	1 310 124	6 998.1
2003	10 492.0	1 314 639	7 980.7
2004	11 416.0	1 319 139	8 653.8
2005	12 323.0	1 323 722	9 309.5
2006	13 801.0	1 328 432	10 389.0

Source: World Bank Development Indicators (2008)

Other indicators of economic development

Some other indicators of economic development include:

- crude birth rate – the total number of births per thousand of the population per year
- crude death rate – the total number of deaths per thousand of the population per year
- dependency rate or ratio – the proportion of the economically dependent part of the population to the labour force
- net migration rate – the difference between immigrants and emigrants in a particular area for a given period of time, per thousand of the population.

Important factors conditioning the size of the labour force in any economy are its crude birth rate, its crude death rate, labour force participation rate and the extent of net migration. For Trinidad and Tobago it is clear that the crude birth rate has fallen. This is a typical feature of economies with increasing per capita growth. There has, however, been a marginal increase in the crude death rate, but this has been very small and virtually constant since 1999. The dependency ratio, which is the ratio of the economically active population to the non-working population, fell from 65.8 in 1990 to 48 in 2004, a decline of 27.1%. In 1990, there was a positive inflow of immigrants to Trinidad and Tobago, as net migration stood at 15 652 persons. In the period thereafter for which data is available, there has been a persistent net outflow (except in 1996 when there was a net inflow) of migrants out of the Trinidad and Tobago economy – see Table 9.4.

Table 9.4 *Selected demographic and employment trends for Trinidad and Tobago, 1990–2005*

Year	Crude birth rate	Crude death rate	Dependency ratio	Net migration
1990	19.7	6.7	65.8	15 652
1991	18.2	6.7	63.3	–1 146
1992	18.6	6.9	60.3	–2 089
1993	16.9	7.1	58.7	–7 012
1994	15.7	7.4	57.2	–4 636
1995	15.3	7.2	54.2	–10 265
1996	14.2	7.4	52.0	1 554

Year	Crude birth rate	Crude death rate	Dependency ratio	Net migration
1997	14.5	7.2	50.2	−24 850
1998	13.4	7.3	50.2	−6 244
1999	14.1	7.8	46.8	−3 709
2000	14.1	7.5	46.8	−3 709
2001	14.1	7.6	46.8	n.a.
2002	14.1	7.6	45.8	n.a.
2003	14.0	7.7	46.5	n.a.
2004	14.2	7.9	48.0	n.a.
2005	13.8	7.7	48.0	n.a.

Sources: Annual Statistical Digest (CSO) and Review of the Economy (various years)

Education as an indicator of human development

Empirical research has shown that, in general, countries with higher levels of education enjoy higher standards of living. The *World Education Report* has noted that:

> ... policies aimed at alleviating poverty, reducing infant mortality and improving public health, protecting the environment, strengthening human rights, improving international understanding and enriching the national culture are essentially incomplete if they are not specifically incorporated into an appropriate educational strategy.

World Education Report (1991)

At the turn of the 21st century, developing countries began to aggressively pursue strategies to facilitate the formation of innovation-driven industries that would enhance sustainable development. The education sector is a critical target facilitator of such development. Improvements in education, especially with regards to access to tertiary education, are positively correlated with higher economic growth rates. Governments in developing countries must, therefore, expedite the establishment of an educational framework that facilitates sustainable development through the meaningful interaction of all stakeholders.

Table 9.5 *Adult and youth literacy rates in CARICOM and some other economies, 1990 and 2002*

Country	Adult literacy rate (% ages 15 and above)		Youth literacy rate (% ages 15–24)	
	1990	2002	1990	2002
Mauritius	79.8	84.3	91.1	94.5
Singapore	88.8	92.5	99.0	99.5
Antigua and Barbuda	–	–	–	–
Bahamas	96.4	–	96.5	–

Barbados	99.4	99.7	99.8	99.8
Belize	89.1	76.9	96.0	84.2
Dominica	–	–	–	–
Grenada	–	–	–	–
Guyana	95.2	–	99.8	–
Jamaica	82.2	87.6	91.2	94.5
Montserrat				
St Kitts and Nevis	–	–	–	–
St Lucia	–	–	–	–
St Vincent and the Grenadines	–	–	–	–
Suriname	–	–	–	..
Trinidad and Tobago	96.8	98.5	99.6	99.8

Source: UNDP, Human Development Report (various years)

Table 9.5 provides some data on adult literacy and youth literacy rates in selected CARICOM economies compared with those of Mauritius and Singapore. Notice that Trinidad and Tobago's adult literacy estimates increased between 1990 and 2002, and, with the exception of Barbados, was higher than the other CARICOM economies, and even higher than Mauritius and Singapore. Notice that the same trend also existed for youth literacy estimates.

Table 9.6 *Public expenditure on education, percentage of all levels, various years*

Country	Pre-primary and primary		Secondary		Tertiary	
	1990	1999–2001	1990	1999–2001	1990	1999–2001
Mauritius	37.7	32.0	36.4	38.3	16.6	15.6
Norway	39.5	48.3	24.7	20.6	15.2	25.4
Singapore	29.6	–	36.5	–	29.3	–
US	–	39.2	–	34.5	–	26.3
UK	29.7	34.4	43.8	48.4	19.6	17.2
Antigua and Barbuda	–	36.9	–	37.3	–	15.1
Bahamas	–	–	–	–	–	–
Barbados	37.5	33.4	37.6	33.9	19.2	29.9
Belize	61.0	44.9	20.2	35.1	8.1	16.2
Dominica	–	64.4	–	30.1	–	–
Grenada	64.1	–	31.7	–	0.0	–
Guyana	–	–	–	–	–	–
Jamaica	37.4	36.8	33.2	33.8	21.1	19.2
Montserrat						

Country	Pre-primary and primary		Secondary		Tertiary	
	1990	1999–2001	1990	1999–2001	1990	1999–2001
St Kitts and Nevis	–	28.5	–	31.5	–	21.2
St Lucia	48.2	–	23.3	–	12.8	–
St Vincent and the Grenadines	–	48.9	–	25.5	–	5.2
Suriname	60.5	–	14.5	–	8.8	–
Trinidad and Tobago	42.5	59.6	36.8	32.3	11.9	3.7

Source: UNDP, Human Development Report, 2004

The Caribbean has traditionally placed significant emphasis on education and as such this sector has received moderately large portions of social sector expenditure – see Table 9.6. Notice that for Trinidad and Tobago, as with all the other countries, investment has focused at the primary and secondary school levels.

Table 9.7 *Public expenditure on education as a percentage of GDP, 1990 and 1999–2001*

	1990	1999–2001
Mauritius	3.5	3.3
Antigua and Barbuda	–	3.2
Bahamas	4.0	–
Barbados	7.8	6.5
Belize	4.7	6.2
Dominica	–	5.0
Grenada	5.1	–
Guyana	3.4	4.1
Jamaica	4.7	6.3
St Kitts and Nevis	2.7	7.7
St Lucia	–	7.3
St Vincent and the Grenadines	6.4	9.3
Suriname	8.1	–
Trinidad and Tobago	3.6	4.0

Source: UNDP, Human Development Report (2004)

The UNDP's *Human Development Report* also cites data on the proportion of GDP spent on education. For the period 1999–2001, notice that Trinidad and Tobago spent the least amount (in terms of relative proportion) on education, after Mauritius, Antigua and Barbados. Note too that compared with other CARICOM economies, Trinidad and Tobago spends the lowest proportion of its budgetary outlay on education.

Table 9.8 *Share of education sector in budgetary outlays (%), 2000–03*

	2000	**2001**	**2002**	**2003**
Barbados	20.3	18.5	16.3	n.a.
Dominica	16.7	16.8	17.3	17.2
Grenada	16.4	17.1	17.3	15.9
Jamaica	18.2	18.0	0.0	15.6
St Kitts	14.2	14.4	13.6	13.0
St Lucia	23.5	21.5	22.7	21.3
Trinidad and Tobago	8.1	9.4	11.9	10.7

Source: Hosein et al. (2004)

Structural characteristics of Caribbean economies

Size

Table 9.9 gives some of the details of several CARICOM economies, compared with three of its main trading partners. Notice that based on population, GDP and land mass, these CARICOM economies are small.

Table 9.9 indicates that the economy with the largest GDP per capita in CARICOM is that of Trinidad and Tobago, and even this is only 40% of the GDP of Canada, and 27% of that of the US. Even in terms of land mass, Caribbean economies are typically small (although Guyana and Suriname are relatively large).

Trade openness

Trade openness can be measured in a variety of ways. Some of the more common approximations used in the economics literature include:

- imports as a percentage of GDP
- exports as a percentage of GDP
- average of imports and exports as a percentage of GDP.

Using Guyana as a reference point, Table 9.10 shows that the Guyanese economy is very open, with a trade to GDP ratio very much in excess of unity.

Table 9.10 *Exports and imports of Guyana, 1995–2005*

	Exports of goods and services (% of GDP)	**Imports of goods and services (% of GDP)**	**Trade (% of GDP)**
1995	101.2	112.1	213.3
1996	102.6	108.7	211.3
1997	99.7	109.5	209.1
1998	95.9	107.9	203.8
1999	96.5	104.6	201.1
2000	96.1	110.7	206.8
2001	95.0	111.4	206.4

Table 9.9 *Comparing GDP, land area and population of Canada, the US and selected CARICOM economies, 2006*

GDP per capita (constant 2000 US$)	
Canada	25 894.2
Guyana	1 043.8
Jamaica	3 357.1
Suriname	2 745.6
Trinidad and Tobago	10 388.7
US	37 791.4
Land area (sq. km)	
Canada	9 093 510
Guyana	196 850
Jamaica	10 830
Suriname	156 000
Trinidad and Tobago	5 130
US	9 161 920
Population, total	
Canada	32 649 000
Guyana	739 065
Jamaica	2 667 300
Suriname	455 273
Trinidad and Tobago	1 328 432
US	299 398 000

Source: CIA Factbook

	Exports of goods and services (% of GDP)	Imports of goods and services (% of GDP)	Trade (% of GDP)
2002	92.8	105.5	198.2
2003	89.8	99.8	189.6
2004	95.8	105.7	201.5
2005	87.9	123.9	211.8

Source: World Bank Development Indicators

Composition of exports

The composition of the export basket of any economy is very important. A country that exports an agriculture-intensive basket of exports would have a different structure of employment to, say, an economy with an export basket concentrated in manufactured goods. Table 9.11 shows the exports of Trinidad and Tobago.

Table 9.11 *The composition of Trinidad and Tobago exports (US$ million), 1990–2004*

Year	sitc0	sitc1	sitc2	sitc3	sitc4	sitc5	sitc6	sitc7	sitc8	sitc9	Total exports
1990	85.6	24.6	12.4	1275.4	3.9	295.4	190.1	40.4	31.6	2.4	1961.9
1991	90.2	23.5	3.4	1061.9	3.3	335.3	185.0	18.7	27.9	2.2	1751.3
1992	88.0	25.3	3.9	992.8	2.4	286.3	203.5	23.1	34.7	1.9	1661.9
1993	93.2	31.5	3.7	832.3	2.6	276.8	206.3	45.3	33.3	1.5	1526.6
1994	107.4	39.8	3.7	750.4	4.3	522.5	236.2	15.5	30.8	59.3	1769.9
1995	146.2	52.3	8.1	1108.9	5.5	609.5	341.0	48.8	51.7	0.1	2372.1
1996	136.4	57.7	9.2	1125.6	6.3	567.3	314.3	93.3	49.5	0.4	2360.0
1997	158.0	76.1	10.2	1087.1	8.0	616.3	360.9	97.9	53.6	0.5	2468.4
1998	152.7	88.9	7.9	922.8	9.3	505.7	376.5	69.4	59.0	0.5	2192.6
1999	149.6	78.3	6.5	1523.2	5.6	536.0	349.4	104.1	62.7	0.2	2815.6
2000	154.2	86.1	6.7	2816.5	3.6	747.7	383.7	51.4	64.1	0.7	4314.7
2001	145.2	94.7	9.2	2468.8	5.1	816.4	436.5	75.3	68.4	0.3	4119.8
2002	143.6	100.5	9.3	2313.1	5.8	643.0	474.2	93.3	66.4	0.3	3849.7
2003	125.5	101.3	11.7	3477.6	6.0	908.6	449.1	72.2	63.2	0.5	5215.7
2004	141.5	83.3	15.6	3873.4	7.3	1526.9	577.1	130.1	66.9	0.6	6422.8
% structural change	65.3	238.6	25.8	203.7	87.2	416.9	203.6	222.0	111.7	–75.0	227.4

Note: The single digit sitcs are: sitc0: food and live animals; sitc1: beverages and tobacco; sitc2: crude materials and inedible oils except fuels; sitc3: minerals, fuels, lubricants and related materials; sitc4: animal and vegetable oils and fats; sitc5: chemicals; sitc6: manufactured goods classified by materials; sitc7: machinery and transport equipment; sitc8: miscellaneous manufactured articles; sitc9: miscellaneous transactions and commodities.

Source: Hosein et al. (2004)

Referring to Table 9.11, total exports from Trinidad and Tobago increased from US$1 961.9 million in 1990 to US$6 422.8 million in 2004. This is a phenomenal increase of 227.4%. Sitc 1 (239%) and sitc 5 (417%) were the two sections in which the growth rate for the time interval 1990–2004 were in excess of the overall aggregate export growth performance. Observe that these two-export sections (sitc 3 and sitc 5, hereafter petroleum exports) accounted for the majority of Trinidad and Tobago's exports. In particular, petroleum exports accounted for 80.1% of total exports in 1990 and by 2004 its share of total exports increased even further to 84.1% (see Table 9.12).

Table 9.12 *Share of sitc 3 and sitc 5 in total exports (%), 1990–2004*

Year	Share of sitc 3 in total exports	Share of sitc 5 in total exports	Share of sitc 3 + sitc 5 in total exports
1990	65.0	15.1	80.1
1991	60.6	19.1	79.8
1992	59.7	17.2	77.0
1993	54.5	18.1	72.7
1994	42.4	29.5	71.9
1995	46.7	25.7	72.4
1996	47.7	24.0	71.7
1997	44.0	25.0	69.0
1998	42.1	23.1	65.2
1999	54.1	19.0	73.1
2000	65.3	17.3	82.6
2001	59.9	19.8	79.7
2002	60.1	16.7	76.8
2003	66.7	17.4	84.1
2004	60.3	23.8	84.1

Source: Hosein et al. (2004)

The composition of the export basket in terms of market destination is also an important consideration in analysing a country's trade pattern. Ideally an economy should try to sell to economies with the ability to pay. It should also try and sell to as broad a category of countries as possible so that a recession in any one export market does not trigger a recession in its own market.

As Table 9.13 shows, the US is an important export market for the Trinidad and Tobago economy, absorbing approximately 70% of total exports from Trinidad and Tobago in 2004. Although CARICOM absorbed 12.9% of total exports from Trinidad and Tobago in 2004, this was still much lower than the 30% which the regional block imported from Trinidad and Tobago in 1998.

Table 9.13 *The direction of Trinidad and Tobago's exports, 1990–2004*

Year	Level of exports (US$ million)				Share (%)				
	Total	US	EU	CARICOM	Total	US	EU	CARICOM	Rest of world
1990	1961.9	1144.0	110.4	259.8	100	58.3	5.6	13.2	22.9
1991	1751.3	965.3	168.2	220.5	100	55.1	9.6	12.6	22.7
1992	1661.9	879.0	99.2	257.4	100	52.9	6.0	15.5	25.6
1993	1526.6	742.2	69.8	328.2	100	48.6	4.6	21.5	25.3
1994	1769.9	859.6	166.2	371.7	100	48.6	9.4	21.0	21.0
1995	2372.1	955.2	212.4	503.3	100	40.3	9.0	21.2	29.5
1996	2360.0	1092.9	183.3	610.4	100	46.3	7.8	25.9	20.0
1997	2468.4	998.3	208.7	573.9	100	40.4	8.5	23.2	27.9
1998	2192.6	826.4	140.9	656.8	100	37.7	6.4	30.0	25.9
1999	2815.6	1097.1	184.2	726.7	100	39.0	6.5	25.8	28.7
2000	4314.7	1849.2	255.2	970.0	100	42.9	5.9	22.5	28.7
2001	4062.5	1764.8	192.2	978.0	100	43.4	4.7	24.1	27.8
2002	3809.4	1792.2	180.6	767.4	100	47.0	4.7	20.1	28.1
2003	5101.1	2791.1	160.9	1008.0	100	54.7	3.2	19.8	22.4
2004	6382.9	4420.2	193.2	822.4	100	69.3	3.0	12.9	14.8
Average	2970.1	1478.5	168.4	603.6	100	48.3	6.3	20.6	24.8
% change	4421.0	3276.2	82.8	562.6	0	11.0	−2.6	−0.3	−8.0

Source: Central Statistical office for Trinidad & Tobago

Resource base and export basket

Different Caribbean islands have different types of resource advantages. Thus Guyana has a resource advantage in gold, diamonds, bauxite and natural forest products. Trinidad and Tobago has a resource advantage in hydrocarbon-based minerals, while Jamaica has resource abundance in bauxite and its beautiful beaches. The patterns of trade for these countries show that each of the respective export baskets is significantly dependent on the country's resource base.

Poverty

The headcount poverty index, which shows the proportion of the population living below the poverty line, varies from 5% in The Bahamas to 43% in Guyana. Even in oil (and gas) rich Trinidad and Tobago, some 20% of the population is estimated to be below the poverty line. The Gini coefficient, which is used in studies to illustrate income inequality, provides a useful insight into social conditions in Caribbean countries. The Gini coefficient has a theoretical range between 0 and 1. The closer the coefficient is to 1, the greater the extent of inequality. For CARICOM countries in 1997, every member state had a Gini coefficient score in excess of 0.42 (see Figure 9.1, opposite).

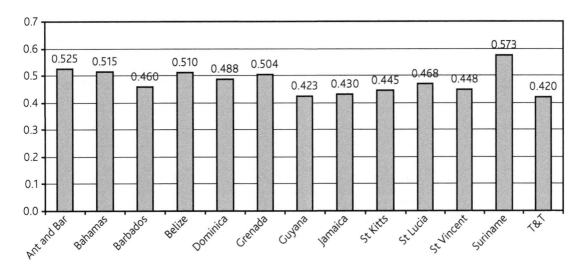

Figure 9.1 *Gini coefficients of CARICOM member states, 1997*

Source: Baker (1997)

Economic dependence

Many Caribbean economies are very dependent on the international community for their survival. Some economies are dependent on a particular export market as a principal export destination. Others are dependent on some foreign economy for an inflow of foreign direct investment, while others are dependent on the foreign economy for aid.

Table 9.14 (overleaf) provides an indication of the increasing economic dependence of the Trinidad and Tobago economy on the petroleum sector. Observe that the share of petroleum foreign direct investment (FDI) in total FDI averaged 86.9% in the period 1994–2006. The average for the years 2000–06 is in excess of the average for the 1990s. The share of the petroleum sector in total output also increased considerably in the time interval under consideration: in total output it increased from 28% in 1994 to 42.1% in 2006, an increase of 14.1 percentage points. Petroleum products are produced in Trinidad and Tobago and exported to the international community, so the rise in the share of petroleum GDP in total GDP coincides with an increase in the share of petroleum exports in total exports. Petroleum exports as a share of total exports increased from 60.8% of total exports in 1994 to 84.2% in 2006, an increase of approximately 24 percentage points. The final variable considered as an indicator of increasing economic dependence is that of petroleum revenues as a percentage of total revenues. This increased from 25.1% in 1994 to 43.2% in 2006, an increase of 18.2 percentage points. (A fifth indicator of dependence on the petroleum sector can be found in the share of petroleum FDI in domestic gross capital formation. This increased from 52.8% in 1994 to 72.7% in 1999. The unavailability of data after 1999 for gross capital formation by composition prevented a further analysis of this variable.)

Table 9.14 *Indicators of resource dependence, 1994–2006*

Year	(PFDI/FDI) %	(PGDP/GDP) %	(Petroleum export/total exports) %	(Petroleum revenue/total revenue) %
1994	52.8	28.0	60.8	25.1
1995	89.9	28.1	63.4	30.0
1996	93.9	26.4	60.1	32.7
1997	95.5	26.8	56.6	19.9
1998	76.5	29.8	50.0	14.7
1999	72.7	31.3	60.3	19.0
2000	90.3	31.7	73.3	35.9
2001	97.8	33.3	70.1	32.8
2002	93.4	38.3	66.0	23.5
2003	91.4	38.4	74.4	36.9
2004	93.9	39.3	74.3	37.0
2005	91.2	42.5	81.7	46.1
2006	91.3	42.1	84.2	43.2

Sources: Review of the Economy; author computations

Implications for regional economies

Dependence on aid

Many developing economies are dependent on foreign aid for their economic survival. There are three principal reasons why countries give economic aid to other sovereign nations: humanitarian, political and economic. From a purely humanitarian perspective, people in more fortunate economies provide humanitarian aid to people in less fortunate economies. In the Caribbean region, for example, when an economy is hit by a hurricane, other economies that have been spared often provide economic aid in the form of food relief.

From a political perspective some economies also provide aid. This was especially the case in the past when both communist and non-communist regimes provided aid to various types of economy in an attempt to win political support for their respective agendas.

From an economic perspective, some economies provide aid to other countries to help strengthen their own markets. This is especially the case when a country that has been struck by some form of disaster is an important export market destination for the economy giving the aid.

When an economy is dependent on aid it can sometimes slow the pace at which it implements economic reform. This is dangerous, as important types of administrative and bureaucratic changes that can initiate economic growth may be stalled.

Preferential trade agreements

Significantly, CARICOM member states have been able to negotiate for special non-reciprocating relationships with other countries and blocs of countries. Consequently, the Caribbean has evolved with an inbuilt dependency nurtured by acknowledgement of its geopolitical significance, and recognition of the fact that it is an underdeveloped postcolonial entity. In fact, it may be argued that preferential trading agreements have encouraged and maintained firms in a static comparative advantage position based on such commodities as sugar, bananas, rice and rum and in so doing have limited the diversification of Caribbean economies into greater value-added products. Caribbean countries pounced upon these margins of preference offered by the old economic and social order and in many member states these preferences have become institutionalised.

As Owen Arthur, the former Prime Minister of Barbados noted:

> Old and long-standing forms of economic activity have been perpetuated on the presumption that a system of international trade preferences will continue to underwrite their survival and their viability.

Arthur 2001, p.383

However, the new trend seems to be for the formation of preferential trading arrangements that is based on the principle of reciprocation. This means that preferences are given to member states but they are also expected to provide preferences to the other members within the preferential trading arrangement.

Foreign direct investment

For many capital-starved developing economies, including those of the Caribbean, foreign direct investment (FDI) is an important and critical part of their economic development process. Table 9.15 shows the importance of FDI to the gross capital formation (GCF) process (total investment) in various host regions and economies.

Table 9.15 *Inward FDI flows as a percentage of gross fixed capital formation, by host region and economy, 1970–2003*

	1970	1975	1980	1985	1990	1995	2000	2001	2002	2003
World	2.49	2.35	2.28	2.39	4.50	5.41	19.77	11.96	10.13	7.46
Developed countries	2.16	1.96	2.71	2.38	4.77	4.45	21.29	11.50	9.96	6.65
Developing countries	4.48	3.81	1.17	2.48	3.63	7.98	14.86	13.09	9.85	10.02
Latin America and the Caribbean	5.20	4.31	3.16	4.84	4.17	9.24	21.12	19.79	14.90	11.16
Antigua and Barbuda	0.00	0.00	51.13	27.78	47.70	17.29	8.80	23.64	17.91	22.30
Bahamas	0.00	23.32	2.38	–7.92	–2.64	15.29	38.94	15.72	31.23	22.64
Barbados	18.27	29.94	1.46	2.61	3.46	4.46	3.83	3.48	3.45	23.96
Belize	0.00	0.00	0.00	21.82	17.93	15.45	12.41	27.42	11.79	17.98
Dominica	0.00	0.00	0.00	10.69	19.01	78.36	14.22	18.70	25.25	23.58
Grenada	0.00	0.00	–0.05	11.43	16.55	22.57	22.26	46.09	38.67	40.09
Guyana	14.66	0.48	0.34	1.88	4.71	26.36	41.59	36.67	27.43	16.54
Jamaica	36.80	9.16	7.15	–1.94	15.03	8.95	22.16	26.07	17.74	21.76
St Kitts and Nevis	0.00	0.00	5.46	33.83	55.33	19.19	58.93	45.00	52.42	30.69
St Lucia	0.00	0.00	67.45	37.23	47.64	24.12	30.21	13.15	20.37	19.00

	1970	1975	1980	1985	1990	1995	2000	2001	2002	2003
St Vincent and the Grenadines	0.00	0.00	4.73	6.38	13.08	38.35	31.85	20.45	29.97	37.30
Trinidad and Tobago	48.43	18.59	10.53	0.08	15.66	29.97	42.32	41.73	47.36	36.87

Source: World Investment Report (various years)

Activity 9.2

1 List THREE structural characteristics of a Caribbean economy with which you are familiar.

2 Outline THREE factors that constrain the economic development in Caribbean economies.

Feedback

1 Three structural characteristics of a Caribbean economy are:
- small size
- high degree of openness
- high economic dependency.

2 Three factors that constrain the economic development in Caribbean economies are:
- dependency on aid
- vulnerability to natural and man-made change
- changes in world prices.

Activity 9.3

For any named CARICOM economy, evaluate the various sources and destination sectors of FDI.

Feedback

Main sources of FDI (US$ millions)

	US	UK	Canada	Germany	Japan	India	Other
1991	98.5	38.5	0.1	22.8	0.1	0.0	−15.9
1992	123.1	40.4	0.1	0.0	0.0	0.0	7.4
1993	339.3	31.0	0.2	3.7	0.1	0.0	−1.7
1994	398.0	8.7	0.0	47.0	0.0	70.1	−2.8
1995	275.4	15.9	1.2	6.6	0.0	0.0	−3.4
1996	328.6	21.6	0.8	10.1	0.0	0.0	−4.8
1997	482.6	55.2	158.8	116.1	0.0	150.0	36.9
1998	524.8	99.6	10.9	11.9	0.0	34.0	50.7
1999	274.6	232.1	9.3	7.5	0.1	57.0	62.7
2000	315.9	254.7	1.8	14.0	0.0	11.1	82.0
2001	372.3	307.1	7.1	36.5	0.1	20.8	91.1
2002	352.7	290.9	7.2	34.8	0.1	19.8	85.2

Source: Central Bank of Trinidad and Tobago

FDI flows to the petroleum sector, of which US$ millions

	Petroleum	Mining and exploration and production refineries, petrochemicals	Service contractors, marketing and distribution	Food, drink and tobacco	Chemicals and non-metallic minerals	Assembly-type and related industries	Distribution	All other sectors	Total
1991	125.1	118.2	6.9	2.7	−0.5	0.4	−0.3	16.7	144.1
1992	153.2	144.6	8.6	−0.5	0.3	0.3	1.6	16.1	171.0
1993	348.9	348.7	0.2	1.9	0.1	−0.4	4.2	17.9	372.6
1994	275.1	290.0	−14.9	5.7	128.7	−1.9	1.0	112.4	521.0
1995	266.0	253.6	12.4	3.2	1.7	−0.4	6.2	19.0	295.7
1996	334.7	320.6	14.1	4.3	2.3	0.7	4.4	9.9	356.3
1997	952.2	947.6	6.6	8.4	2.3	−0.7	3.1	31.7	999.6
1998	599.7	585.3	14.4	9.1	2.2	−0.1	2.0	119.0	731.9
1999	467.7	449.0	18.7	3.8	2.9	0.1	−0.5	169.3	643.3
2000	613.7	613.9	−0.2	−21.3	1.8	−18.4	1.7	102.0	679.5
2001	816.3	787.2	29.1	−18.1	−0.3	5.5	0.5	31.0	834.9
2002	738.2	694.8	43.4	3.6	1.5	8.1	−0.7	40.0	790.7

Source: Central Bank of Trinidad and Tobago

Table 9.15 indicates that FDI flows as a percentage of GCF increased between 1970 and 2000 for all of the economies listed. Observe that after 2000, FDI/GCF fell for most of these economies. Within CARICOM, all of the CARICOM economies had an FDI/GCF ratio in excess of 15% in 2003. Note that in Grenada, St Kitts and Nevis, St Vincent and Trinidad and Tobago, more than 30% of the GCF was accounted for by FDI inflows.

In terms of the stock of FDI as a percentage of GDP, this has persistently improved in the world, as well as in developed and developing economies as entire blocks. By 2003, all CARICOM economies had stocks of FDI as a percentage of GDP, which were in excess of 18%. Dominica, Grenada, St Kitts and Nevis, St Lucia and St Vincent and the Grenadines carried FDI stocks in excess of 100% of GDP (see Table 9.16).

Table 9.16 *Inward FDI stock as a percentage of GDP, by host region and economy, 1980–2003*

	1980	1985	1990	1995	2000	2001	2002	2003
World	6.60	8.34	9.30	10.23	19.31	20.94	22.96	22.94
Developed countries	4.85	6.21	8.22	8.90	16.60	18.01	20.51	20.67
Developing countries	12.45	16.32	14.70	16.30	29.26	31.69	31.86	31.45
Antigua and Barbuda	21.26	46.47	74.48	88.57	84.43	86.73	90.58	94.35
Bahamas	40.99	23.41	18.86	21.18	32.26	34.33	37.33	39.23

	1980	1985	1990	1995	2000	2001	2002	2003
Barbados	12.06	10.46	10.02	12.48	12.27	13.29	14.07	18.35
Belize	6.36	9.36	22.12	26.46	38.06	43.82	41.64	43.51
Dominica	0.14	10.73	42.88	89.87	100.39	106.37	116.96	123.09
Grenada	1.54	9.83	31.74	60.71	84.96	101.64	111.63	124.47
Guyana	4.18	8.57	10.63	71.59	106.63	114.67	121.14	125.89
Jamaica	21.28	25.02	18.65	29.84	45.04	50.64	57.26	62.41
St Kitts and Nevis	2.08	40.51	100.62	105.49	147.23	166.43	183.77	189.01
St Lucia	70.08	104.25	80.21	92.10	116.52	125.02	126.70	125.68
St Vincent and the Grenadines	1.99	7.53	24.33	67.89	145.41	146.02	150.17	155.43
Suriname	−3.40	5.33	−167.68	−92.93	−80.77	−97.59	−86.05	−81.10
Trinidad and Tobago	15.66	23.30	41.29	68.77	85.82	86.12	92.48	92.40

Source: World Investment Report (various years)

Table 9.17 Highest-ranked countries using Briguglio's composite vulnerability index

Rank	Country
1	Antigua and Barbuda
2	Tonga
3	Seychelles
4	Vanuatu
5	St Kitts and Nevis
6	St Lucia
7	Chad
8	Singapore
9	St Vincent and the Grenadines
10	Grenada
11	Bahamas
12	Jamaica
13	Kiribati
14	Mauritius
15	Belize

Source: Briguglio (1995)

Vulnerability to natural and man-made change

In regional and international trade discussions, the governments of CARICOM countries have been underscoring the point that despite middle-income status, their economies remain extremely vulnerable, and poverty is a serious concern. These economies are vulnerable not only to natural factors, for example hurricanes, but also to 'man-made' market developments affecting their major exports.

Economic vulnerability in particular can be defined as the risk of harmful unforeseen events associated with exogenous shocks. These shocks can have a negative impact on welfare, growth and development. They can be grouped into three categories:

1 Environmental shocks, which include natural disasters such as earthquakes, hurricanes, typhoons, drought

2 External trade and exchange related shocks, such as global interest rate fluctuations, severe decreases in demand, instability of commodity prices and the like

3 Non-environmental domestic shocks, such as political instability, uprisings and so on

Briguglio (Small Island States and their Economic vulnerabilities, *World Development*, 23:1615–1632, 1995) derived a composite vulnerability index for small island states and their economic vulnerabilities. Briguglio attempted to show that small states are typified by a special set of disadvantages, which makes them very vulnerable to a number of external forces. Based on three variables – economic exposure, a transport index and a disaster prone index – Briguglio determined that the 15 most vulnerable economies in the world were those listed in Table 9.17. Note that eight of these 15 countries are CARICOM member states.

Changes in world prices

When an economy is heavily dependent on a particular commodity in the international market place and the price of this commodity changes, then this can create adverse economic outcomes in the benefiting economy.

Some developmental economists such as Raul Prebisch and Hans Singer argued that the production of goods along comparative advantage lines will cause developing countries to continue to produce mainly primary goods for exports. However, primary goods generally have low price and income elasticity of demand, which in turn translates into low levels of relative incomes compared with economies producing manufacturing goods.

End test

1   Distinguish between economic growth and economic development.

2   What is endogenous growth theory?

3   List five indices of human development.

4   How can the degree of trade openness be measured?

5   What are the main reasons why countries give economic aid?

End test feedback

1   Economic growth refers to the expansion in a country's national income, output and employment. It is the quantitative increase in national income and results from an increase in either the quantity or quality of factors of production, and the efficiency with which it is utilised.

   Economic development refers to the more qualitative changes associated with growth. Note that economic growth is a prerequisite condition for development, as development essentially implies an improvement in the standard of living of the population.

2   Endogenous growth theory attempts to take growth theory beyond the traditional models and develop models that explain how technological progress occurs. These growth theories have been collectively referred to as endogenous growth models and they include the work of Paul Romer and Robert Lucas. Endogenous growth theorists emphasise the importance of physical capital accumulation, research and development and human capital development in driving the economic growth process in modern economies.

3   Life expectancy, literacy, crude death rate, dependency rate, infant mortality rate.

4   Trade openness can be measured in a variety of ways. Some of the more common approximations used in the economics literature include:

- imports as a percentage of GDP
- exports as a percentage of GDP
- average of imports and exports as a percentage of GDP.

5   There are three principle reasons why countries give economic aid to other sovereign nations: humanitarian, political and economic.

   From a purely humanitarian perspective, people in more fortunate economies provide humanitarian aid to people in less fortunate economies. In the Caribbean region, for example, when an economy is hit by a hurricane, other economies that have been spared often provide economic aid in the form of food relief.

   From a political perspective, some economies also provide aid. This was especially the case in the past when both communist and non-communist regimes provided aids to various types of economy in an attempt to win political support for their respective agendas.

   From an economic perspective, some economies provide aid to other countries to help strengthen their own markets. This is especially the case when a country that has been struck by some form of disaster is an important export market destination country for the economy giving the aid.

10 International trade

Specific objectives

You should have an understanding of:

the role of exports in creating domestic income and the role of imports in generating income for foreigners

the factors that determine exports and imports including: international price, domestic production, domestic prices and exchange rates, international economic activity as it affects the tourism market in the Caribbean, shifts in international demand and the emergence of substitutes, changes in international income

foreign exchange earnings from exports: access to capital goods, the export multiplier, access to consumer goods, increased domestic production

the Theory of Comparative Advantage

arguments for protection including: infant industries, employment, food security

arguments for trade liberalisation including access to technology, availability of cheaper goods and services, application of the Theory of Comparative Advantage

methods of protection including: tariffs, quotas and other non-tariff methods

explanation of the commodity terms of trade

The role of exports in creating domestic income and the role of imports in generating income for foreigners

When an economy sells goods and services to the foreign economy it generates both employment and income for factors of production in the home economy. In the same way, imports by the foreign economy from the home economy provide employment and income for the factors of production from the foreign economy.

The factors that determine exports and imports

International price

Other things being constant, the goods and services exported and imported by an economy depend on its relative international price. To illustrate this, consider Figure 10.1 (the black arrows show conditions that are the same between the home country and the foreign country; the white arrows show conditions that are different): in this simple model the main distinction between the home country and the foreign country is the differences in the endowment of supply of factors of production, which explains the Heckscher-Ohlin (HO) model as the basis for trade. In the lower right-hand segment the demand for final commodities is established by both the tastes of households and the distribution in the ownership of factors of production (or distribution of income). The demand for factors of production is derived from the demand for commodities. The derived demand for factors and the supply of factors together determine factor prices. Commodity prices are influenced by both the state of technology and the prices of factors of production. In summary, therefore, the HO model indicates that the economy with the cheaper good will sell that good to other economies and, in turn, import the goods produced cheaply by these other economies.

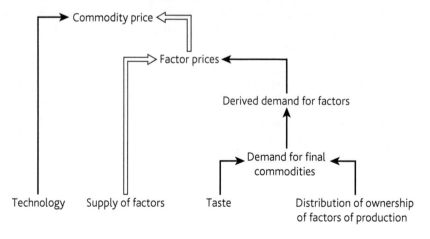

Figure 10.1 *A general equilibrium illustration of the HO model*

Domestic production

This is also linked to Figure 10.1. The goods and services that an economy produces in abundance are linked to its abundant factors of production. The economics literature has emphasised in various places that a nation produces and exports those commodities in which it has an abundance of factors of production and imports those commodities that call for factor proportions in the opposite direction.

Domestic prices and exchange rates

Although an economy may have an abundance of a particular block of factors of production, if its exchange rate is overvalued then it may make its commodity relatively unattractive to the consumers in the foreign economy. To illustrate what is meant by an overvalued exchange rate, assume that the true exchange rate of the Trinidad and Tobago dollar to the US dollar is TT$8 = US$1. If, for a variety of reasons, the exchange rate is kept at TT$6.25 to US$1, then this exchange rate is overvalued. An overvalued exchange rate makes it easier for domestic consumers to buy goods and services produced in the foreign economy but more difficult for the domestic economy to export.

International economic activity as it affects the tourism market in the Caribbean

The correlation between tourism and economic development must be considered by policy-makers, especially in economies with a buoyant tourism sector. One key impact of tourism is the extent to which it can help to ease balance of payments constraints. In the context of the two-gap model, tourism can provide valuable foreign exchange which can be used to import capital goods necessary for the economic development of the host nation.

Tourism activity can also bring into 'commercial' use formerly unemployed resources from which the host economy can derive rents. When tourists visit a country, the portfolio of goods and services that they consume includes non-tradables and unpriced natural resources. These unpriced natural resources help to generate a valuable source of economic rents for the host economy via the tourism industry. In Mexico, for example, the government has utilised tourism to enhance regional growth by establishing instant resorts in such peripheral locations as Cancun and Puerto Villata. In a similar manner, the Jamaican government has utilised tourism as an instrument to accelerate the growth of the Montego Bay district on the north coast of Jamaica.

In small, highly open developing economies, such as those of the CARICOM sphere, the predominant type of unemployment is structural and stems mainly from the inability of the existing capital endowment to absorb the entire labour force even in the best of times. In such economies, tourism can create niche opportunities for employment in craft industries and for workers in the construction, utilities, restaurants and hotel and guesthouses subsectors of the economy. Collectively, these potential benefits of tourism (including its contribution to the balance of payments), the development of hitherto unused natural resources, and the creation of employment opportunities, create further economic gains when their multiplier effects are taken into consideration. However, the economic potential of such sectors is matched by its vulnerability to international shocks. Consider Table 10.1 (overleaf), which shows the trends in tourism arrivals to various CARICOM destinations. Notice that for most of the listed countries tourism flows between 2001 and 2002

Specific objectives

interpretation of changes in the commodity terms of trade

export price index divided by import price index multiplied by 100.

were less than the estimates for 2000 (recall the terrorist attack on the World Trade Center on 11 September 2001). Notice though that tourism flows thereafter began to recover.

Table 10.1 *International tourism, number of arrivals (thousands)*

	1995	2000	2001	2002	2003	2004	2005	2006
Antigua and Barbuda	220	230	215	218	239	268	267	273
Bahamas, The	1598	1544	1538	1513	1510	1561	1608	1600
Barbados	442	545	507	498	531	552	548	563
Belize	131	196	195	200	221	231	237	247
Dominica	60	70	66	69	73	80	86	92
Grenada	108	129	123	132	142	134	99	n.a.
Guyana	106	105	99	104	101	122	117	113
Jamaica	1147	1323	1277	1266	1350	1415	1479	1679
St Kitts and Nevis	79	73	71	69	91	118	128	132
St Lucia	231	270	250	253	277	298	318	303
St Vincent and the Grenadines	60	73	71	78	79	87	96	97
Suriname	43	57	54	60	82	138	160	n.a.
Trinidad and Tobago	260	399	383	384	409	443	463	n.a.

Source: World Bank Development Indicators (2008)

Shifts in international demand and the emergence of substitutes

When an economy is heavily dependent on exports of a particular commodity, the production of which is made redundant by the emergence of a substitute commodity, then that economy can experience significant adverse changes in its export revenue earnings. In the last five decades technical progress has magnified the substitution of natural primary commodities with synthetic substitutes, to the detriment of primary-producing developing economies, for example nylon replacing cotton, and the fall in world demand for copper as fibre-optic cables replace traditional telecoms infrastructure.

Changes in international income

Some commodities have low income elasticity of demand. This means that when there is an increase in international incomes the export revenues of economies exporting low income elasticity commodities would realise a relative decline in export revenues.

Foreign exchange earnings from exports

Access to capital goods

When a country exports its goods and services to the international community it earns valuable foreign exchange, which it can use to purchase capital goods produced in foreign economies. Capital goods imports are critical to developing economies as they help to produce all types of goods including goods for aiding development.

The export multiplier

The export multiplier provides an indication of the expansion in overall economic activity occasioned by an increase in exports. As with the simple multiplier, the export multiplier depends on the availability of spare capacity in the economy.

Access to consumer goods

Apart from capital goods, an increase in export revenue earnings also allows domestic consumers to purchase foreign consumer goods and so improve their consumption welfare.

Increased domestic production

When constraints on the imports of capital goods are eased, as occurs when an economy has an adequate flow of export revenues, this facilitates an increase in the production of goods and services in the domestic economy.

The Theory of Comparative Advantage

Absolute advantage

As early as 1776, Adam Smith noted that nations can be analysed in the same way that households can and that free trade among nations with specialisation would improve the welfare of all nations. In *The Wealth of Nations*, Adam Smith argued that free trade offered the best portfolio of opportunities for all countries. Smith's main suggestion was that with free trade the nations of the world could specialise in the production of those commodities in which they had an absolute advantage and import those commodities in which they had a disadvantage. International specialisation would therefore lead to an increase in world output and all nations would benefit.

The Theory of Absolute Advantage set out in this section is based on the following list of assumptions:

1 We assume two countries, two commodities and two factors of production.
2 Factors are easily substitutable between productive options.
3 The analysis is for a particular period of time with a given level of technology.
4 Constant cost economies of scale are assumed so that changes in production have no effect on the costs of production.
5 There are no barriers to trade in existence between trade partners.

To portray Smith's thinking on absolute advantage, this section proceeds with an example. Table 10.2 shows the output per man-hour for the Jamaican and Trinidad and Tobago economy as concerns the production of methanol and sugar.

Observe that Trinidad and Tobago can produce methanol six times as efficiently as Jamaica, while Jamaica can produce sugar three times as efficiently as Trinidad and Tobago. Suppose that Trinidad and Tobago exchanged 12 barrels of methanol (the equivalent of 2 tonnes of sugar) with Jamaica to obtain 6 tonnes of sugar. These 4 extra units of sugar

Activity 10.1

1 Distinguish between exports and imports.

2 Give ONE example of an export from the Caribbean community (CARICOM).

Feedback

1

Export	Import
Sale of goods and services to a foreign country	Purchase of goods and services from a foreign country

2 Sugar

Table 10.2 *Output per man-hours*

	Trinidad and Tobago	Jamaica
Methanol (barrels/ man-hour)	12	2
Sugar (tonnes/ man-hour)	2	6

are available to Trinidad and Tobago and represent a gain of 2 hours of Trinidad and Tobago time. Jamaica will also benefit, for the 12 units of methanol it receives would have taken it 6 hours to produce. These 6 hours, however, could be used by the Jamaicans to produce 36 tonnes of sugar. So, by exchanging 6 units of sugar for 12 units of methanol Jamaica can gain 30 tonnes of sugar or save 5 man-hours.

Smith, therefore, argued for greater specialisation on an international basis to improve global resource allocation and, by extension, global output. Note though that world output is only increased in Smith's argument if each nation holds an absolute advantage in the production of at least one commodity.

David Ricardo, a British economist, was able to expand on some of Smith's ideas by explaining the conditions under which an economy with no absolute advantage could trade and gain.

The Theory of Comparative Advantage

Smith's analysis left an unanswered question: Why would trade occur between two countries if one had an absolute advantage in the production of both goods? In the late 18th and 19th centuries, the UK was the most advanced country in the world with an absolute advantage in the production of most goods. Given this situation, why would the UK trade with less productive areas such those in the Americas? David Ricardo developed the answer. Expanding upon Adam Smith's work based on absolute advantage, Ricardo formulated the Theory of Comparative Advantage.

Comparative advantage theory was first introduced by Robert Torrens in 1815 in an essay on the corn trade. However, a systematic explanation was developed by David Ricardo in 1817 in the book *On the Principles of Political Economy and Taxation*. The Theory of Comparative Advantage states that it is beneficial for two countries to trade, although one country may be able to produce all of the items traded more cheaply than the other. Emphasis is placed on the ratio between how easily two countries can produce different kinds of goods. In this case the absolute cost of production is not emphasised.

Table 10.3 *Output per man-hour*

	Trinidad and Tobago	Jamaica
Methanol (barrels/hr)	12	2
Sugar (tonnes/hr)	6	4

Let us assume we had a situation such as that shown in Table 10.3, where Trinidad and Tobago can produce more of both methanol (M) and sugar (S) than Jamaica per man-hour. (This is not an unusual position as many developed economies have factor endowment attributes that enable them to produce more of all commodities at lower per unit costs than developing economies.)

Observe that if Trinidad and Tobago were to exchange 12 units of methanol for 12 units of sugar with Jamaica, then Trinidad and Tobago would be giving up 1 hour's worth of effort but receiving 2 hours' worth of its productive capability in sugar, so that it benefits by 6 tonnes of sugar. In turn, if Jamaica were to produce 12 units of methanol, Jamaica would need to deploy 6 hours of labour, so that it saves 3 hours when it exchanges 12 tonnes of sugar for 12 barrels of methanol with Trinidad and Tobago, as the Jamaicans utilise only 3 hours of labour to produce 12 tonnes of sugar.

So, with an exchange of 12 methanol for 12 sugar, Trinidad and Tobago gains 6 tonnes of sugar and Jamaica 12 units of methanol. $12M = 12S$ is called the international terms of trade, but it is not the only terms of trade at which both nations benefit. Let us investigate this point a bit further.

Recall that in Trinidad and Tobago 1 man-hour can produce either $12M$ or $6S$, which means that it will not be in Trinidad and Tobago's best interest to give up $12M$ for less than $6S$. If this were the case, Trinidad and

Tobago could simply take 1 man-hour and produce 6S. In a parallel vein of reasoning, Jamaica can utilise 1 man-hour to produce 2 units of M or 4 units of S. In this scenario, it will not be practical for Jamaica to give up more than 24S to obtain 12M. If such were the case, it would be best for Jamaica to produce its own methanol as it would be too costly to import.

So, we have established some boundaries within which trade will be beneficial for both economies:

- Trinidad and Tobago must get more than 6S for 12M.
- Jamaica must not be required to give up more than 24S for 12M.

The international terms of trade must, therefore, be such that 12M trade for at least 6S for Trinidad and Tobago and less than 24S for Jamaica to gain: 6S < 12M < 24S.

Observe that 18S (24S – 6S) represents the total gain from trade. The distribution of the gains from trade depends upon the actual values at which the terms of trade settles. The closer the terms of trade settles to 6S for 12M, the more Jamaica gains from trade. Similarly, if 12M settles close to 24S then Trinidad and Tobago reaps the larger share of trade.

Adam Smith and David Ricardo based their theories on the assumption that output is a function of a single factor of production, labour. Using this argument, we can express the cost of producing methanol in terms of the cost of producing sugar.

Let initial conditions be such that in Trinidad and Tobago 1 man-hour can be used to produce 12M or 6S; alternatively 1M requires 1/12 man-hours and 1S requires 1/6 man-hours. In Jamaica 1M requires 1/2 man-hour while 1S requires 1/4 man-hour. This information is summarised in Table 10.4.

Table 10.4 *Man-hours to produce methanol and sugar*

	Trinidad and Tobago	Jamaica
Cost in man-hours to produce 1M	$\frac{1}{12}$	$\frac{1}{2}$
Cost in man-hours to produce 1S	$\frac{1}{6}$	$\frac{1}{4}$

Let $\left(\frac{PS}{PM}\right)T$ and $\left(\frac{PS}{PM}\right)J$ represent the price/cost relation in Trinidad and Tobago and Jamaica respectively.

$$\left(\frac{PS}{PM}\right)T = \left(\frac{\left(\frac{1}{6}\right)}{\left(\frac{1}{12}\right)}\right) = 2$$

$$\left(\frac{PS}{PM}\right)J = \left(\frac{\left(\frac{1}{4}\right)}{\left(\frac{1}{2}\right)}\right) = \frac{1}{2}$$

Since $\left(\frac{PS}{PM}\right)J < \left(\frac{PS}{PM}\right)T$ then in Jamaica sugar is relatively cheaper to produce. Trade needs to take place somewhere between Jamaica's price and Trinidad and Tobago's price, i.e. $\frac{1}{2} < \frac{PS}{PM} < 2$. As long as a terms of trade holds within this range of values, Trinidad and Tobago can buy sugar from Jamaica and trade will be initiated.

Activity 10.2

Consider Figure 10.2 which shows the demand and supply conditions for a single commodity A in two countries, X and Y.

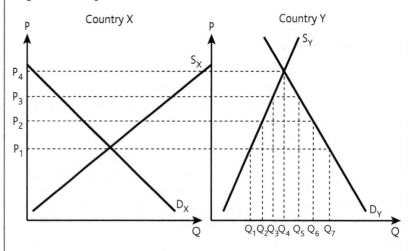

Figure 10.2

1 Which country will export commodity A?

2 At a price of P_2, how much of commodity A will be demanded by country Y, how much will be imported.

Feedback

1 Country X will engage exports.

2 Q_6 will be demanded – Q_2 will be imported.

Arguments for protection

Infant industries

The infant industry argument was introduced in 1791 by Sir Alexander Hamilton in his *Report on Manufactures*, and Friedrich List, a German economist, applied it in the early 19th century as the basis of an argument to shield German industries from British industries. A country may sometimes implement protectionist measures to allow its infant industries the opportunity to mature under protected market conditions, until its firms can effectively participate in international trade. However, some economists have argued that the successful maturity of an infant does not constitute proof that the industry would not have emerged on its own.

Employment

Some economies implement protectionary measures to protect their domestic economy. This argument is invalid in the sense that the wages of labour alone does not condition the employment of labour, as the productivity of labour also has to be considered. If productivity levels in any Caribbean economy are higher than in, say, China, then that Caribbean economy would need no protection from cheap Chinese labour.

Food security

An economy that is concerned about its domestic food security situation may wish to impose protectionary measures so that its farmers can run a profitable business that allows a lower level of dependence on the foreign economy for food.

Activity 10.3

Class discussion

Discuss some drawbacks associated with protectionism.

Feedback

Discussion topics can include the following:

- Lack of competition results in greater inefficiency

- High bureaucratic and administrative costs associated with maintaining protection

- Retaliation from trade partners

Methods of protection

Tariffs

Tariffs are the most popular form of protection. They act in the same way as taxes. Tariffs may be *ad valorem* or specific. An *ad valorem* tariff is the portion of the market price of an imported good, paid to the government, while a specific tax is on the weight or physical quantity imported of a commodity.

The economic effects of a tariff may be discussed as follows. Let the world price of the commodity be W_p (see Figure 10.3). With a tariff, the domestic price is now the original world price plus the tariff. Specifically, if W_p is the world price and we impose an *ad valorem* tariff t, the domestic price level becomes $W_p (1 + t)$. The imposition of a tariff, by virtue of providing a rise in the price of the foreign commodity on the domestic market, benefits domestic producers of this commodity, whose output would now be competing against a higher-priced substitute. Note that higher price levels reduce the consumer surplus of consumers.

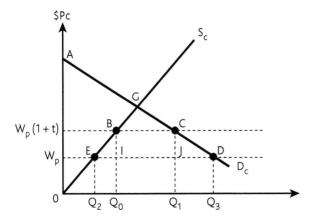

Figure 10.3 *The economic effects of a tax on a small economy*

At W_p the consumer surplus of the small economy is ADW_p. Producer surplus associated with a domestic production level of Q_2 is W_pE0. Given that the HC would like to consume Q_3 units of this commodity and produces only Q_2 units, then $Q_3 - Q_2$ units of this commodity is imported. Table 10.5 provides a summary.

Table 10.5 *Economic effects of the tariff in Figure 10.3*

	Pre-tariff	Post-tariff
Price to consumer	W_p	$W_p (1 + t)$
Domestic consumption	Q_3	Q_1
Domestic production	Q_2	Q_0
Imports	$Q_3 - Q_2$	$Q_1 - Q_0$
Consumer surplus	$W_p A D$	$W_p (1 + t) AC$
Producers' surplus	$0 W_p E$	$0 W_p (1 + t) B$
Government revenue	0	IBCJ
Deadweight consumption loss	0	JCD
Deadweight production efficiency loss	0	EBI

To evaluate more specifically the welfare effects in a tariff, a trapezium extract of Figure 10.3 is used. Figure 10.4 is divided into four parts:

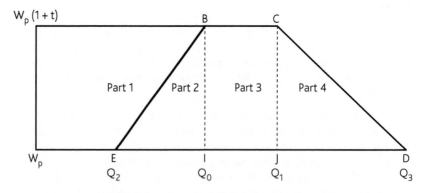

Figure 10.4 *Decomposition of the fall in consumer surplus associated with a tariff*

■ **Part 1:** The increase in domestic price results in an expansion on domestic supply. Part 1 in Figure 10.4 therefore represents a decrease in consumer surplus which is transferred to producers as an increase in producer welfare.

■ **Parts 2 and 4:** These are those parts of consumer surplus that society as a whole loses. These two triangles are known as deadweight losses. Part 2 is associated with a deadweight production loss, and part 4 a deadweight consumption loss.

■ **Part 3:** This area represents the tariff revenues, where $W_p (1 + t) - W_p$ is the magnitude of the tariff and $Q_1 - Q_0$ represents imports.

Therefore, when a country implements a tariff, the overall level of consumer welfare falls and society carries a deadweight cost. Note that the slope of the demand and supply curves conditions the size of these deadweight losses.

Non-tariff measures cover a broad range including:

■ quotas

■ embargoes

■ exchange controls

■ import deposit schemes

■ voluntary export restraints

■ product standard regulation

■ complex customs procedures

■ indirect measures

■ subsidies

■ campaigns against imports.

Quotas

Quotas are limits on the amount of goods that can enter a country. They can be of a physical nature, for example, 10 cars per month; or they may take the form of a value, for example, no more than $500 000 in imports of item X per month. Governments implement quotas for a variety of reasons, including the following:

■ To protect small infant industries from large-scale competition: Since quotas limit the amount of a commodity entering a country, the interest of local industries and small infant industries will be protected.

■ To act as a measure to reduce competition against local products: In some cases quotas give local industries some level of monopoly power to ensure their survival. This is necessary, especially in the case of small developing countries that sometimes utilise suboptimal production techniques with an associated high cost of production, making it very difficult for local firms to compete with products from more efficient foreign firms.

- As a form of retaliation against trading policies set by other countries: If, for example, country A imposes tariffs on products from country B, country B may restrict goods from country A from entering country B's market, thus reducing country A's exports.

Figure 10.5 outlines the economic implications of imposing a quota in an economy.

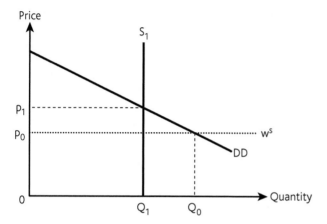

Figure 10.5 *Illustration of a quota*

A quota restricts output from Q_0 to Q_1 and price increases from P_0 to P_1. With a quota there is a fixed import level of imports of Q_1.

Embargoes

An embargo is the most extreme form of a quota. It represents a zero import volume for a commodity. All economies have an embargo on the import of some types of drugs, for example, marijuana or cocaine.

Exchange control

A government can require that its exporters declare all of the foreign exchange that they earn with the central bank. In this way, importers requiring foreign exchange will have to go to the central bank to buy it. As a result the central bank and the government can effectively control the amount of foreign money leaving the country and, therefore, the amount of imports.

Import deposit schemes

Some governments limit the amount of goods imported by requiring importers to make a deposit at the central bank before they can import goods from abroad. The objective of the import deposit is to limit the liquidity of the importers so as to restrict the amount of goods they can afford to import.

Export subsidies

Governments may also subsidise the production of exports to make them cheaper and more competitive on the world market. Subsidies can also be given to producers for domestic consumption to make them cheaper than imports.

Example

The superscripts 99 and 00 represent the years 1999 and 2000 respectively. The base year is 1999.

$$P \times 99 = 100$$

$$P \times 00 = 95$$

$$Pm99 = 100$$

$$Pm00 = 110$$

$$NBTT99 = \frac{P_x^{99}}{P_m^{99}} = \frac{100}{100} = 100$$

(expressed as a percentage)

$$NBTT00 = \frac{P_x^{00}}{P_m^{00}} = \frac{95}{110} = 86$$

representing a 14% decline.

Table 10.6 *Terms of trade in developed and developing economies, 1990–2003*

Year	Terms of trade	
	Developed countries	Developing countries
1990	103	101
1991	104	101
1992	104	100
1993	104	101
1994	105	102
1995	105	102
1996	103	102
1997	104	103
1998	105	100
1999	105	99
2000	100	100
2001	102	98
2002	103	98
2003	105	97

Source: UNCTAD Statistical Handbook (various years)

Voluntary export restraint

A voluntary export restraint is an agreement between governments for one country, say country A, to limit its exports of a particular good to the other country, say country B.

Arguments for trade liberalisation

On purely economic grounds, it is difficult to support most of the reasons advanced for restrictions on free trade. This section outlines and discusses some of the reasons advanced for freer international trade.

When a country engages in free trade, it benefits from a more efficient allocation of scarce resources. This means that there is less economic wastage as domestic firms have to compete with efficient foreign firms for the domestic market. A strategy of trade liberalisation that encourages foreign direct investment would also help to accelerate the developmental process, as the exploitation of some natural resources – for example, crude oil deposits in deepwater areas – is very expensive and generally needs financially well-endowed foreign firms to assist. Trade liberalisation in this regard enables easier access to technology and cheaper goods and services including raw materials.

With trade liberalisation and a larger amount of imports, the domestic economy can benefit from the imports of much-needed physical capital equipment. The import of physical capital is critical to the economic development process because it helps to deepen capital-to-labour ratios in developing economies and this can help to promote the level of economic output.

Exports by domestic firms help to provide the domestic economy with valuable foreign exchange that can in turn be used to help purchase much-needed foreign capital and goods and services.

In summary, what trade liberalisation does is facilitate the domestic firm producing at one level but consuming at another level. Trade liberalisation in the context of the Theory of Comparative Advantage allows an economy to specialise production and increase overall output levels.

The commodity terms of trade

The commodity terms of trade index (also called the net barter terms of trade index) presented in this chapter, can be represented as:

$$\text{Net barter terms of trade (NBTT)} = \left(\frac{\text{EPi}}{\text{MPi}}\right) \times 100$$

where

EPi = export price index

MPi = import price index

A value of this index above 100 indicates an improvement in the NBTT and a fall below 100 indicates a worsening of the NBTT.

A change in the terms of trade affects the command of one unit of export on imports. Assume that initially 1 metric tonne of methanol produced for export in country A purchased 1 tonne of sugar produced in country B. A favourable change in country A's net barter terms of trade, however, say because of an increase in the price of methanol, may result in this same metric tonne of methanol fetching more than 1 tonne of sugar.

Table 10.6 illustrates the terms of trade of both developed and developing economies for the period 1990–2003. Observe that while the terms of trade for developed economies improved from 1990 to 2003, for developing economies it actually fell.

Feedback

The terms of trade index for country A $= \dfrac{\text{export price index}}{\text{import price index}} \times \dfrac{100}{1}$

$$= \dfrac{148}{125} \times 100 = 118.4$$

Activity 10.4

The table below shows the import and export price indices for country A in the year 2002.

Year	Import price index	Export price index
2002	125	148

Calculate, to one decimal place, the terms of trade index for country A.

End test

1 What is the Theory of Absolute Advantage?
2 What are the assumptions on which the Theory of Absolute Advantage is premised?
3 What is the Theory of Comparative Advantage?
4 Why would a country engage protectionist policies?
5 List 10 non-tariff barriers to trade that a country may wish to impose.

End test feedback

1 The Theory of Absolute Advantage advocated that with free trade the nations of the world could specialise in the production of those commodities in which they had an absolute advantage and import those commodities in which they had a disadvantage. International specialisation would therefore lead to an increase in world output and all nations would benefit.

2 • We assume two countries, two commodities and two factors of production.
   • Factors are easily substitutable between productive options.
   • The analysis is for a particular period of time with a given level of technology.
   • Constant cost economies of scale are assumed so that changes in production have no effect on the costs of production.
   • There are no barriers to trade in existence between trade partners.

3 The Theory of Comparative Advantage states that it is beneficial for two countries to trade, although one country may be able to produce all of the items

traded more cheaply than the other. Emphasis is placed on the ratio between how easily two countries can produce different kinds of goods. In this case the absolute cost of production is not emphasised.

4 Protectionist policies might be used:
   • to protect infant industries
   • to protect employment
   • to maintain or enhance food security.

5 • Quotas
   • Embargoes
   • Exchange controls
   • Import deposit schemes
   • Voluntary export restraints
   • Product standard regulation
   • Complex customs procedures
   • Indirect measures
   • Subsidies
   • Campaigns against imports

Balance of payments and exchange rates

Specific objectives

You should have an understanding of:

the meaning of the balance of payments

capital items and current items

the causes and consequences of balance of payments – disequilibria

policy responses to balance of payments crises including: devaluation, expenditure switching and expenditure reducing measures

the meaning of exchange rates

determination of exchange rates

fixed and floating exchange rate systems: fixed, free floating, managed float

the effects of exchange rate changes.

Explanation of the balance of payments

A country that is engaging in foreign trade will both make and receive payments from its trading partners. The balance sheet on which these transactions are accounted is referred to as the balance of payments (BOP).

The 'ABC' of the BOP

It is essential to understand the classification system of debits and credits in the BOP. As a general rule, debit items in the BOP reflect transactions that give rise to a payment outward from the home country (HC). Thus imports, gifts made to a foreign country (FCs) and investments made in FCs by domestic nationals are debit items. By convention, debit items are recorded with a minus (–) sign.

Credit items are recorded with a plus (+) sign. Credit items refer to those items that lead to an inflow of foreign currency. These include exports, foreign direct investment (FDI) into the HC and gifts made to the HC.

The categories of the BOP

The BOP has five main categories:

1 Goods and service accounts
2 Unilateral transfer account
3 Long-term capital account
4 Short-term private capital account
5 Short-term official capital account

The transaction in categories (1) and (2) are easy to determine, but those in (3), (4) and (5) are a bit more difficult but nonetheless can de discerned if reference is made to two simple rules:

1 Debit items generally give rise to an outflow of foreign currency.
2 Credits generally give rise to an inflow of foreign currency.

Additionally, as the amount of foreign assets owned by residents of the HC decreases, the net claims of the HC against the FC also decreases. This is credited. A decrease in the ownership of HC assets by residents of the FC decreases the net claims of foreigners on the HC. This item is debited.

Classification system of debits and credits in the BOP accounts

Table 11.1 (opposite) summarises the various categories in the BOP account.

The rest of this chapter discusses the various sub-accounts of the BOP, commencing with the current account.

Table 11.1 *Categories of the BOP account*

Debits (–)	Credits (+)
Category I Imports of goods Imports of services	Exports of goods Exports of services
Category II A. Unilateral transfer (gifts) made	A. Unilateral transfer (gifts) received
Category III Increase in long-term foreign assets owned by HC private citizens and government Decrease in long-term home country assets owned by foreign private citizens and governments	Decrease in long-term foreign assets owned by HC private citizens and government Increase in long-term home country assets owned by foreign private citizens and governments
Category IV Increase in short-term foreign assets owned by HC private citizens Decrease in short-term home country assets owned by foreign private citizens	Decrease in short-term foreign assets owned by HC private citizens Increase in short-term home country assets owned by foreign private citizens
Category V Increase in short-term foreign assets owned by HC government (official monetary authorities) Decrease in short-term home country assets owned by foreign governments (official monetary authorities)	Decrease in short-term foreign assets owned by HC government (official monetary authorities) Increase in short-term home country assets owned by foreign governments (official monetary authorities)

Source: Appleyard (2001)

Current account and capital account

Current account

The current account of the BOP includes trade in merchandise goods, trade in services, investment income and current unrequited transfers. Inflow of investment income has been identified as accruing to the central bank, the commercial banks, the central government and state enterprise in the form of interest on investment, deposits and foreign currency account balances held abroad. These tables have been designed to provide a counterpart to flows of goods, services and income provided to or received from the rest of the world without any *quid pro quo*, in an effort to conform to the system of double-entry bookkeeping.

Table 11.2 (overleaf) shows the debit and credit items for the current account of the BOP of the Trinidad and Tobago economy for the period 1999–2001. As indicated above, the credit items are those transactions that give rise to an inflow of currency, while the debit items are those transactions that lead to an outflow of currency.

For this period there was an increase in the credit receipts of Trinidad and Tobago on the current account from US$3 556.1 million to US$5 050.7 million. In the same interval of time the total debit recordings on the current account of the balance of payments increased from US$3 525.5 million in 1999 to US$4 634.7 million in 2001.

Table 11.2 *Trinidad and Tobago's current account (US$ million) – debit and credit entries 1999–2001*

Item	1999 Credit	1999 Debit	2000 Credit	2000 Debit	2001 Credit	2001 Debit
Current account	3556.1	3525.5	4988.9	4444.6	5050.7	4634.7
Merchandise	3815.8	2752.2	4290.3	3321.5	4304.2	3586.1
Services	603.1	274.0	533.8	387.7	573.8	370.0
Transportation	204.4	123.6	207.6	173.2	207.3	116.6
Travel	209.6	82.8	212.8	147.1	20.9	151.0
Communication	111.4	8.6	36.3	5.5	29.8	5.6
Insurance	27.9	3.9	45.8	0.1	78.6	8.1
Other government	10.8	20.9	10.6	24.5	10.6	30.9
Other services	39.1	34.2	40.7	37.3	46.6	57.8
Investment income	68.3	468.2	80.9	709.4	108.7	648.0
Current unrequited transfers	68.9	31.2	63.9	26.0	64.0	30.6
Private	56.2	28.6	40.6	22.3	49.3	25.5
Government	12.7	2.6	23.3	3.7	14.7	5.1
Capital (exc. reserves and related items)	1155.6	1115.2	1077.2	842.5	1119.9	783.7

Source: Balance of Payments (2001)

Activity 11.1

The daily newspaper headline read, 'Country Y has a current account balance of payment deficit'.

1 Explain the term *current account balance of payment deficit*.

2 The table below shows the balance of payments current account for country Y for the year 2002 (US$ millions).

Year	Merchandise exports	Merchandise imports	Balance of services	Balance on transfers	Balance on investment income account
2002	1500	1815	450	30	–100

a Calculate the balance of trade (BOT).
b Calculate the current account balance and state whether it is a surplus or a deficit.

Feedback

1 Current account balance of payment deficit is where the total of the international flow of goods, services and transfer payment is negative.

2 a The balance of trade (BOT) for country Y:

Merchandise export – merchandise import + balance on services

$1500 million – $1815 million + $450 million = $135 million

b Current account balance :

Net merchandise exports	−315
Balance on services	450
Balance on transfers	30
Balance on investment income account	−100
	65

There is a current account surplus.

Capital account

The capital account records financial transactions between residents of one country and residents of other countries. These transactions include private and official transactions, and portfolio and direct investment. The investment can be either short term or long term in nature.

Direct investment transactions are those transactions for which the controlling majority for the asset is obtained at the point of purchase. Such transactions can occur between residents of two countries or between companies, such as multinational corporations.

In contrast, portfolio investment is the acquisition of an asset that does not give the purchaser control. An obvious example is the purchase of shares in a foreign company or of bonds issued by a foreign government. Loans made to foreign firms or government come in the same broad category. Such portfolio investment is often also distinguished by the period of the loan (short, medium or long are conventional distinctions, although in many cases only the short and long categories are used). The distinction between short-term and long-term investment is often confusing but usually relates to the specification of the asset rather than to the length of time for which it is held. The net value of the balance of direct and portfolio investment defines the balance on the capital account. Table 11.3 provides some key definitions associated with the capital account of the balance of payments of Trinidad and Tobago.

Table 11.3 *Some definitions of key terms encountered in the capital accounts of Trinidad and Tobago*

Capital (excluding reserves and related items)	The capital account has been divided into the monetary and non-monetary sectors, each of which has been further disaggregated: the non-monetary sector may also be divided into the public and private sectors and the monetary sector into the central monetary institutions and other institutions. The monetary sector has been recorded separately, since these transactions play a prominent role in the settlement of international transactions.
Monetary sector	The documentation of capital movements, particularly from direct investment enterprises, is of great importance to a developing country like Trinidad and Tobago. In the Trinidad and Tobago BOP, a direct investment enterprise is defined as an enterprise (branch or subsidiary) in which 10% or more of the voting stock is held or controlled by non-residents.
Non-monetary sector	
Private sector	These entries cover loan drawdowns and repayments by direct investment firms, other private capital flows identified from the direct foreign investment survey and the survey of local companies.

Public sector	This may be split into loans received, loans to other Caribbean governments, state enterprise borrowing, other official sector assets, other liabilities.
	Loans received reflects the international capital transactions of the government of Trinidad and Tobago in the form of loan drawdowns and repayments on the external debt, brought to account on the consolidate Fund of the Comptroller of Accounts, Investment Division.
	Loans to other CARICOM countries: The debit entries of this reflect Trinidad and Tobago's position, in keeping with the Caribbean policy of regional cooperation, to extend loans directly to other Caribbean governments and indirectly to them via loans to international institutions. On the credit side, the repayments are recorded. These loans are considered as non-reserve assets.
	State enterprise borrowing: The credit and debit entries are drawing and repayments on external loans by state enterprises and statutory boards. These items were included in private sector capital but are now shown separately for analytical purposes.
	Other official sector assets: The entries record changes in the sinking fund investments held against external loans and changes in the public sector's assets as a result of the nationalisation of private enterprises.
	Other liabilities: The short-term liabilities of the central government comprise increases in liabilities to international institutions mainly in the form of Trinidad and Tobago dollars, and issued by the government in payment of its membership subscriptions. Also included are any short-term debts incurred by the government as a result of its acquisitions of private enterprise.

Source: Central Statistical Office for Trinidad & Tobago

Long-term capital account

The long-tem capital account provides an indication of the relative attractiveness of the HC in relation to the FC. These longer-term influences are separated from the shorter-term influences that appear in categories IV and V and which are conditioned by the flows of hot money. For most small developing economies, a significant part of the capital account is FDI flows. Figure 11.1 shows the trends in long-term capital flows to the Trinidad and Tobago economy.

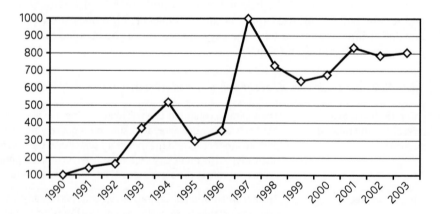

Figure 11.1 *FDI inflows to Trinidad and Tobago, US$ million, 1990–2003*

The sum of the Current Account Balance (CAB) and the long-term capital account in the economy is referred to as the basic balance. This is to emphasise that this balance reflects basic long-term forces at work in the economy. The current account balance, for example, provides an indication of the quality and quantity of exports and also provides an indication of the influence of the international terms of trade and the import habits of residents.

Short-term capital flows

Category IV of the BOP has the largest number of entries. It is in category IV that the majority of financing entries in category I to III are recorded. Capital transactions involving hot money flows are also carried in this account.

Official reserve transactions balance

The official financing account measures the changes in the short-term and long-term liquid and non-liquid assets of a nation in terms of changes in the official reserves during the period.

The causes and consequences of balance of payments – disequilibria

A current account deficit (CAD) implies that a larger amount of goods and services is flowing into an economy than is flowing out. A capital account surplus means that more money is flowing into the economy than is flowing out.

A CAD is sometimes regarded suspiciously by the public because it is associated with the perception that jobs are being exported. Some degree of caution should be exercised here, however, as:

$$Y = C + I + G + X - M$$

which indicates that $X - M$ is but one facet influencing Y, so that there is no reason why an $X - M$ value that is negative should imply an overall loss of jobs as C, I and G also influence Y and hence employment in an economy.

When foreign firms acquire domestic assets, it is sometimes conceived by members of the public as a potentially harmful event. However, if we consider a foreigner buying TT$1 million in financial units from the Unit Trust Company of Trinidad and Tobago, although this investor will receive investment income, the Unit Trust can invest this foreign investor's money (in Trinidad and Tobago or elsewhere) and generate for Trinidad and Tobago an even greater productive use of the investment outlay.

A second perception is that if foreigners own domestic assets then this compromises national sovereignty. There may be some truth in this for very large foreign firms employed in the most productive sector of the economy, but it is generally incorrect. In particular, how can the purchase of a bond sold by the government influence national sovereignty, as all this allows the foreigner is to benefit from a particular level of return on a specific date?

Policy responses to balance of payments crises

Most of the economies of the Caribbean sphere run current account deficits. The governments have a number of policy responses that they can make to correct these deficits. These include devaluation, expenditure switching and expenditure reducing measures.

Devaluating a country's currency effectively makes exports cheaper and imports more expensive. All else held constant, this would increase the demand for exports and reduce the demand for imports, which improves the balance of payments situation.

Expenditure-switching policies also improve the balance of payments position, encouraging consumers to switch demand from imported goods to locally produced goods and services.

Expenditure-reducing policies are aimed at encouraging a reduction in imports. Reducing the marginal propensity to import will also have the effect of improving the balance of payments position.

The marginal propensity to import shows the proportion of any increase in income that goes to imports. Consider Table 11.4 which provides the trends in GDP and imports for selected CARICOM member states.

Table 11.4 *GDP and imports for selected CARICOM economies (current US$ billion)*

	Trinidad and Tobago		Barbados		Guyana		Jamaica		Suriname	
	GDP	Imports of goods and services	GDP	Imports of goods and services	GDP	Imports of goods and services	GDP	Imports of goods and services	GDP	Imports of goods and services
1990	5.07	1.45	1.71	0.88	0.40	0.32	4.59	2.38	0.40	0.18
1991	5.36	1.77	1.69	0.85	0.34	0.43	4.11	2.11	0.44	0.20
1992	5.53	1.83	1.59	0.73	0.37	0.56	3.54	2.24	0.40	0.14
1993	4.58	1.79	1.64	0.85	0.44	0.61	4.89	2.72	0.44	0.10
1994	4.95	1.62	1.73	0.86	0.54	0.64	4.94	2.84	0.60	0.16
1995	5.33	2.09	1.86	1.05	0.62	0.70	5.81	3.53	0.69	0.19
1996	5.76	2.38	1.98	1.12	0.71	0.77	6.53	3.61	0.86	0.26
1997	5.74	3.29	2.19	1.29	0.75	0.82	7.47	3.88	0.93	0.32
1998	6.04	3.25	2.36	1.30	0.72	0.77	7.83	3.89	0.95	0.50
1999	6.81	3.01	2.47	1.40	0.69	0.73	7.83	3.83	0.89	0.30
2000	8.15	3.71	2.54	1.45	0.71	0.79	8.03	4.33	0.89	0.30
2001	8.82	3.94	2.53	1.36	0.70	0.78	8.22	4.47	0.76	0.42
2002	9.01	4.03	2.46	1.36	0.72	0.76	8.60	4.75	1.08	0.43
2003	11.24	4.26	2.68	1.51	0.74	0.74	8.29	4.79	1.27	0.58
2004	12.67	5.24	2.80	1.71	0.79	0.83	8.89	5.32	1.49	0.71
2005	15.09	6.56	3.04	1.93	0.79	0.98	9.71	5.91	1.78	0.81
2006	18.14	–	3.43	–	0.90	–	10.02	6.32	2.11	–

Source: World Bank Development Indicators (2008)

The following are some other measures:

- **Price competitiveness:** To improve price competitiveness, countries can devalue their currencies. Devaluation makes the price of the domestic good cheaper in the foreign market. The presumption here is that if foreign consumers can get goods from, say, Jamaica, because it has devalued its currency, it will sell more to the outside world.

- **Education:** One of the reasons for the persistence of current account deficits among Caribbean economies is probably because the quality of export goods may be low. One way to improve on the quality of the export goods is to improve on education and training options in the region.

- **Types of goods produced:** It is possible that the economy may be producing the wrong types of goods. In particular, if an economy is producing goods that are not in high demand by the world economy, then this can lead to a current account deficit as exports may not be able to pay for imports. This may require the government to help sunrise firms with various forms of financial assistance so that they can mature.

Exchange rates

There are a number of reasons why Trinidad and Tobago dollars are demanded:

1 Foreign consumers may wish to buy goods from Trinidad and Tobago and so will require Trinidad and Tobago dollars to facilitate the transaction.

2 Trinidad and Tobago entrepreneurs owning assets in foreign countries will need to convert any foreign income earned into TT$ and so will demand TT$.

3 When people send gifts to Trinidad and Tobago from abroad they will need to purchase Trinidad and Tobago dollars.

4 Another source of demand for Trinidad and Tobago currency comes from foreign firms wishing to buy domestic assets.

Trinidad and Tobago dollars in turn are supplied in a number of instances, for example:

- to purchase foreign goods and services

- by foreign firms sending remittances from their investment incomes in Trinidad and Tobago to their parent companies located in a foreign economy

- as remittances by non-residents working in Trinidad and Tobago to their home country

- by Trinidad and Tobago entrepreneurs wishing to buy assets in other economies.

Types of exchange rates

There are essentially three types of exchange rate regime:

1 **Flexible exchange rate regime:** The exchange rate is determined by the interaction of the demand and supply for currency arising out of the need to engage in international transactions.

2 **Fixed exchange rate regime:** The exchange rate is maintained through the interventions (via the purchase or sale of currency) of the central bank at a particular level.

3 **Managed float regime:** Under this type of regime, the central bank seeks to stabilise the exchange rate within a predetermined range for a given period of time, but does not fix it at a particular level.

Determination of exchange rates

Flexible exchange rates

As noted above, flexible exchange rates are determined through the interaction of demand for and supply of a particular currency, and as such the rate fluctuates as a result of changes in the conditions of demand and supply (see Figure 11.2).

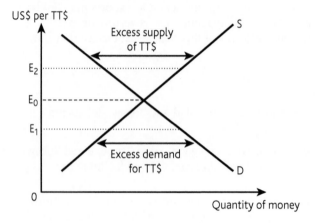

Figure 11.2 *Illustration of flexible exchange rates*

Notice in Figure 11.2 that the value of TT dollars is shown in terms of US dollars. The equilibrium rate adjusts to equate the level of official financing on the balance of payments account. With a balance of payments account equal to zero, the balance of the official financing account will also be zero and as such the exchange rate will occur at the point E_0 where demand is equal to supply. If the exchange rate falls below this equilibrium level, the demand for TT currency exceeds the supply of TT currency. Consequently the exchange rate will rise – that is, there will be an appreciation of the TT dollar, until equilibrium is restored at E_0. If the exchange rate rises above the equilibrium level, then the supply of TT currency exceeds the demand for TT currency. This situation will cause a fall in the exchange rate – that is, the TT dollar depreciates until equilibrium is restored at E_0.

Activity 11.2

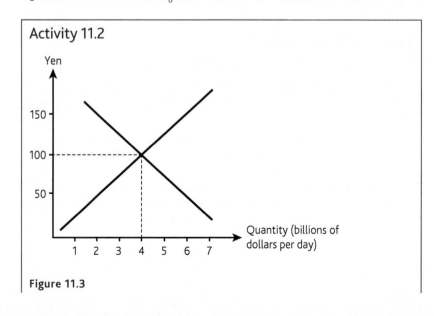

Figure 11.3

Use the information in Figure 11.3 to answer the following questions.

1 What is the exchange rate in terms of the following:
   a Yens per dollar
   b Dollars per yen
2 What type of exchange rate system is used in Figure 11.3?
3 What will happen to the value of the yen with respect to the dollar for the following?
   a At prices below equilibrium level
   b At prices above equilibrium level

Feedback

1 a 100 yen per dollar
   b 0.01 dollar per yen
2 Flexible exchange rate
3 a Appreciate
   b Depreciate

Fixed exchange rates

Fixed exchange rates are maintained using official financing transactions – that is, when a particular rate is set given that the balance of payments account is not usually zero, the central bank must correct for either the balance of payments deficit or the surplus. For example, referring to Figure 11.2, if the central bank fixes the rate at E_1 there will be a balance of payments surplus. The central bank will therefore accumulate foreign reserves in order to meet the excess demand for TT dollars.

If the rate is fixed at E_2, however, the balance of payments will be in deficit as the receipt of foreign exchange is less than the payments. The central bank will, therefore, have to draw down on its foreign reserves in order to correct for the excess supply of TT currency.

The managed float

The managed float regime occurs between the two extremes of a purely flexible exchange rate and a purely fixed rate. The central bank intervenes in the foreign exchange market to stabilise the volatility associated with continuous changes in the conditions of demand and supply for currency. In this regard, managing the exchange rate between a particular range has the benefit of allowing policymakers to plan with some degree of certainty the macroeconomic affairs of a country.

The foreign exchange rate

The exchange rate between two currencies, for example the US$ and TT$, refers to how many Trinidad and Tobago dollars are required to obtain one US dollar, and vice versa.

As Figure 11.4 (overleaf) shows, in 1960 TT$1.71 = US1$, although by 2007 this had depreciated to TT$6.31 = US$1. The figure also shows the amount of US dollars per unit of Trinidad and Tobago dollars. Specifically, observe that corresponding to TT$6.31 = US$1 in 2004, we could have also written US$0.16 = TT$1. Similar exchange rates between Trinidad and Tobago and its other bilateral trading partners can also be determined.

The effects of exchange rate changes

There are two effects in play once a currency is devalued:

■ **The price effect:** The price effect is associated with the relative price of exports to imports. With currency devaluation the price of exports effectively falls while the price of imports rises. No doubt this results in the deterioration of an economy's current account balance.

■ **The volume effect:** The fact that exports become cheaper should encourage an increased volume of exports and the fact that imports become more expensive should lead to a decreased volume of imports. The volume effect clearly contributes to an improving current account.

The net effect depends upon whether the price or volume effect dominates.

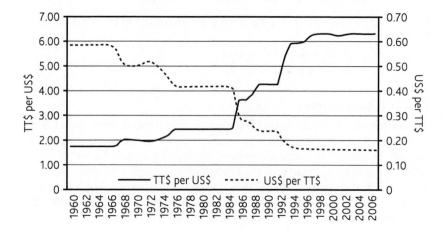

Figure 11.4 *Official exchange rate between T&T and the US*

Reasons for the J-curve effect

With a devaluation the current account balance worsens initially and only then improves. In the long run, a devaluation gives rise to the J-curve effect, an illustration of which is provided in Figure 11.5.

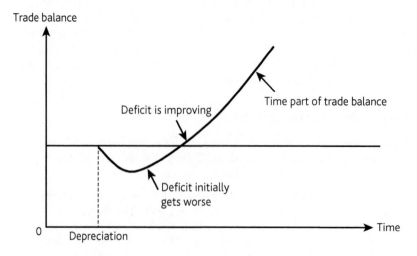

Figure 11.5 *The J-curve*

In particular, when the HC devalues, the cost of its imports increases.

There are a number of reasons cited in the literature for the J-curve effect:

■ **Time lag in consumer response:** Consumers may take time to adapt their tastes away from the generally more expensive foreign good. Consumers may also be concerned about the reliability of domestic producers both from a quantity and quality perspective and so may continue to buy the foreign product in the short run, while observing domestic producers.

- **Time lag in producer responses:** Producers too may take some time to adapt to an increase in demand for exports as they need to change the scale of their plant and so on to accommodate a new higher level of demand.

- **Imperfect competition:** It takes time for a firm based in an FC to produce and successfully penetrate the markets of the HC. If the HC were to undergo depreciation then this firm from the FC, rather than lose its market share in the HC, may lower its prices to partly influence the effects of the depreciation of the HC. Similarly, in regards to import-competing firms, the FC may react to the devaluation by the HC by reducing the price level it charges for commodities in its domestic market. In so doing, these import-competing firms from the FC would prevent foreign penetration of their home market. The requirement that foreign firms be able to decrease their prices implicitly requires some degree of imperfect competition in the supply of the relevant good. This point, especially as relates to small developing economies, is relevant. In particular, when the HC devalues its currency, the cost of its imports increases. Because imports are an important part of the consumption bundle in open economies, the rise in import prices will trigger an increase in wages which in turn would reduce the competitive edge that the devaluation in the HC, triggered in the first instance.

End test

1   What are the sub-accounts included in the balance of payments account?

2   What types of transaction does the current account record?

3   What types of transaction does the capital account record?

4   What are the main types of exchange rate regime?

5   What factors account for the J-curve?

End test feedback

1   The sub-accounts of the balance of payments (BOP) account include:

- goods and service account

- unilateral transfer account

- long-term capital account

- short-term private capital account

- short-term official capital account.

2   The current account of the BOP includes trade in merchandise goods, trade in services, investment income and current unrequited transfers.

3   The capital account records all international transactions that involve a resident of the country exchanging either their assets or their liabilities with a resident of another country.

4   There are essentially three types of exchange rate regime:

- Flexible exchange rate regime: The exchange rate is determined by the interaction of the demand and supply for currency arising out of the need to engage in international transactions.

- Fixed exchange rate regime: The exchange rate is maintained through the interventions (via the purchase or sale of currency) of the central bank at a particular level.

- Managed float regime: Under this type of regime, the central bank seeks to stabilise the exchange rate within a predetermined range for a given period of time, but does not fix it at a particular level.

5   There are a number of reasons cited in the literature for the J-curve effect:

- Time lag in consumer responses

- Time lag in producer responses

- Imperfect competition

12 Economic integration

Specific objectives

You should have an understanding of:

the main forms of economic integration, including: free trade area, customs union, common market, economic union

the costs and benefits of economic integration including trade creation and trade diversion

the objectives of CARICOM and the rationale for the CARICOM Single Market and Economy (CSME)

the significance of integration movements, for example European Union (EU) and the North American Free Trade Agreement (NAFTA) for Caribbean Economies.

Main forms of economic integration

There are several forms that regional economic integration agreements can adopt:

- **Free trade areas (FTA):** This is where member states remove all barriers to trade between themselves and their integration partners. However, members of an FTA retain the right to have their own independent commercial policies. Examples include the Latin American Free Trade Area (LAFTA) and European Free Trade Association (EFTA).
- **Customs union (CU):** These are similar to FTAs but also have a common commercial policy – that is, it includes a common external tariff. Examples are the Central American Common Market (CACM) and CARICOM Community.
- **Common market (CM):** This is a customs union that has graduated to the stage of allowing the free intra-regional movement of factors of production. The CARICOM integration agreement graduated to the stage of a single market in January 2006.
- **Complete economic union (CEU):** This is a common market that carries a common block of fiscal and monetary policies.
- **Complete political union (PU):** This is where the member states involved actually become one nation, for example, the political union of East and West Germany in the 1980s to form Germany.

Table 12.1 provides summary information on the various attributes of regional trading agreements.

Table 12.1 *Categories of regional trading agreements*

FTA	CU	CM	EU	PU
1	1	1	1	1
	2	2	2	2
		3	3	3
			4	4
				5

where:

1 = removal of intra-group tariffs
2 = common external tariff
3 = intra-group capital and labour mobility
4 = common economic policy and common currency
5 = one government

Economic integration schemes occur at various levels and once the integration process itself is started, one form can evolve into another form.

Activity 12.1

Class discussion

Countries may engage different forms of preferential trading agreements with each other in order to foster free trade. There are five main types of preferential trading arrangement. Using Figure 12.1, identify the level of integration illustrated at each circle and discuss the associated characteristics.

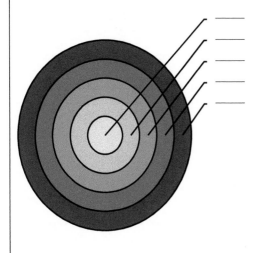

Figure 12.1

The benefits and costs of economic integration include trade creation and trade diversion.

- **Trade creation and trade diversion:** In general terms, trade creation refers to the process by which the establishment of a free trade area 'creates' or increases the amount of trade between member countries. On the other hand, trade diversion refers to the fact that the formation of a free trade area often 'diverts' trade away from relatively efficient trade partners outside the FTA towards relatively inefficient suppliers from within the FTA.

- **Greater specialisation and economies of scale:** When a customs union is formed there is an expansion in the preferential market base of the home country (HC) firm beyond that of the HC economy towards that of the market base represented by the customs union. This greater target market base can encourage domestic firms to specialise and benefit from economies of scale. Thus, whereas the maximal target population for a firm in Trinidad and Tobago is only 1.3 million, the population of CARICOM is 12.6 million. This means that firms in Trinidad and Tobago under the umbrella of the CARICOM regional integration arrangement now have a larger market base, with protection, to which its firms can cater (see Table 12.2).

Table 12.2 *CARICOM population, 2006*

CARICOM country	Population 2006	Population as a % of total CARICOM population
Antigua and Barbuda	84 097	0.52
Bahamas, The	327 279	2.03
Barbados	292 930	1.81
Belize	297 612	1.84

CARICOM country	Population 2006	Population as a % of total CARICOM population
Dominica	72 396	0.45
Grenada	108 148	0.67
Guyana	739 065	4.57
Jamaica	2 667 300	16.51
Montserrat	4 800	0.03
St Kitts and Nevis	48 393	0.30
St Lucia	166 014	1.03
St Vincent and the Grenadines	119 772	0.74
Suriname	455 273	2.82
Trinidad and Tobago	1 328 432	8.22
Haiti	9 445 947	58.46
Total	16 157 458	100.00

Source: World Bank Development Indicators, 2008

- **Greater competition:** With the larger number of firms that would exist in a regional trade bloc as a whole, compared with the number in any single member of that trade bloc, there is naturally a fiercer amount of rivalry among firms, especially those in the same industry. Increased competition helps to minimise economic wasting by improving factor allocation.

- **Higher levels of investment:** RTAs, by virtue of representing larger markets, help to stimulate investment by both domestic and foreign firms. Domestic firms invest more within RTAs as the larger market requires greater volumes of output. Larger markets also potentially offer higher levels of profits. Foreign firms may invest in RTAs so as to escape any tariff barriers that are enacted with the formation of the RTA.

- **Possible dynamic losses:** Economic integration among economies often results in some inequitable distribution of benefits. In general, the advanced countries gain benefits and the less advanced ones tend to lose out. In order to avoid the fragmentation of any RTA as a consequence of an inequitable distribution of the material gains, suitable policy measures should be established to assist those economies that tend to lose out. Assistance can be provided in the form of financial and technological investments.

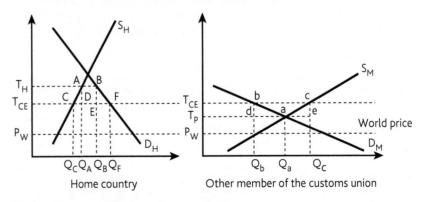

Figure 12.2 *Welfare effects of economic integration*

Consider Figure 12.2: without integration the world price is P_w. Both countries will impose a tariff on imports of P_wT_H in the HC and P_wT_p in the other member country. The HC will import AB from other countries. The other member country will produce for the domestic economy. It will not have to import because at Q_a domestic consumption equals domestic production. When the countries establish a customs union they will implement a common external tariff of T_{CE}. In the HC the price is reduced. Domestic consumption increases from Q_B to Q_F while domestic supply decreases from Q_A to Q_C. The amount of imports will increase from AB to CF. There is trade creation of CD to EF. Imports will come from the other member of the customs union. There is trade diversion of DE. Consumer surplus increases by THBFTCE. Producer surplus is reduced by THADTCE. Government revenue is reduced. In the other member country price increases. Domestic consumption decreases from Q_a to Q_b and domestic production increases from Q_a to Q_c. Producers will now have a surplus of bc to export to member countries of the customs union. Consumers will lose surplus equal to $T_{CE}bT_p$. Producers will gain surplus of $T_{CE}caT_p$.

CARICOM single market and economy (CSME)

The formation of the CARIFTA (Caribbean Free Trade Area) 1965–72 marked a milestone in the regional integration process in the Caribbean. It was formed to provide continued economic linkages among the English-speaking countries of the Caribbean following the dissolution of the West Indian Federation.

The Caribbean Community (CARICOM) came into existence in 1973, after CARIFTA had failed to fully integrate the region. CARIFTA failed to fully develop, partly because members relied heavily on tariff revenue and thus were reluctant to reduce tariffs, and trade between the members was extremely limited. In short, national interests of member states were allowed to dominate. Although CARIFTA failed, it provided the basis for the formation of CARICOM. CARICOM had matured into a single market and economy (CSME) by 2006.

CARICOM existed in the range between a custom union and a common market, allowing the free movement of capital and some categories of skilled persons. A common external tariff (CET) has been implemented by all member states of CARICOM. CARICOM had as its objectives economic integration, the coordination of foreign policy and function cooperation in areas such as health, education and industrial relations.

The Caribbean Single Market and Economy (CSME) entails the integration of all CARICOM states into a single economic unit, and the subsequent removal of the tariff barriers within the region. This attempt at unification serves to address challenges that small developing CARICOM economies face in light of increasing globalisation. It is anticipated that the CSME will stimulate growth and hence enhance the international competitiveness of the CARICOM member states.

The main objectives of the CSME include the following:

- **Freer intra-regional movement of capital:** This entails the movement of capital from one intra-regional state to another CARICOM state. The freer intra-regional movement of capital is to be facilitated through the elimination of foreign exchange controls, the convertibility of currencies and, with time, a regional stock exchange.
- **The free movement of labour:** This involves the uninhibited movement of labour, particularly university graduates, within the region.
- **The establishment of a common external tariff to goods originating from non-member states.**

- **Harmonisation of economic policy, especially monetary and fiscal policies:** This entails the coordination of exchange rate and interest rate policy within the region as well as agreed targets for budgetary deficits.
- **Formation of a common currency:** In time it is hoped that a common currency can be formed that can facilitate the easier comparison of key prices among the member states. This would also facilitate a reduction in intra-regional transaction costs.

The CSME promises a number of benefits for CARICOM economies, including:

- access to a larger regional market of just over 15 million people, if Haiti is included, thus providing more opportunities for production and trade for CARICOM members; the CSME will help diversify the range of markets in which CARICOM goods and services will be traded
- creation of more opportunities for investment, both by CARICOM residents and in attracting foreign direct investment (FDI) flows
- the opportunity for improved services at the regional level
- opportunities for artistes to display and advertise their talents in all member states
- opportunities for CARICOM nationals to gain employment in any CARICOM member state they wish
- more opportunities for nationals to study in CARICOM countries of their choice
- pooling of talents to improve the participation in international debates and negotiations with one voice.

The significance of integration movements for CARICOM economies

Free Trade Area of the Americas

The pending Free Trade Area of the Americas (FTAA) is in the spirit of open regionalism. The FTAA was launched in 1994 at the Summit of Americas in Miami. The summit's objective was to create an FTAA by 2005. However, the FTAA missed this deadline due to the negotiations associated with the WTO Ministerial Conference in 2005. Since then, some of the economies of the western hemisphere have begun to independently pursue bilateral trade agreements. It should be noted, however, that plans are in place for a future summit, titled the Sixth Summit of the Americas, intended to be held in Cartegena, Columbia in 2012. The envisioned purpose of the FTAA is to liberalise intra-hemispheric trade. This would involve the progressive removal of both tariff and non-tariff barriers within the hemisphere. The FTAA would address the following nine areas:

- Market access
- Agriculture
- Services
- Investment
- Intellectual property rights
- Subsidies, anti-dumping and countervailing duties
- Government procurement
- Competition policy
- Dispute settlement

At the summit the following objectives of the FTAA were expressed:

- To enhance the prosperity of the hemisphere through economic integration and free trade.
- To remove poverty and discrimination in the hemisphere.
- To preserve and strengthen the democracies within the hemisphere.
- To guarantee sustainable development and preservation of the environment.

The interest in an FTAA was sparked in part by a similar development that had taken place on 14 November 1994 (three weeks before the announcement of the FTAA) in Bogor, Indonesia. Here a group of leaders from Asia and the Pacific endorsed the attainment of free trade by 2010 for its developed country membership and by 2020 for its developing country membership. Fearing falling behind, Latin American countries pushed at the summit for the progressive elimination of intra-hemispheric barriers to trade by 2005.

The FTAA, when established, would include 34 out of the 35 countries in the Western Hemisphere (the only exclusion is Cuba). It would involve the progressive removal of barriers to trade and investment among the member states. Two of the member states of the proposed FTAA arrangement, Canada and the US, are classified as developed nations, while four of them – Argentina, Mexico, Brazil and Chile – have at various points in the recent past been classifiable as newly industrialising countries. The small member states of CARICOM constitute 14 of the 34 states in the FTAA. These states are very open and depend on foreign trade and investment for a substantial part of their economic activity.

Table 12.3 shows some key macroeconomic aggregates of the various economies or group of economies in the Western Hemisphere. In particular, the population of the countries of the Western Hemisphere in 2000 tallied to 813.2 million out of a world total of 6.05 billion – that is, the population of the FTAA represents approximately 13.4% of the total world population. Another indicator of the size of the FTAA can be obtained by looking at its contribution to world Gross Domestic Product (GDP). In 2000, the FTAA member states accounted for 40% of world GDP, or US$12.47 trillion out of a world total of US$31.4 trillion. The countries of the FTAA also accounted for 22% of world exports, determined by an FTAA merchandise export value of US$1.41 trillion out of a world export package of US$6.43 trillion in 2000. Significantly, though, this block of countries, which represents just over one-tenth of the world's population, imports just under one-third (28.4%) of total world imports.

Table 12.3 *Some macroeconomic aggregates on FTAA members, 2000*

	GDP growth (annual %)	Total population (million)	GDP (current US$ million)	Merchandise exports (current US$ million)	Merchandise imports (current US$ million)
NAFTA	5.11	410.27	11 105 410	1 224 977	1 686 718
Mercosur	1.56	231.49	976 245	102 708	107 447
Andean com	2.73	113.11	279 875	58 027	42 100
Cacm	3.25	35.83	66 242	14 315	24 133
Caribbean	2.64	22.54	48 807	13 829	21 830
of which CARICOM	2.64	14.17	29 220	8 092	12 351

	GDP growth (annual %)	Total population (million)	GDP (current US$ million)	Merchandise exports (current US$ million)	Merchandise imports (current US$ million)
Antigua and Barbuda	0.41	0.07	660	10	355
Bahamas, The	4.49	0.30	4 818	910	1730
Belize	11.15	0.24	773	194	450
Dominica	0.20	0.07	268	53	147
Grenada	7.97	0.10	407	50	230
Guyana	−1.38	0.76	713	570	660
Haiti	1.12	7.96	3 951	164	1036
Jamaica	3.15	2.63	7 709	1296	3 216
St Kitts and Nevis	5.33	0.04	328	30	160
St Lucia	0.70	0.16	707	60	370
St Vincent and the Grenadines	2.13	0.12	337	47	163
Suriname	−14.47	0.42	846	435	526
Trinidad and Tobago	8.89	1.30	7 703	4 273	3 308
FTAA (1)	–	813.24	12 476 579	1 413 856	1 882 228
WORLD (2)	–	6 057.97	31 498 070	6 425 577	6 626 593
(1/2)	–	13.42	39.61	22	28.4

Source: World Bank (2002); author derivations

CARICOM and the FTAA

The small size of CARICOM within the pending FTAA can also be gleaned from Table 12.3. CARICOM's GDP in 2000 was US$29.2 billion, or 0.23% of the GDP of the pending FTAA. CARICOM's merchandise exports and imports of US$8.1 billion and US$12.4 billion, are a mere fraction of the total exports and imports of the FTAA nations ranking at 0.57% and 0.66% respectively. The population of CARICOM represents 1.74% of the FTAA total.

Benefits and costs of the FTAA for CARICOM countries

But what are the benefits and costs to a small regional trade agreement like CARICOM in a trade bloc such as the FTAA? In a very real way the pending FTAA offers CARICOM countries access to the markets of North America, and it also offers access to the markets of Latin America. The FTAA arrangements would provide CARICOM more stable access to Latin American countries as compared with countries outside of the pending FTAA.

Traditional trade theory suggests that trade agreements can have two predominant types of influence: trade diversion and trade creation effects. With the formation of an FTA there is a shift from the most efficient producer towards the lowest-cost intra-regional producer; this is trade diversion. The second effect is the creation of trade by allowing the high-cost intra-regional producers to supply the intra-regional market. Whether or not the FTAA will be beneficial depends on the relative magnitudes of the trade diversion and trade creation effects.

The increased competition from extra-CARICOM members within the FTAA can potentially lead to a loss in employment in inefficient industries. At the same time, the more dynamic CARICOM firms would lower operational costs and improve their efficiency in the context of the wave of import competition that the FTAA is expected to bring on stream.

However, a number of reasons have been cited by UNECLAC (2001) as to why the adjustment costs of CARICOM member states in an FTAA would be higher than for other countries.

The member states of the CARICOM sphere produce a narrow range of primary commodities, which are targeted at a few principal markets. These commodities are produced mainly by a group of small firms with characteristically low resource endowments and small profit margins, so it would be difficult for them to make significant changes.

Many of the main export items from CARICOM member states are sold in markets that offer them margins of preference, for example: the US through the Caribbean Basin Expansion Recovery Act (CBERA) and Caribbean Basin Trade Partnership Act (CBTPA); Canada through the Caribcan arrangement; Europe through the various Lomé agreements; and within CARICOM where the common external tariff exists. These margins of preference have allowed CARICOM firms to subsist with inefficient production functions. The FTAA would lead to a dissipation of some of these margins of preference, with serious implications for income and employment in the affected member states.

Many CARICOM member states, especially those of the OECS sub-regional blocs, depend on international trade taxes for the bulk of their fiscal revenues. The formation of an FTAA and the removal of intra-hemispheric tariffs would lead to substantial erosion of their fiscal revenues with immediate and serious implications for their economic development. As the data in Table 12.4 reflects, by 1999, apart from Barbados, Dominica, Jamaica and Trinidad and Tobago, every other CARICOM member state extracted more than 34% (and in most cases over 40%) of their fiscal revenues from import taxes.

Table 12.4 *Import taxes as a percentage of fiscal revenues, 1990–99*

Country	1990	1991	1992	1993	1994	1995	1996	1997	1998	1999
Antigua and Barbuda	52.08	54.84	54.75	54.12	51.48	51.83	51.08	49.70	50.36	48.08
Anguilla	n.a.	65.97	67.84	48.33	54.92	53.23	58.25	57.04	65.57	63.18
Bahamas, The	65.94	62.23	55.62	54.97	53.65	52.62	52.77	52.10	49.79	52.67
Barbados	13.21	9.44	8.08	8.08	8.63	8.61	8.08	9.26	9.35	9.57
Belize	51.54	51.86	47.82	49.20	49.70	52.97	34.41	31.60	33.50	34.80
Dominica	17.80	18.20	17.40	17.60	14.70	14.30	14.00	15.00	13.50	14.60
Guyana	11.04	10.20	9.50	12.60	12.80	11.60	11.70	11.80	12.10	n.a.
Jamaica	n.a.	13.40	13.70	13.60	10.90	11.90	10.80	11.30	10.60	10.40
St Kitts and Nevis	53.50	50.30	48.30	26.20	49.10	45.60	45.30	44.20	42.00	43.50
St Lucia	51.90	50.50	50.01	50.60	48.30	48.00	47.90	44.70	48.60	47.10
St Vincent and the Grenadines	51.10	49.60	48.70	47.60	45.90	48.90	43.60	44.90	42.70	43.30
Trinidad and Tobago	8.20	8.10	9.40	9.40	7.70	5.80	5.20	6.30	7.20	7.20

Source: Hosein et al. *(2002)*

EU and Caribbean economies

The Treaty of Rome established the European Economic Community (EEC) in 1957. At that time it was also agreed that those African economies that held colonial ties to France would benefit in terms of the economic treatment it received from the EEC. In 1958, the first European Development Fund (EDF) was established, with the primary aim of assisting the former francophone colonies. With the emergence of independence in some of these francophone economies, a wave of negotiations was undertaken with the EEC for the continuation of the preferential treatment to these colonies. This provided the basis upon which the EU–Africa Partnership was built. This partnership was formalised by the signing of the Yaoundé Convention in 1963, between the EEC and 18 other colonies, most of which were former French colonies. Significantly, this first partnership agreement was premised on reciprocating trade. In the first Yaoundé Agreement the emphasis was on agriculture. A second Yaoundé Convention was signed in July 1969 and this continued the reciprocal non-discriminatory trading agreement with the EU and the African economies.

The first Lomé Convention was signed in 1975. One of the new members of the EEC at this point was the United Kingdom (UK). With the coming on board of the UK, preferential trading privileges similar to those offered to the francophone colonies were offered to UK's former Caribbean and Pacific colonies. Table 12.5 provides a summary fn the various trade and development assistance agreements between the European Economic Commission (currently known as the European Union) and its former hinterlands. The list spans the Yaoundé Conventions to Lomé Conventions 1 through Lomé 4.

Table 12.5 *Conventions between the EEC/EU and the AASM/ACP*

Year	Convention
1963	Yaoundé I: Agreement between the EEC and 18 former francophone African colonies, providing the colonies with commercial advantages and financial aid.
1969	Yaoundé II: Renewal of Yaoundé I, including Kenya, Tanzania and Uganda, introducing preferential trade arrangements for developing countries and access to raw materials for the EEC.
1975	Lomé I: Convention included preferential trade agreements on most ACP products, each individual state having the right to decide on its policies, a cooperation system ensuring the security of relations, impartiality, respect for sovereignty, common interests and interdependence existing and the STABEX system for stabilisation of agricultural export earnings as well as direct development aid.
1979	Lomé II: SYSMIN system providing stabilisation aid to mining industries in ACP countries.
1984	Lomé III: Attention shifts from industrial development towards food security and self-reliance.
1990	Lomé IV: Focus on structural adjustment and crosscutting themes such as the encouragement of democracy, good governance, human rights; fortifying women's role; environmental safety; intensified regional cooperation and a greater role of the private sector, in response to debt crises and famines.
1995	Lomé IV rev: Underlining the importance of human rights, democracy and good governance, as well as regional cooperation. Decentralised cooperation via participatory partnerships was also fostered, with the inclusion of an assortment of civil society actors.
2000	Cotonou: Removal of most tariffs on imports from ACP group with sugar and beef and veal to be covered by proposed REPAs, and a new tariff-only banana regime, to be phased in. Shift towards participatory development paradigm.
2001	EBA: Immediate removal of all tariffs on all imports from LDCs except arms, with three-stage removal of tariff and quotas on sugar, rice and bananas.

The Lomé Conventions were characterised by two major dimensions: development and trade. The development aspect of the Lomé Conventions involved the transfer of resources from the EU via the Economic Development Funds (EDF), for the development of socio-economic infrastructure in ACP (Africa, Caribbean and Pacific) economies. The trade dimensions of the EU–ACP relationship hovered around the preferential access of commodities from the ACP economies into the EU market. However, there were a variety of limitations to these EU–ACP relations, including:

- the type of products that could enter the EU market
- the extent of value added: the more processed the good, the higher the level of tariff that was imposed
- the type of commodity: some commodities, like rice and sugar, for example, had quotas
- the EU had in place a series of non-tariff barriers, for example sanitary and phyto-sanitary (SPS) measures, particularly on the import of food items
- commodity protocols on selected commodities: sugar, banana, meats and veal, textiles, rum and spirits.

The EU–ACP relationship also carried two compensatory mechanisms, STABEX and SYSMI.

The negotiations for change in EU–ACP relations began in September 1998. A new arrangement, the Cotonou Agreement, was signed by the EU and ACP delegates in Benin in 2000.

The Lomé Conventions: reasons for failure

One of the main reasons for the failure of the Lomé trading regime was its incompatibility with the rules of the World Trade Organization (WTO) and the EU's Banana Trade Regime. The latter in particular provided the centre-stage for a confrontation. Specifically, the various Lomé trade preferences extended to bananas via the Banana Protocol, which gave preferential access to the EU market, but there was a limit to the amount of Latin American bananas that could gain access to the EU market. This prompted these Latin American economies to challenge the Banana Trade Regime. The Latin American states argued that the Banana Trade Regime was in contravention of Articles I, II, III, X and XIII of the GATT (General Agreement on Tariffs and Trade). This clause in the GATT provisions excluded any GATT members from discriminating against other GATT members, in terms of its trading rules. In this regard, given that the ACP and Latin American economies were signatories of the GATT, the Most Favored Nation (MFN) clause implied that both the ACP and Latin American economies needed to have equal market access to the EU. The Banana Protocol clearly violated this. The dispute was taken up with the WTO and on 19 April 1999, after much deliberation, the WTO ruled that the EU's Banana Trade Regime was inconsistent with its MFN clause and so the US could retaliate by imposing tariffs on the import of products from the EU, until such time as the EU modified its trade arrangements to comply with WTO regulations.

Another important reason for the change in EU–ACP relations was the need by the EU to provide increased accountability to the taxpayers of the EU against the backdrop of the emergent socio-economic problems in some of the EU economies. As a consequence, the EU initiated a system of partial or in some cases complete suspension of preferential treatment to those ACP economies with a weak track record for human rights and the principle of democracy. Europe's economic and political priorities were clearly changing. The change in the structure of Europe's economy also led to a shift in economic and political interest from the ACP countries, to those economies geographically closer to Europe.

The Lomé Conventions were also characterised by a complex administrative regime that created long delays, which increased economic inefficiency. In particular, financial aid from the EU did not take sufficient account of the weak institutional fabric of the ACP countries. This lack of an institutional and policy context in the ACP membership often hampered the effective use of EDF funds, the consequence of which was a retardation effect in the impact of the Convention on the economic development prospects of the ACP economies.

In addition, the Lomé Agreements did not stimulate the types of change that were anticipated. Even though the EU provided as much as 99% preferential market access, the share of ACP imports in EU imports decreased from 8% in 1975 to 2.8% in 2000. Additionally, as much as 50% of ACP exports to the EU are still concentrated in just eight commodities. More disturbing was the fact that the ECPDM (2006) notes that non-ACP economies, which did not benefit from trade preferences, were able to outperform the ACP economies in the EU market.

Economic Partnership Agreement (EPA) the Caribbean

In 1995 the World Trade Organization (WTO) was formed, providing a platform for the European Union (EU) to enter into negotiations for the formation of a new signature agreement with the ACP economies. These negotiations matured into the Cotonou Agreement. The Cotonou Agreement is a development cooperation agreement, which encompasses a series of formal arrangements outlining political cooperation and preferential trade agreements between the EU and the ACP group.

The EU proposes to achieve these objectives by using Economic Partnership Agreements (EPAs) with six blocs of the ACP group. The relevant EPA for the Caribbean is called CARIFORUM. CARIFORUM comprises 15 sovereign nations, including Antigua and Barbuda, The Bahamas, Barbados, Belize, Dominica, Dominican Republic, Grenada, Guyana, Haiti, Jamaica, St Lucia, St Vincent, St Kitts and Nevis, Suriname, and Trinidad and Tobago. EPAs can also provide a stable basis for the future developmental planning of CARIFORUM states, especially in the context of WTO compatibility. Specifically, this will reduce the need for recourse to waivers and other concessions (see Burnette and Manji (2005) *Economic Partnership Agreements: Territorial conquest by economic means?*). Negotiations for an EPA between the EU and CARIFORUM is now in its fourth stage. If the proposed EPA schemes are to help develop the economies of CARIFORUM, they would have to consider the specific needs of the region.

Since the announcement of the proposed EPA, the EU Commission has supported a number of studies to investigate the impact of these regional integration arrangements on the ACP economies. However, these studies all generally show a loss of fiscal revenues. Because of the fiscal dependence of most Caribbean economies on international trade taxes, the fiscal consequences of adjustment is a sensitive issue. Greenaway and Milner (A Grim REPA, GEP Research Paper 03/30, 2003) estimate the following losses in customs revenues in CARICOM economies – see Table 12.6.

Inevitably, any large decrease in fiscal earnings would adversely affect the ability of the CARIFORUM economies to finance some of their key expenditures regarding developmental areas such as health care, education and poverty reduction. The removal of tariffs has to be countered by the introduction of a business-friendly fiscal system, so that

Table 12.6 *Changes in customs revenue by country*

	EC$ million
Barbados	182.4
Belize	52.8
Dominica	21.8
Grenada	31.2
Jamaica	635.1
St Kitts	25.9
St Lucia	60.4
St Vincent	27.3
Trinidad and Tobago	390.1

Source: Greenaway and Milner (2003)

firms will not be afraid to make the transition from the informal to the formal sector. A familiar approach is to replace the taxes on imports with a consumption tax or a tax on factors of production.

In many developing economies there is a lack of competition amongst suppliers and as a consequence some domestic firms have become inefficient. In this type of environment, what may happen is that CARIFORUM economies may be forced to streamline their production structures towards the production of primary goods. In this regard the EPA can significantly hamper economic diversification in these economies. A potential consequence of this, given the general backward and forward economic linkages that the manufacturing sector typically fosters, is a rise in unemployment in CARIFORUM economies. Economic development throughout history has occurred with some degree of protectionism for small firms in manufacturing and processing. The tariff structure needs to be responsive to the dynamism of the economic environment nationally, regionally and internationally.

There is the need to improve the delivery and structure of the education system within these CARIFORUM economies as well as an empowerment of the civil society movement in ACP states. Human capital formation in the region needs to be improved. In several member states primary school enrolment is low – less than 90%. At the secondary school level enrolment rates fall below 70% in some member states.

Building tertiary education capacity is critical for the development of CARIFORUM economies. While basic literacy and numeracy skills are critical to help ensure that citizens can function in modern-day economies, there is a need for a high level of tertiary education output as economies mature. Tertiary education helps a nation to tap into the global pool of knowledge. It also assists with scientific development of economies and with the development of critical support institutions such as the government and financial systems. An improvement in the stock of tertiary level education in an economy also helps to improve its overall competitiveness and enhance its trading capacity. Critically, development of the tertiary education skills of a nation helps to reduce the dependence on externally secured enterprise. Further, as the World Bank (2002) notes:

> Tertiary education is also important for the construction of the institutional regime through the training of competent and responsible professionals needed to achieve sound macroeconomic and public sector management. Moreover, tertiary institutions often provide the backbone of a country's informational infrastructure, frequently the main repository of information (libraries, etc.), computer network host and internet service provision. Tertiary level education is also recognised as critical to capacity building, particularly in countries with a severe shortage of high level skills

> Constructing Knowledge Societies:
> New Challenges for Tertiary Education, 2002

EU funding can help improve capacity and the availability of equipment to tertiary-level institutions in the CARIFORUM sphere at both the face-to-face and distance learning modes.

To enhance the development of CARIFORUM economies there is a critical need to improve on the functioning of their various data-collecting institutions. In all CARIFORUM economies, critical and basic data for the developmental planning process is issued with substantive time lags. Even more, there is a need to extend this facility to a regional level, probably housed within the existing CARICOM Secretariat. The availability of a wide cadre of high-quality data will be of vital significance in helping to improve the intra-CARICOM decision-making process and would also be central to any further negotiations the regime will have to undertake with third parties.

There will also be the need at the CSME level to hasten the intra-CSME movement of workers. Trinidad and Tobago experienced consistent positive real growth for the period 1994–2006. As a consequence the unemployment rate decreased to 7% in 2006 and all indications are that the economy has moved towards full employment. The EU, by providing resources to help strengthen the CSME process, can help to accelerate the intra-regional movement of factors of production. The unrestricted movement of labour within the regional bloc can help to promote a faster pace of economic growth. There has been some progress towards an enhanced intra-regional movement of skilled labour, but capital markets within the Caribbean sphere still remain relatively undeveloped.

In a similar regard, there is the need within the region for a regional marketing company of some sort. UNECLAC (2001) identifies with this type of reasoning and has noted that within the Caribbean there is:

> … a need for better trade promotion mechanisms including trade shows, trade expose and direct market-making through customer surveys and dealing with brokers and retailers. In all instances, efforts must be made to ascertain the tastes, preferences of consumers, technical, health and safety standards that exported products must meet. This limits rejection of products and saves time and money. Better use must also be made of information technology, especially the internet, to advertise regionally the products of different countries and firms and to promote information and exchange between producers and consumers.

> Trade, environment and development: implications for Caribbean countries, UNECLAC, 2001

The EPA has as one of its objectives, deepening of the regional integration process. However, while negotiations for the EPA are progressing there is still room for a deepening of the regional integration process amongst the participating ACP bloc. Concerning the CARICOM, the Dominican Republic's Secretary of Foreign Relations, Carlos Morales Troncoso, in a recent speech to the Council of Ministers in CARIFORUM noted:

> We do not yet have the common rules required to consolidate our Caribbean bloc. We signed the Free Trade Agreement between the Caribbean Community and the Dominican Republic in 1998, thanks to the leadership of our Heads. This agreement was a big step at the time. But it is far from representing the set of rights and obligations that would ensure the free circulation of goods, services and capital in the region. To try to amend it to achieve such freedom is not a viable option in the short term, in spite of the progress made to date and to the positive impetus behind the ongoing efforts. It is urgent, therefore, that we be bold and ambitious, because it is obvious that there is another alternative that could provide immediate results. What if we considered the Dominican Republic's accession to the Caribbean Single Market and Economy (CSME)? Wouldn't this be a more logical option to consolidate our regional integration and to create the enabling environment for negotiating with the European Union as a unified bloc?

> Morales T.C. 'Welcome Remarks', 14th Meeting of Cariforum Ministers, 2005. Santo Domingo, Secretariat of State for Foreign Relations

The North American Free Trade Agreement

The North American Free Trade Agreement (NAFTA) was formally implemented on 1 January 1994, with the expressed purpose of removing all barriers to trade among the US, Canada and Mexico. Under the NAFTA agreement thus far, all agricultural trade barriers have been removed between the US and Mexico. With regards to agricultural trade between the US and Canada, most of the trade tariffs were removed by 1 January 1998.

Mexico and Canada engaged in separate negotiations on market access for agricultural goods (tariffs on dairy, poultry, eggs and sugar have not been removed). Some tariffs were immediately removed while others were allowed a transition period of 5 to 15 years. This facility ensured that Mexico entered into free trade with the US and Canada beginning 1 January 2008.

End test

1 What are the various forms of economic integration?

2 What are the main objectives of the Caricom Single Market and Economy (CSME)?

3 What is the Cotonou Agreement? When was the Cotonou Agreement signed?

4 Which countries make up CARIFORUM?

5 When was NAFTA implemented?

End test feedback

1 The various forms of economic integration are:
- free trade area
- customs union
- common market
- economic union
- political union.

2 The main objectives of the CSME include the following:
- Freer intra-regional movement of capital: this entails the movement of capital from one intra-regional state to another CARICOM state. The freer intra-regional movement of capital is to be facilitated through the elimination of foreign exchange controls, the convertibility of currencies and, with time, a regional stock exchange.
- The free movement of labour: this involves the uninhibited movement of labour, particularly of university graduates (list other category of work) within the region.
- The establishment of a common external tariff to goods originating from non-member states.
- Harmonisation of economic policy, especially monetary and fiscal policies: this entails the coordination of exchange rate and interest rate policy within the region as well as agreed targets for budgetary deficits.
- Formation of a common currency: in time it is hoped that a common currency can be formed which can facilitate the easier comparison of key prices amongst the member states. This would also facilitate a reduction in intra-regional transaction costs.

3 The Cotonou Agreement is a development cooperation agreement that encompasses a series of formal arrangements outlining political cooperation and preferential trade agreements between the EU and the ACP group. The agreement takes its name from the capital of the West African state of Benin, where it was signed in 2000.

4 CARIFORUM comprises 15 sovereign nations, including Antigua and Barbuda, The Bahamas, Barbados, Belize, Dominica, Dominican Republic, Grenada, Guyana, Haiti, Jamaica, St Lucia, St Vincent, St Kitts and Nevis, Suriname, and Trinidad and Tobago.

5 NAFTA was formally implemented on 1 January 1994, with the expressed purpose of removing all barriers to trade between the US, Canada and Mexico.

13 International economic relations

Specific objectives

You should have an understanding of:

the role and functions of the World Trade Organization

the role of the International Monetary Fund and World Bank in the international financial system

multinational (transnational) corporations

the nature of foreign direct investment

potential benefits and disadvantages, including: access to technology and capital, access to markets, access to management skills, repatriation of profits, transfer pricing, crowding out of domestic businesses

the concept of globalisation

forces driving globalisation, for example, technological innovation, trade liberalisation, and liberalisation of capital markets

implications of globalisation for developing countries with particular reference to the greater Caribbean (greater competition, access to markets, access to technology, cheaper prices and greater variety of goods, loss of preferential markets).

The role and functions of the World Trade Organization

The World Trade Organization (WTO) was founded on 1 January 1995, providing a replacement for the General Agreement on Tariffs and Trade (GATT). Basically, the WTO has the following functions:

1 It facilitates enhanced powers for the settlement of trade disputes.
2 It is a multilateral trade organisation covering goods, services and intellectual property rights.

The WTO has a common disputes procedure. It is charged with the responsibility of developing and policing the development of the multilateral trading system along the principles built by the eight rounds of negotiations, which were concluded under the GATT. The WTO provides the resources for trade dispute resolution through various independent dispute panels. Member states have to abide by the rulings of the WTO or face the possibility of trade sanctions. The WTO is financed by contributions from its various member states.

The role of the International Monetary Fund and World Bank in the international financial system

After the end of the Second World War in 1945, the allied nations met in Bretton Woods, US to discuss the rebuilding of the global economy. The Bretton Woods Agreement led to the establishment of two critical institutions to help with the economic development process: the International Monetary Fund (IMF) and the International Bank for Reconstruction and Development (IBRD, now commonly referred to as the World Bank).

The IMF commenced operations in 1947 with 40 members, but it has grown considerably since then with well over 160 member states.

The objectives of the IMF included:

1 **Helping to promote world trade by facilitating the full convertibility of all currencies:** When all currencies can be freely converted one into the other, then this helps to facilitate the growth of multilateral trade as one economy does not then need to strike a trade balance with other countries, which is difficult to attain. By 1965 all the major currencies were convertible one into the other.

2 **Promoting the stability of exchange rates:** The founders of the IMF were in search of a system of exchange rates that had more flexibility than the gold standard but at the same time also provided a high degree of stability. The founders chose an adjustable peg system and all members of the IMF had to define their currencies in terms of gold. As it stood then, under the adjustable peg system exchange rates of member states were not to deviate more than 1% from the declared parities.

Thus if the declared parity of the Trinidad and Tobago dollar was say, TT\$6.25 = US\$1, then it was the duty of the central bank to ensure that the TT\$ to the US\$ maintained an exchange rate in the range TT\$6.25 ± 1% = US\$1.

This system allowed for some flexibility as the IMF permitted both devaluations and revaluations of currencies to occur. Today, however, most countries have floating exchange rates.

Financial assistance

The members of the IMF contribute to a pool of foreign currencies, which are conditioned by the size of the member state's national income and also by its relative importance in international trade. This pool of currencies forms the basis from which member states in balance of payments difficulties could get assistance.

In recent times the IMF has laid down a variety of rules and conditions that member states need to follow in the management of floating exchange rates. The IMF has also borrowed from its member states in recent times to expand its resource base.

The World Bank is the sister institution to the IMF and it was established in 1944. The main purpose of the World Bank is to provide long-term assistance to economies to help them in their economic reconstruction and developmental progress. Since the World Bank was formulated it has increased considerably in size and today it has 185 members.

In the early years, the World Bank lent mainly to European countries to help them reconstruct their economies. However, today it lends mainly to developing economies. Although initially it lent to help build up physical infrastructure, the World Bank now lends a considerable amount to build up social expenditures in the area of education and health care.

The World Bank also provides developing economies with a wide range of technical research advice. In general it does not finance the full amount of a project but requires that the developing economy has some financial input.

Multinational (transnational) corporations

A multinational corporation (MNC) has its headquarters in one country and multiple operations in other countries. Examples include Royal Bank of Canada, and Cable and Wireless. These companies can be huge and in some instances their annual turnover will be in excess of the GDP of many developing countries.

When MNCs set up operations in a country it is a one-time injection of foreign exchange into the economy. For this reason many governments of developing countries have welcomed MNCs by offering incentives such as tax-free holidays. These MNCs generate employment not only at the company level but for firms to which they subcontract services.

Foreign direct investment

Foreign direct investment (FDI) includes all capital transactions that are made to acquire a lasting interest (usually 10% or more of voting stock) in an enterprise operating in a country other than that of the investor. FDI is the sum of equity capital, reinvested earnings and other long-term and short-term capital as shown in the balance of payments. FDI can be defined as investment of long-term duration from a foreign country into a domestic 'host' country. It may take the form of a 'composite bundle of capital stocks, know-how and technology'. The implication of this long-term investment is that there is a long-term relationship between the investor and the host country's enterprise. Direct investment comprises not only the initial amount of investment between the investor and the enterprise but also all subsequent transactions.

The nature of FDI

In the essay entitled 'Imperialism, the Highest Stage of Capitalism' Lenin (1917) explained that the Western World would export their capital to the less developed countries in order to extract the highest profitability from the indigenous labour force. This line of reasoning formed the backbone of the policy to restrict the inflows of foreign direct investment in the less developed economies. By the 1980s, however, the global economic environment had changed so negatively as a consequence of the international debt crisis that these economies began to re-evaluate their position on FDI and indeed began to lobby for the inflow of more foreign investment.

This increase in FDI flows acted as the engine of growth for several developing countries. Some economies, where FDI acted as the main or important sources of growth, include Taiwan, Singapore, Indonesia and China. CARICOM member states have realised the importance of FDI in the development process and attempts have been made to maintain the competitiveness of the regional economies in terms of attracting FDI.

Benefits of FDI

There are a number of potential benefits to a country of FDI:

- **Build-up of physical capital:** The small economies of the CARICOM sphere are characterised by high levels of structural unemployment, indicating that the existing capital stock is insufficient to absorb the entire labour force. In these small capital-starved developing economies an increase in the physical capital stock is always a welcome development. FDI in these economies can lead to an increase in the stock of physical capital per person.

- **Human capital, management and organisational skills:** Foreign firms usually make substantial contributions to the host economy in terms of helping to improve its stock of human capital. Many MNCs now practise corporate social responsibility and so routinely offer scholarships and bursaries to deserving students from the geographical area in which their productive operations are located. These foreign companies also offer staff upgrade opportunities. Labour training and skills acquisition are supposed to improve the stock of knowledge in the host economy. FDI also facilitates the introduction of alternative (superior) managerial and organisational practices. Even in the absence of significant amounts of physical capital accumulation with FDI, licensing and other such quasi-investment arrangements tend to promote knowledge transfers from the foreign economy to the host economy.

- **Access to technology:** The transfer of technology has been shown to be the impetus for the economic development of many economies. Consider that before the industrial revolution, Europe doubled its per capita incomes over a period of 350 years; during the industrial revolution, Britain did likewise in 60 years; but for countries such as such as Botswana, Chile, China, Ireland, Japan and Thailand, FDI-led growth resulted in the virtual doubling of their GDP in about 10 years.

  FDI also improves the extent of technical progress in the host economy via a 'contagion effect'. There are two main ways in which FDI helps to transfer technology from the foreign country to the home country: via backward linkages, and through labour mobility. When foreign MNCs engage in backward linkages with local firms along their value chain they often assist them by advising on the appropriate technology to use. FDI also helps to transfer foreign technology to the host economy via labour mobility. So when a worker is employed with an MNC, the worker is likely to gain access to superior management practices and may also gain knowledge of superior technology. When employees leave these MNCs for other firms within the domestic economy, some of the technological knowledge embodied with the movement of human capital spills over to the new firm.

It is also possible that the presence of foreign MNCs may encourage domestic firms to upgrade their technology and know-how and improve their research and development so that FDI may promote the output of domestic firms.

- **Market access:** Sir Arthur Lewis, in 1949, proposed that 'every inquiry into industrialisation must commence with the market'. Lewis argued that indeed the market access was a critical success factor to the development of the region's industrialisation drive, and as such should be the main reason why foreign investment should be 'wooed and fawned upon'.

  Lewis suggested that marketing of these goods should be focused on the extra regional markets, given that the domestic market was too small to provide the necessary impetus needed to support the industry. The prospect of the intra-regional market as a potential launching pad to allow fledgling industries to develop their capacity to penetrate extra regional markets, however, was viewed as a feasible development strategy in this regard.

- **FDI and financial crises:** FDI also carries the advantage, as compared with other types of capital flow, of offering protection against financial crises in the global economy. This in turn will reduce the extent of volatility experienced in the growth process.

- **FDI and poverty reduction:** Because FDI can influence the economic growth performance of an economy, it carries serious implications for the reduction of poverty. Specifically, FDI can help to generate economic returns for the government, which in turn could be used to build up safety nets for the poor. By helping to reduce poverty, FDI creates room for benefiting economic agents to invest greater amounts in their stock of skills and in improving their health status, both of which could lead to an improvement in their individual productivity and hence national productivity.

Disadvantages of FDI

There are, too, a number of potential disadvantages to a country of FDI:

- **Repatriation of profits:** The repatriation of profits to the MNCs' home economies represents a drain of foreign exchange. Repatriation of profits is accounted for in the balance of payments account as an outflow of resources and represents a leakage from the domestic economy.

- **Transfer pricing:** The practice of transfer pricing allows the multinational firms to lower their tax burden to host economies by reporting their profitability levels away from high tax economies towards lower tax economies. As a consequence, profit levels in high-tax economies are understated. This translates into lower-than-potential tax revenues.

- **Environmental damage:** Some foreign firms sometimes operate in a manner that may destroy important aspects of the environment in host economies. For example, firms drilling for crude oil may sometimes, through oil spills, be responsible for significant coastal damage.

Another example can be found in Guyana where multinational logging companies, especially those from Malaysia and South Korea, have begun an intensive attack on South American forests. This situation is made worse where local governments are unable to effectively control the activities of these companies. The consequence is that unsustainable logging has destroyed the natural habitats of the forests and driven the indigenous peoples from the land.

- **FDI and wage inequality:** Foreign firms tend to promote wage inequality in host economies. They may offer workers a higher wage rate then those in the domestic workforce, which can lead to a dualistic wage structure. In Trinidad and Tobago the various residential areas where the oil sector workers live are noticeably better than those for workers in other segments of the economy.

- **FDI and domestic investment:** FDI can crowd out domestic firms in the same line of business because they typically have a superior level of technology and managerial expertise.

- **FDI and decision-making:** Because foreign firms are usually involved at higher levels of the economy they may be able to influence key decisions made by the government. This compromise of national sovereignty can become a source of discontent among the population depending on how and when it occurs.

The concept of globalisation

Globalisation may be defined as the process of intensification of the interconnectivity of economic, political and social activities across borders, which tends to stimulate the world economy and result in human innovation and technological progress.

The process of globalisation can be broken up into three distinct stages. The first lasted until around 1914, during which time the majority of trade took place between large cities and their hinterlands. The second phase of globalisation lasted until just after the Second World War. It was characterised by a period of consolidation and expansionism after the Great Depression of the 1930s, which led to a reassessment of the virtues and benefits of international trade. During this period the world economy also witnessed the emergence of the Bretton Woods system of global, economic and financial management, which began to operate through the establishment of the IMF, the World Bank and GATT.

The third round of globalisation started after the Second World War. This stage of globalisation is the most intense and expansive thus far and is characterised by the internationalisation of production and technological improvements on a scale previously to unknown, in a wide range of areas from information to biotechnology. In this phase of globalisation there has also been a considerable amount of trade liberalisation and a substantial removal of barriers to FDI, accompanied by a generally diminished role for the state and the formation of mega trade blocks in both hemispheres. In this phase, the WTO was established to oversee the acceleration of free trade on a global scale.

Forces driving globalisation

The process of globalisation is driven by a number of forces. One of these is the greater movement of capital across sovereign borders. Corporations invest abroad for several reasons:

- To exploit technology, managerial, financial or marketing strengths
- To exploit natural resources, usually employing specialised and often technologically sophisticated methods
- To take advantage of low wages but sufficiently skilled labour to serve as a base for exporting to other countries
- To sell services, in which case a local presence is normally required

The traditional theories on FDI assume that a firm operating in a foreign country must have comparative advantage in certain factors to counterbalance the additional costs that arise from differences in culture, language, legal system, and other factors such as increased costs for communication and lack of knowledge of local conditions.

Political stability and the role of the state are no doubt factors that influence FDI inflows. Other factors include an economy's trade regime, investment regime and its infrastructure platform.

Other determinants of the pace of globalisation include institutional factors such as government subsidies, tax breaks, alien land-holding regulations and the provision of warehouses and other infrastructural amenities such as electricity and water.

Implications of globalisation for developing countries, with reference to the greater Caribbean

Globalisation provides a number of threats and opportunities for Caribbean economies. In the first instance, globalisation provides firms operating in the Caribbean sphere with a greater degree of competition. What are the benefits of a greater degree of competition? A greater degree of competition minimises the amount of economic wastage that is engaged. In particular, if firms operating in the Caribbean sphere were only exposed to competition among themselves, then this may allow firms with inefficient production functions to subsist. By reducing economic wastage and improving resource allocation, a greater degree of competition can lead to a higher level of economic welfare.

A deepening of the globalisation process implies that economies will generally have greater market access to the markets of other economies. The implication of this is that Caribbean firms can now sell more goods and services in previously closed foreign markets and so may be able to realise a greater degree of export revenues. Note though that an increased element of globalisation can, by the removal of tariffs in the Caribbean, threaten the amount of tax revenues collected by those Caribbean economies that are dependent on international trade taxes for a significant amount of their tax revenues.

An explicit part of the globalisation process is an improved movement of international capital. A greater degree of FDI is associated with a number of benefits for developing economies, including a greater access to foreign markets, a greater degree of financial investment, and access to foreign technology. Foreign technology can help to increase the output levels of those Caribbean firms that are using outdated technological processes. It can also, in some cases, help to encourage domestic firms to invest in a greater degree of research and development and to engage in joint venture arrangements that will benefit from technological and other spillover benefits.

A significant facet of the globalisation process is associated with access to cheaper goods and services produced in the foreign market. China stands out as a major trading partner to most of its trading partners. Because of its large pool of labour China has been able to mass-produce a vast range of labour-intensive and skilled labour-intensive goods at relatively cheap prices.

China and globalisation

The growth in China's exports and imports has been nothing short of phenomenal. For example, exports from China increased from US$13.7 billion in 1979 to US$952.1 billion in 2006. In the same period, imports into China increased from US$15.7 million to US$798 million, an increase of 4983% (see Table 13.1).

Table 13.1 *China's world trade (US$ billion), 1979–2005*

Year	Exports	Imports	Trade balance
1979	13.7	15.7	−2.0
1980	18.1	19.5	−1.4
1985	27.3	42.5	−15.3
1990	62.9	53.9	9.0
1995	148.8	132.1	16.7
2000	249.2	225.1	24.1
2001	266.2	243.6	22.6
2002	365.6	295.2	30.4
2003	435.4	412.8	25.6
2004	593.4	561.4	32.0
2005	762.0	660.1	101.9
2006	952.1	798.0	154.1

Source: IMF, Directory of Trade Statistics Yearbook (various years)

During the late 1970s and early 1980s, China's government undertook an intensive strategy towards 'awakening a dormant economic giant'. Through various stages of economic policy reform, China began to stimulate capital formation, alongside a culture of entrepreneurship that was complemented by an array of trade liberalisation and investment fundamentals. A reduction in state intervention in the market was complemented by supply-side augmentations to the domestic industrial production base and quality of the workforce.

The benefits of such an intensive and directed development strategy have no doubt made China the powerhouse it is today and, in particular, into an economy with such tremendous growth potential that the international community as a whole is affected by even minute changes in the patterns of demand or supply of this economy. Figure 13.1 (opposite) compares population growth, real GDP growth and real per capita GDP growth. Notice that for the entire period, real GDP growth exceeded population growth, which consequently resulted in an expansion in per capita GDP.

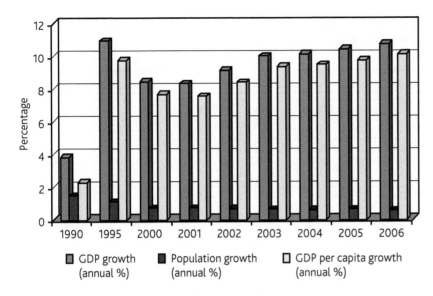

Figure 13.1 *GDP growth rate, GDP per capita growth rate and population growth, 1990–2006*

China is emerging as one of the driving forces of global economic growth. Its share in world GDP has been steadily increasing (Figure 13.2). The average share over period 1989–95 was 7.64% which increased to approximately 10.9% by 2004.

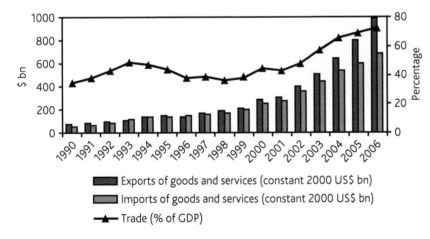

Figure 13.2 *China's exports and imports and trade as a percentage of GDP*

China's consumption of goods and services is also phenomenal. Consider the data in Table 13.2 (overleaf), which shows how significant China is as a consumer in the international economy.

The amount of trade that China engages in has also been increasing. Notice in Figure 13.2 that exports have traditionally been higher than imports, indicating a positive trade balance. By 2006 the level of trade engaged was approximately 72% of GDP.

Table 13.2 *China and the rest of the world: growth in consumption of selected primary commodities, 2002–05 (%)*

Consumption of goods			Contribution of China to global consumption growth
	China	Other countries	World	
Copper	31.6	3.4	8.6	67.3
Cotton	59.5	3.0	19.6	89.2
Natural rubber	46.6	11.9	18.0	45.2
Oil	32.0	5.8	7.5	27.6
Soybeans	49.9	5.2	10.9	58.7

Source: UNCTAD, Trade and Development Report (2006)

End test

1   When was the World Trade Organization (WTO) established? What is its role in international trade?

2   When was the International Monetary Fund (IMF) established? What is its role in international trade?

3   What is foreign direct investment (FDI)?

4   What is globalisation?

5   What are some of the forces driving globalisation?

End test feedback

1   The WTO was founded on 1 January 1995, providing a replacement for the General Agreement on Tariffs and Trade (GATT). It has the following functions:

   • It facilitates enhanced powers for the settlement of trade disputes.

   • It is a multilateral trade organisation covering goods, services and intellectual property rights.

2   The IMF commenced operations in 1947 with 40 members, but has since grown considerably to well over 160 member states. The objectives of the IMF included:

   • helping to promote world trade by facilitating the full convertibility of all currencies

   • promoting the stability of exchange rates.

3   FDI includes all capital transactions that are made to acquire a lasting interest (usually 10% or more of voting stock) in an enterprise operating in a country other than that of the investor. FDI is the sum of equity capital, reinvested earnings and other long-term and short-term capital as shown in the balance of payments. The investment in the host country may consist of a package that includes technology, capital stocks and expertise.

4   Globalisation may be defined as the process of intensification of the interconnectivity of economic, political and social activities across borders, which tends to stimulate the world economy and result in human innovation and technological progress.

5   Forces driving globalisation include technological innovation, trade liberalisation, and liberalisation of capital markets.

References

Appleyard, D. R., and Field, A. J. (2001) *International Economics*. Boston: McGraw-Hill.

Arthur, O. (2001) *The Promise and the Peril: A Caribbean Perspective on the FTAA*. In: CLAA Miami Conference on Free Trade and Integration Implications for the Caribbean Basin.

Baker, J.L. (1997) Poverty Reduction and Human Development in the Caribbean. *World Bank Discussion Paper Number 366*. Washington DC: The World Bank.

Briguglio, L. (1995) Small Island Developing States and their Economic Vulnerabilities. *World Development*, 23(9), pp1615–1632.

Burnett, P., and Manji, F. (2005) Economic Partnership Agreements: Territorial Conquest by Economic Means? *Pambazuka News*, 216.

Business Monitor International (2006) *The West Caribbean Business Forecast Report Q4*. London: Business Monitor International.

Business Monitor International (2007) *The Trinidad and Tobago Business Forecast Report Q3*. London: Business Monitor International.

Central Bank of Trinidad and Tobago (Various years) *Balance of Payments Yearbook of Trinidad and Tobago*. Port of Spain: Central Bank of Trinidad and Tobago.

Central Bank of Trinidad and Tobago (Various years) *Annual Statistical Digest*. Port of Spain: Central Bank of Trinidad and Tobago.

Clark, J.M. (1981 [1923]) *Studies in the Economics of Overhead Costs*. Chicago: University of Chicago Press.

Eatwell, J., and Taylor, L. (2000) *Global Finance at Risk*. New York: New Press.

Economic Commission for Latin America and the Caribbean (2001) *Trade, Environment and Development: Implications for Caribbean Countries*. Port of Spain: ECLAC Subregional Headquarters for the Caribbean.

Economic Commission for Latin America and the Caribbean (2001) *Overview of the Integration of Latin America*. Santiago: ECLAC.

Economic Commission for Latin America and the Caribbean (2002) *Selected Statistical Indicators of Caribbean Countries*. Port of Spain: ECLAC.

European Centre for Development Policy Management (2006) *Redefining ACP-EU Trade Relations: Economic Partnership Agreements*. In: ECDPM Seminar 'The Cotonou Partnership Agreement: What Role in a Changing World?', Maastricht, 18–19 December 2006.

Food and Agriculture Organization of the United Nations (2008) *The State of Food Insecurity in the World 2008*. Rome: FAO.

Fisher, I. (1911) *The Purchasing Power of Money, Its Determination and Relation to Credit, Interest and Crises*. New York: Macmillan.

de Foville, A. (1907) *La Monnaie*, Paris: J. Gabalda.

Friedman, M. (1956) The Quantity Theory of Money: A Restatement. *Studies in the Quantity Theory of Money*. Friedman, M. Ed. Chicago: University of Chicago Press.

Grambsch, A.E., Michaels, R.G. and Peskin, H.M. (1993) Taking Stock of Nature: Environmental Accounting for Chesapeake Bay. *Toward Improved Accounting for the Environment*. Lutz, E. Ed. Washington DC: The World Bank.

Greenaway, D. and Milner, C. (2003) *Caribbean Preferences and Reciprocity: A Grim REPA?* Nottingham: University of Nottingham.

Hamilton, A. (1957 [1791]) Report on Manufactures. *Alexander Hamilton's Papers on Public Credit, Commerce, and Finance*. New York: New York Liberal Arts Press.

ul Haq, M. (1989) The Human Development Paradigm. *Reflections on Human Development*. New York: Human Development Report Office, UNDP.

Hosein, R. and Tewarie, B. (2004) Service Exports and Economic Growth in an Oil Rich Economy: A Case Study of Tourism in Trinidad and Tobago, *Journal of Eastern Caribbean Studies*, 29(1), pp42–68.

Hosein, R. and Tewarie, B. (2003) Regional Economic Partnership Agreements and their implications for CARICOM Sugar Exporting Economies. *Journal of Caribbean Agro-Economic Society*, 6(1), pp165–87.

http://data.worldbank.org/indicator

http://publications.worldbank.org/wdi

http://www.central-bank.org.tt

http://www.commonfund.org

http://www.cso.gov.tt

http://www.eia.gov/countries

Hume, D. (1999 [1748]) *An Enquiry Concerning Human Understanding*. Beauchamp, T.L. Ed. Oxford: Oxford University Press.

Hutton, W. (1986) *The Revolution That Never Was: An Assessment of Keynesian Economics*. London: Longman.

International Monetary Fund (2007) The Price Level, Inflation and Exchange Rates. *Financial Programming and Policies*. Washington DC: IMF.

International Monetary Fund (Various years) *Direction of Trade Statistics Yearbook*. Washington DC: IMF.

Keynes, J.M. (1936) *The General Theory of Employment Interest and Money*. London: Macmillan.

Lewis, W.A. (1949) *Economic Survey: 1919–1939*. London: George Allen & Unwin.

Lewis, W.A. (1955) *The Theory of Economic Growth*. London: George Allen & Unwin.

List, F. (1991 [1841]) *The National System of Political Economy*. New Jersey: Augustus M. Kelly.

Mäler, K.G. (1991) National Accounts and Environmental Resources. *Environmental and Resource Economics*, 1(1), pp1–15.

Marchesi, S. (2000) Adoption of an IMF Programme and Debt Restructuring: An Econometric Analysis. *CSGR Working Paper No. 56/00*.

Mill, J.S. (1920 [1848]) *Principles of Political Economy*. London: Longman, Green.

von Mises, L. (1980 [1912]) *Theory of Money and Credit*. Indianapolis: Liberty Classics.

Morales, T.C. (2005) *Welcome Remarks*. In: 14th Meeting of Cariforum Ministers, Santo Domingo.

Newcomb, S. (1886 [1966]) *Principles of Political Economy*. New York: A.M. Kelley.

Okun, A.M. (1962) Potential GNP: Its Measurement and Significance. *American Statistical Association, Proceedings of the Business and Economics Statistics Section*, pp98–104.

Peskin, H.M., and Marian, S.D.A. (2001) Accounting for Environmental Services: Contrasting the SESA and the ENRAP Approaches. *Review of Income and Wealth*, 47(2), pp203–219.

Phillips, A.W. (1958). The Relation Between Unemployment and the Rate of Change of Money Wage Rates in the United Kingdom, 1861–1957. *Economica*. London: LSE.

Ricardo, D. (1951 [1817]) On the Principles of Political Economy and Taxation. *The Works and Correspondence of David Ricardo, Volume 1*. Sraffa P. Ed. Cambridge: Cambridge University Press.

Say, J.B. (1855 [1803]) *A Treatise on Political Economy*. Philadelphia: Lippincott, Grambo and Co.

Smith, A. (1981 [1776]) *An Inquiry into the Nature and Causes of the Wealth of Nations, Volumes 1 and 2*. Campbell, R. H. and Skinner, A.S. Eds. Indianopolis: Liberty Fund.

Thirlwall, A. P. (1978) Ed. *Keynes and Laissez-Faire*. London: Macmillan.

Torrens, R. (1815) *An Essay on the External Corn Trade*. London: Hatchard.

Trinidad and Tobago (1980) *Population and Housing Census, 1980, Volume II*. Port of Spain: Central Statistical Office.

Trinidad and Tobago (1990) *Population and Housing Census of the Commonwealth Caribbean. Volume of Basic Tables of Sixteen CARICOM countries*. Port of Spain: Central Statistical Office.

Trinidad and Tobago (2000) *Population and Housing Census: Community Register*. Port of Spain: Central Statistical Office.

Trinidad and Tobago (Various years) *Continuous Sample Survey of the Population*. Port of Spain: Central Statistical Office.

Trinidad and Tobago (Various years) *Review of the Economy*. Port of Spain: Ministry of Finance.

United Nations Conference on Trade and Development (2006) *Trade and Development Report*. Geneva: UNCTAD.

United Nations Conference on Trade and Development (Various years) *Statistical Handbook*. Geneva: UNCTAD.

United Nations Conference on Trade and Development (Various years) *World Investment Reports*. Geneva: UNCTAD.

United Nations Development Programme (Various years) *Human Development Report*. New York: UNCTAD.

United Nations Education, Scientific and Cultural Organization (1991) *World Education Report*. Paris: UNESCO.

World Bank (2006) Global Development Finance. *The Development Potential of Surging Capital Flows*. Washington DC: The World Bank.

Acknowledgements

The author and the publisher would also like to thank the following for permission to reproduce material:

Table 1.2 *from Continuous Sample Survey of the Population (various years)* by Central Statistics Office, Trinidad & Tobago; Table 1.3 *from Continuous Sample Survey of the Population (various years)* by Central Statistics Office, Trinidad & Tobago; Table 1.5 from Review of the Economy (various years) copyright © 2010 Ministry of Finance, Trinidad & Tobago; Table 1.6 copyright © TTCrime.com; Table 1.7 from The West Caribbean Business Forecast Report 2006 by Business Monitor International. Copyright © Business Monitor International Ltd; p36 from W. Hutton, The Revolution That Never Was: An Assessment of Keynesian Economics, 1986, Longman. Reproduced with the permission of Pearson Education; p36 from A. P Thirwall, Keynes and Laissez Faire, 1978, Palgrave Macmillan reproduced with the permission of Palgrave Macmillan; Table 3.1 International Bank for Reconstruction and Development/The World Bank: World Development Indicators (2008); Table 3.2 from Central Statistical Office for Trinidad & Tobago: Population and Housing Census (1980) (1990) (2000); Table 3.5 from International Bank for Reconstruction and Development/The World Bank: World Development Indicators (2008); p62 reprinted with permission from *The Encylopaedia Britannica*, © 1999 by Encyclopaedia Britannica, Inc; Table 5.1 copyright © 2007, Caribbean Development Bank; Table 5.2 from International Bank for Reconstruction and Development/The World Bank: World Bank Data (1960–2004); Table 5.3, 5.4, 7.2, 9.13, 11.3 copyright © Central Statistical Office of Trinidad & Tobago, 2011; Table 6.1, 6.2, 7.3, fig. 11.1 from Central Bank of Trinidad and Tobago: Balance of Payment Yearbook (various years); p89 from Bank of Guyana Annual Report (2007). Reproduced with permission from the Bank of Guyana; p90 from Central Bank of Trinidad and Tobago: Monetary Policy Report (2008); Table 6.4 from Central Bank of Trinidad and Tobago: Annual Statistical Digest (various years); Table 7.1, 8.2, 8.4, 9.3, 9.11, 10.1, 11.4, 12.2 from International Bank for Reconstruction and Development/The World Bank: World Development Indicators (2008); p105 adapted from Jamaat al Muslimeen Coup Attempt' from Wikipedia, the free encyclopedia http://en.wikipedia.org/wiki/Jamaat_al_Muslimeen_coup_attempt; Table 8.1 from UNELAC: Selected Statistical Indicatiors of Caribbean Countries, LC/CAR/P.O.S, (2002); p112 from F.C Gueye, M. Vaugeois, M. Martin, and A. Johnson, 'Negotiating Debt Reduction in the HIPC Initiative and Beyond' (2007) from Debt Relief International Ltd. Copyright © DFI Group; Table 8.3 from Country Reports (various years) © 2011 The Economist Intelligence Unit Limited. All rights reserved; Table 9.1, 9.5 from Human Development Report (various years). Copyright © United Nations Development Programme (UNDP). All rights reserved; Table 9.2 from Human Development Report (2007). Copyright © United Nations Development Programme (UNDP). All rights reserved; Table 9.4 from Central Statistical Office for Trinidad & Tobago: Annual Statistical Digest (various years); Table 9.6, 9.7 Human Development Report (2004). Copyright © United Nations Development Programme (UNDP). All rights reserved; Table 9.8, 9.11, 9.12 from R. Hosein and B. Tewarie, 'Service Exports and Economic Growth in an Oil Rich Economy: A Case Study of Tourism in Trinidad and Tobago', *Journal of Eastern Caribbean Studies* 29 (1): 42–68 (2004). Reproduced with the permission of the author; Table 9.9 from *The World Factbook* 2009 Washington, DC: Central Intelligence Agency, 2009; Figure 9.1 from International Bank for Reconstruction and Development/The World Bank: Poverty Reduction and Human Development in the Caribbean, Discussion Paper 366 by J.L. Baker (1997); Table 9.14 from Review of the Economy (various years) copyright © 2010 Ministry of Finance, Trinidad & Tobago; Table 9.15, 9.16 from UNCTAD: World Investment Reports (various years); pp130–131 from Central Bank of Trinidad and Tobago: Annual Statistical Digest (various years); Table 9.17 reproduced from World Development, 23: 1615–1632, L. Briguglio, Small Island States and their Economic Vulnerabilities, 1995, with permission of Elsevier; Table 10.6 from UNCTAD: Statistical Handbook (various years); Table 11.1 from D. R Appleyard and A.J Field, International Economics, McGraw Hill (2001); Table 11.2 from Central Bank of Trinidad and Tobago: Balance of Payments (2001); Table 12.3 from International Bank for Reconstruction and Development/The World Bank (2002); Table 12.4 from R. Hosein and B. Tewarie, 'Regional Economic Partnership Agreements and its implications for CARICOM Sugar Exporting Economies', *Journal of Caribbean Economic Society*, 6 (1): 165–87 (2003); Table 12.6 from D. Greenaway & C. Milner, 'A Grim REPA' (2003). Copyright © Leverhulme Centre for Research on Globalisation and Economic Policy, Universtiy of Nottingham; p170 from UNECLAC: Trade Environment and Development: Implications for Caribbean Countries, LC/CSR/G.669 (2001a); p170 from Morales T.C., 'Welcome Remarks', from 14th Meeting of Cariforum Ministers (2002). Copyright © 2011 Caribbean Community (CARICOM); Table 13.1 from International Monetary Fund. Statistics Dept, Direction of Trade Statistics Yearbook, IMF (various years); Table 13.2 from UNCTAD: Trade and Development Report (2006).

Every effort has been made to contact copyright holders and we apologise if any have been overlooked. Should copyright have been unwittingly infringed in these course notes, the owners should contact the publishers, who will make the correction at reprint.